GUIDE TO
Homeland Security Careers

Donald B. Hutton
Anna Mydlarz

BARRON'S

For
Victoria Haley Hutton & John Bradley Hutton

and

In Memory of
September 11, 2001 Victims and Heroes
&
Lt. General Vernon Walters
U.S. Army Veteran Anthony Mydlarz

You will be remembered in the hearts of good Americans always . . .

All inquiries should be addressed to:
Barron's Educational Series, Inc.
250 Wireless Boulevard
Hauppauge, NY 11788
http://www.barronseduc.com

International Standard Book No. 0-7641-2375-0

Library of Congress Catalog Card No. 2002035611

Library of Congress Cataloging-in-Publication Data

Hutton, Donald B.
   Barron's guide to homeland security careers / Donald B. Hutton and Anna Mydlarz.
      p.   cm.
   ISBN 0-7641-2375-0
      1. United States. Dept. of Homeland Security—Vocational guidance.   2. Civil defense—Vocational guidance—United States.   3. National security—Vocational guidance—United States.   4. Emergency management—Vocational guidance—United States.   5. Law enforcement—Vocational guidance—United States.   6. Terrorism—United States—Prevention.   I. Mydlarz, Anna.   II. Title

HV6432 .H88   2003
363.1'023'73—dc21   2002035611

PRINTED IN THE UNITED STATES OF AMERICA
9 8 7 6 5 4 3 2 1

CONTENTS

SECTION 2 Emergency Preparedness and Response Careers

CHAPTER 4 Federal Emergency Response Agency Opportunities

SECTION 3 Chemical, Biological, Radiological, and Nuclear Countermeasures Careers

SECTION 4 Information Analysis and Infrastructure Protection Careers

SECTION 5 Military Careers

SECTION 6 Your Application and Background Check

ACKNOWLEDGMENTS

A VERY SPECIAL THANKS TO:

- ✪ Frank McCarton, Deputy Director of the City of New York Office of Emergency Management
- ✪ Department of Defense Public Information Office
- ✪ U.S. Department of State Public Information Office
- ✪ U.S. Department of Justice Public Information Office
- ✪ U.S. Department of Homeland Security Public Information Office

---

GUIDE DISCLAIMER

Every effort has been made to provide accurate and complete information in this guide. However, there may be small errors or slightly obsolete information in the content due to changes in U.S. government policy, which seems to be changing every day! Therefore, this book should only be used as a general guide to opportunities and careers and not as a final and permanent information source.

FOREWORD

AMERICA'S NEED FOR HOMELAND SECURITY WILL NOT CHANGE

The concept of Homeland Security is more than just adding another cop on the beat or more soldiers on the border. Terrorism's dark history proves that inflicting the unthinkable upon the unsuspecting creates panic. Security prevents panic. It is achieved when we identify and prevent the terrorists' goals. Preventing terrorism involves the cooperation of many partners focused on protecting the very fabric of American life. It requires a range of skills from traditional law enforcement officers to research scientists, each focused on sensing, identifying, or responding to a potential threat.

The potential threats are many. They range from explosives to economic crime perpetrated by an unknown assailant connected to an obscure Internet site thousands of miles away. The tools of terrorism vary from complex nuclear devices and genetically altered bacteria and viruses to explosives imbedded in an air traveler's shoe. Yet each weapon has in common the ability to produce a disproportionately high share of human misery. The challenge for homeland security lies in acquiring the information necessary to identify each of these threats and to reliably trigger a response that will prevent the consequences of their deployment.

Meeting that challenge will be daunting but absolutely vital. It will also require that the knowledge base among those entrusted with homeland security be broad and highly versatile. Prior backgrounds in various branches of public service as well as experience in science will prove invaluable to the future homeland security officer. For example, the detection of a suitcase bomb can range from the highly labor intensive visual search of each air traveler's suitcase to scanning bags electronically. Automating the process offers improvements in speed and reliability but uncovers serious scientific problems. Is the bomb a crystal or a liquid? Is it packed as a solid lump, or has it been hidden in a suitcase's liner as a sheet explosive? Will it show up on X ray, or will it masquerade as many commonly packed household items? Newer technologies promise to answer these questions. However, they will demand that the homeland security officer understands the scientific principles that govern their function in order to use them effectively.

In terrorism's dark history, there is no greater cause of public panic than the spread of disease. The spread of silent killers that can be passed by a friendly handshake or enjoying a shared meal truly turns friends into enemies. The fact that illness occurs only several days later confuses us as we separate our friends from enemies. Smallpox, long a dreaded disease, was first used as a weapon of terrorism in the United States during the French and Indian War. The soldiers gave winter blankets that they collected from infected people with small-pox to the opposing Native-American warriors. Due to the hardiness of the smallpox virus, it survived on the blankets and decimated the tribes.

Protecting our water supplies from biological agents also presents immense challenges. A range of biological and chemical products could compromise a commodity that we cannot live without for more than a matter of hours—water. Of greater concern is that the quantity of poison needed to contaminate our reservoirs can be small and be dispersed from remote locations. Detecting these weapons will require a synergy of many sciences, ranging from complex computer chips that can function like a miniature underwater laboratory to telecommunication transmitters that will coordinate global positioning system (GPS) data to the time and location of intrusion.

The tragedy of September 11 has taught us that the future home-land security officer will need to be armed with the latest knowledge in secure wireless radio communication. Maintaining the first responders' ability to contain and prevent terrorism is of the highest priority. Systems that provide redundancy of communication as well as encryption assures that rescue efforts are undertaken in an organized manner. Once again, homeland security officers need to understand the science, the limits, and the capabilities of these newer systems.

TERRORISM'S DARK HISTORY

"We . . . have the ability to make and use chemicals and poisonous gas. And those gases and poisons are made from the simplest ingredients, which are available in the pharmacies and we could, as well, smuggle them from one country to another if needed. And this is for use against vital institutions and residential populations and drinking water sources and others."

U.S. v. *Ramzi Ahmed Yousef*, Government Exhibit 528-T, August 26, 1998

The science and technology that will underpin homeland security is not limited to the prevention of terrorism. Discoveries that provide security will also drive progress in other arenas, such as public health and improved communication. Just as the space exploration program of the 1960s truly brought the transistor into home products, the twenty-first century investment in science will not only protect our quality of life but will provide breakthroughs in the diagnosis and treatment of disease.

This *Guide to Homeland Security Careers* recognizes the importance of synergy and builds upon the premise that the future homeland security officer requires a diverse background in order to compete successfully and succeed. It recognizes the interconnection of past careers and gives the reader a practical approach on how to expand or change job paths and to participate in this vital future opportunity. I congratulate the reader for using this outstanding guidebook and wish you success in your future endeavors.

Russell W. Bessette, M.D.

Russell W. Bessette, M.D., is the executive director of the New York State Office of Science, Technology and Academic Research (NYSTAR). He was the director of the Instrument and Devices Clinical Laboratory at the Center of Advanced Technology (CAT) at Buffalo from 1985–1989. He has been a leader in academic research for more than 30 years in the fields of science and technology. Prior to his appointment to NYSTAR, Dr. Bessette rose through the academic ranks and was appointed a clinical professor in the Department of Surgery at the State University of New York at Buffalo's School of Medicine. Dr. Bessette has held numerous leadership roles in organized medicine at the local, state, and national levels. Dr. Bessette served as a member of President George Bush's Transition Team for the National Institutes of Health (NIH). The NIH, which had a budget of $17.8 billion in 2000, is one of the world's foremost medical research centers and the federal focal point for medical research in the United States.

PREFACE

THE HOMELAND SECURITY CHALLENGE: DEFINING THE CAREERS TO PROTECT THE NATION

It is the right kind of people who are willing to be called upon to sacrifice and risk, who will keep the world and this country free.

—Lt. General Vernon Walter, 1917–2002

In the post–September 11, 2001 America, a redefining of agencies and organizations is continuing to evolve. The United States Coast Guard is scrambling to reactivate coastal patrols and port security units. It is establishing a new sea marshal program, launching a deepwater program of new cutters, and recruiting for patrol and intelligence officers.

The U.S. Customs Service and Border Patrol will now be hiring at a record rate. Of course, the biggest change is within the Federal Aviation Administration. New positions of federal air marshal, federal security director, and federal security screener have been instituted.

The preparedness for the fire next time is under way. Will a U.S. Coast Guard unit stop a petroleum tanker from exploding? Will an FBI cyber–task force stop an attack on a data warehouse containing millions of files of critical financial information? Will a CIA or NSA analyst intercept a transmission preventing a dirty bomb attack? Will a CDC scientist develop a protocol to defend against a biological attack? Will an American Red Cross worker help save more victims at a disaster site? How do you fit into the picture?

> "We need a Department of Homeland Security. We've got to defend our homeland, because we have a great navy and a great army and a great marine corps and a great air force. But when it comes to defending America from terrorists, they can respond for us, but here in this country, defending against people like we are dealing with, that is not what we need. We need other formulations."
>
> —Warren Rudman, Former U.S. Senator on CNN's *Larry King Live*, 10/09/01

In 1992, I (Don) wrote a fictional piece called *Glow Worms*. Its premise involved a train carrying nuclear reactor cores cross-country from decommissioned U.S. Navy Trident subs that was hijacked by terrorists. They were seemingly bent on exploding the cargo with a dispersal device in a rail yard of a major American city. What was the twist at the end? It was a planned ruse. The real targets to be exploded were the hundreds of chemical trains across the country loaded with cargo such as hydrocyanic acid, petroleum, and a witches brew of numerous other deadly substances. The terrorists in that fictional world believed that homeland security was a fleeting concept in America—and Americans did not take the threat seriously.

We do now. So, we need to define what these new homeland security jobs and careers are—and who is going to join to defend this great nation. Homeland security will need to be more than adding another cop on the beat or more customs officers on the border. Research scientists are needed at the CDC, cyber-technicians are needed to protect the Web networks, so on and so forth. Various public careers are merging to protect the fabric of American life.

For most Americans, the events of September 11 will never be forgotten. As New Yorkers, the authors of this book (Don, a former member of the Coast Guard and a current law enforcement officer, and Anna, a current law enforcement officer) feel a closeness to the folks on the homeland security front lines.

Frank McCarton, deputy director of the City of New York Office of Emergency Management, met with Don one afternoon at the World Trade Center site. They discussed the terrorist attack and its impact. During this meeting, they watched the families, loved ones, and Americans stopping by to pay their respects to those lost. Frank quietly stated, "We [this country] need to make sure this doesn't happen again." *That* is the key to homeland security.

While reading this book and deciding on a career choice, do something in the meantime. Volunteer. Volunteer for the Red Cross as an emergency responder or, as President Bush has requested, for the U.S. Freedom Corps, such as the Peace Corps, AmeriCorps, Senior Corps, Learn and Serve America, or the newly created Citizen Corps. You can also find local opportunities to volunteer with a service organization or some other related group. The U.S. government has reported the following:

- Of the more than 1 million firefighters in the United States, approximately 750,000 are volunteers.

- More than 155,000 emergency medical technicians are nationally registered.

These are the folks who initially respond and help Americans in their times of need. However, they are not enough. We need more and newer emergency positions, which are waiting to be created. Those who attack the society of the free and proud have failed to realize that regardless of the differences we may have as Americans, we pulled together to protect and serve this great country. Help and volunteer on your path to a homeland security career.

TERRORISM FACTOID

A total of 3,547 persons were killed in international terrorist attacks in 2001, the highest annual death toll from terrorism ever recorded. Ninety percent of the fatalities occurred in the September 11 attacks. In 2000, 409 persons died in terrorist attacks. The number of persons wounded in terrorist attacks in 2001 was 1,080, up from 796 wounded the previous year. Violence in the Middle East and South Asia also accounted for the increase in casualty totals for 2001.

Source: U.S. Department of State

In the years to come, an evolution will occur in many positions ranging from law enforcement officers to medical personnel to transportation workers to engineers as homeland security issues and concerns become incorporated. This guide was prepared to make candidates aware of the real possibilities that exist in the field of homeland security careers.

Donald B. Hutton
Anna Mydlarz
2003

INTRODUCTION

☐ **What Is Homeland Security?**
☐ **How to Use This Book**
☐ **Agency Listings**
☐ **Homeland Security Choices**
☐ **Best Opportunities: A Few Selected Agencies**
☐ **Special Considerations**

WHAT IS HOMELAND SECURITY?

In the months after the September 11, 2001, events, much was discussed about the communication problems between numerous federal agencies that needed information to monitor terrorist activities. The federal government in response to a concentrated effect to fight terrorism was a maze of bureaucratic red tape to say the least. Our intelligence, law enforcement, and military assets were in a state of protocol freeze. Common sense got lost along the way, and worse, a sense of competition arose among various agencies. The chart on the next page shows how complex the matrix of information flow was prior to the realignment of key agencies into the Homeland Security Act.

Homeland security is evolving. Homeland security will mobilize and focus the resources of the federal government, state and local governments, the private sector, and the American people to accomplish its mission to:

- prevent terrorist attacks within the United States,

- reduce America's vulnerability to terrorism, and

- minimize the damage and recover from attacks that do occur.

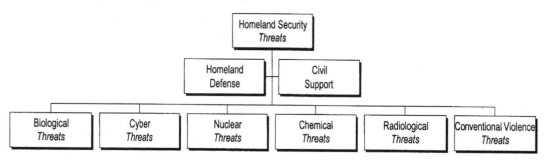

"One has to know that a terrorist can attack at any time and any place using any technique. And it is not physically possible to defend in every place, at every time, against every conceivable method. We just saw the use of aircraft. It could be ships, it could be subways. It could be any number of things. We have been deeply concerned, since I assumed my post with President Bush, about the so-called asymmetrical threats—the problems of the reality that people don't want to contest our armies, navies, or air forces. They know they'll lose. What they can do is use these asymmetrical threats of terrorism, and chemical warfare, and biological warfare, and ballistic missiles, and cruise missiles, and cyber attacks. And we need to continue to work those problems."

Donald Rumsfeld, Interview with Tony Snow of *Fox News*,
September 16, 2001

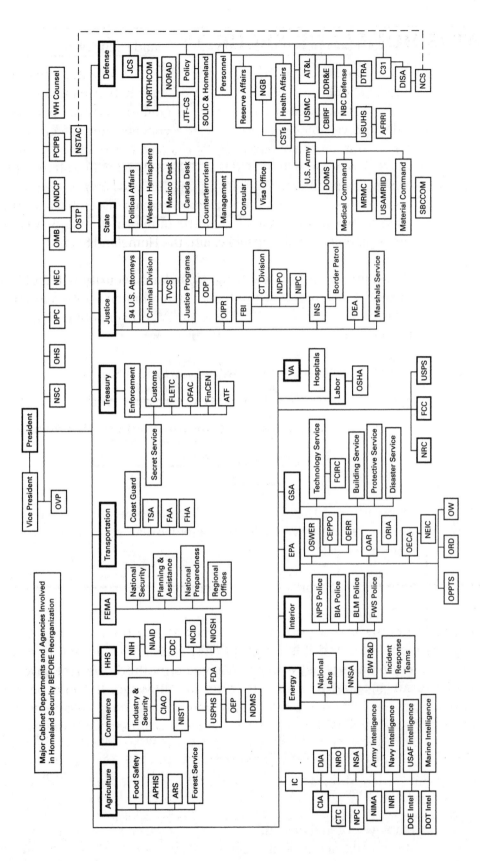

Major Cabinet Departments and Agencies Involved in Homeland Security BEFORE Reorganization

Source: White House Briefing on the Department of Homeland Security, 2002

The key concept is that a chain of homeland security actions or events need to be in place to handle the next attack.

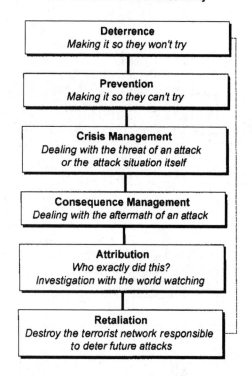

The Chain of Homeland Security

Deterrence
Making it so they won't try

Prevention
Making it so they can't try

Crisis Management
*Dealing with the threat of an attack
or the attack situation itself*

Consequence Management
Dealing with the aftermath of an attack

Attribution
*Who exactly did this?
Investigation with the world watching*

Retaliation
*Destroy the terrorist network responsible
to deter future attacks*

In creation of the U.S. Department of Homeland Security, a single agency would have a clear, efficient organizational structure with four divisions:

- Border and transportation security

- Emergency preparedness and response

- Chemical, biological, radiological, and nuclear countermeasures

- Information analysis and infrastructure protection (threat analysis—intelligence)

The actual Department of Homeland Security will have both oversight and direct command of existing and to-be-established agencies. Employees of the actual Department of Homeland Security would be within these agencies for the most part. Of course, the department will have its own staff, largely at the senior executive levels. In the future, employees could have titles such as homeland security agents. Whether these homeland security agents will be specially designated from agencies under the department remains unclear at this publication.

Department of Homeland Security

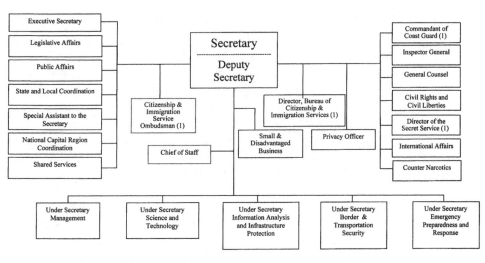

Note (1): *Effective March 1ˢᵗ, 2003*

Department of Homeland Security Headquarters
Nebraska Avenue Center (NAC), Washington, D.C.
www.dhs.gov

Source: White House Briefing on the Department of Homeland Security, 2002

This book will explore the mix of these four career areas. Plus, it will look at the fifth area: U.S. military-related careers. Throughout this book, you will note agencies that have relayed their anticipated positions. The agency planners have a formula of factors, which have given them an anticipated amount of new personnel to be hired for their department or agency. The rationale is to keep the agency at a certain level of workers in order to handle the mission. Planners have to consider the amount of personnel retiring each year and the time needed to test, process, hire, and train new personnel to fill the ranks. Positions in this book for the most part will require extensive background checks, special testing, and a variety of paperwork to be completed by you—the applicant.

By using this book, you can begin the process now, targeting agencies that are looking to hire numerous new personnel over the next four years. Remember that navigating through the hiring maze takes time at some agencies. This time also allows you to enhance your background to be better qualified for consideration.

"These are the times that try men's souls. The summer soldier and the sunshine patriot will, in this crisis, shrink from the service of his country; but he that stands it now, deserves the love and thanks of man and woman."
Thomas Paine, *The American Crisis*, No. 1, December 19, 1776

HOW TO USE THIS BOOK

This book is designed to be a user-friendly guide for homeland security positions. It is segmented into groupings that fit, such as military agencies, municipal agencies, state and federal agencies, and so on. Each listing provides a snapshot of information for the agencies. Many agencies have active recruitment and public information offices that are more than willing to shed some light on their agencies. Whenever possible, a helpful hint or comment has been carefully included. However, the reader is strongly encouraged to conduct follow-up research into the entity he or she is interested in. This book is broken into six sections.

SECTION 1   *Border and Transportation Security Careers*
Border and transportation security agencies are charged with protecting the United States from invaders with evil intent and preventing them from entering our shores. The U.S. Coast Guard, border patrol, and a host of federal law enforcement and transportation agencies will be highlighted.

SECTION 2   *Emergency Preparedness and Response Careers*
Emergency preparedness and response careers deal with disaster assistance. Specialized units of the federal, state, and larger municipalities are listed.

SECTION 3   *Chemical, Biological, Radiological, and Nuclear Countermeasure Careers*
Chemical, biologcal, radiological, and nuclear countermeasures careers need consumer safety officers, special agents, physicians, and scientists. These will work in a host of specialties such as biology, chemistry, and microbiology with agencies like the U.S. Department of Energy, Food and Drug Administration, and the Centers for Disease Control.

SECTION 4   *Information Analysis and Infrastructure Protection Careers (Threat Analysis—Intelligence)*
Information analysis and infrastructure protection careers are involved in defense and intelligence. A variety of careers, such as the CIA, NSA, and others, will be looked at. Source intelligence in threat analysis is critical in preventing the next attack.

SECTION 5   *Military Careers*
General homeland support careers will highlight the military branches. Specific focus will be given to each branch's specialties relating to counterterrorism and homeland protection. Elite units, relating to stealth and covert antiterrorism, are being created in each branch at the time of this writing.

SECTION 6   *Your Application and Background Check*
The application and background checks section provides résumé hints and a sample résumé in the military/federal style. It also shows a sample cover letter. The section gives state and federal application hints with sample announcements, an application for veterans preference, a list of U.S. offices of Personnel Management, locations, phone numbers, Web sites, as well as state civil offices. It describes the federal application process to include the brand-new Optional Form 612 (known as the OF-612) and a federal résumé. Federal pay scales and federal employment information centers (FEIC) are listed.

This section gives you tips on how to handle interviews and background checks. The very nature of interviews and background checks has taken a new, sharper direction. Readers will be instructed about how to conduct themselves and display their backgrounds.

APPENDIX   *Glossaries of Homeland Security, Law Enforcement, and Military Terms*
The glossary includes various words and terms relating to homeland security, law enforcement, the military, and immigration, and will allow the reader to become familiar with meanings for use in examinations and interviews.

AGENCY LISTINGS

Throughout this book, all agencies are highlighted in a special listing format. It displays the key information of the agency so that the reader can determine the agency's profile, the requirements, where to apply, and the actual opportunities that exist.

HOMELAND SECURITY CHOICES

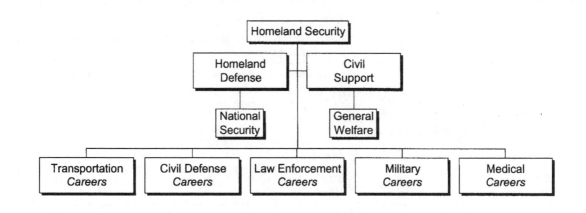

What type of homeland security career do you want? Your interest in seeking a homeland security position has assigned you to a complex investigation that you may find both thrilling and time consuming at the same time. There will be clues on where and how to obtain a homeland security position throughout this book. First, however, you have to make a choice. *What do you want to do?* While you may think you wish to work for only one particular agency, you should consider the options.

For example, years ago, both authors chose to enter law enforcement. However, the decision to become and then actually becoming a law enforcement officer did not happen at the same time. First, they had to gain experience and education so that they could become attractive candidates to the law enforcement administrators who do the actual hiring. You have to decide one thing first: What type of homeland security career do you want? The following table gives you a snapshot of each possible selection.

BORDER AND TRANSPORTATION SECURITY	
Positions	**Basic Mission**
U.S. Coast Guard Member	Law of the sea. Protects U.S. coast from illegal activity; saves lives and maintains air and vessel patrols. Boating safety, drug interdiction, living marine resources, alien migrant interdiction.
Immigration Inspector	Prevents ineligible people from entering the United States.
Border Patrol Agent	Protects the U.S. border from illegal entry from aliens.
FBI Special Agent	Investigates violations of federal criminal law and protects the United States from foreign intelligence activities.
Deputy U.S. Marshal	Provides protection for U.S. courts and judges. Apprehends federal fugitives, and transports federal prisoners.
FAA Air Marshal	Provides protection onboard airplanes as a counterterrorism measure.
Secret Service Agent	Protects the presidents and dignitaries, and investigates threats against them. Investigates counterfeiting crimes.
Bureau of Diplomatic Security Special Agents	Security and law enforcement component of the U.S. Department of State, provides a secure environment for the conduct of U.S. foreign policy on a global scale. Worldwide assignments.
TSA Federal Security Screeners	Inspects and searches air passenger and baggage for safety and security.
TSA Federal Security Directors	Directs and manages federal security programs and policies.

EMERGENCY PREPAREDNESS AND RESPONSE	
Positions	**Basic Mission**
Disaster Coordinator (FEMA & SEMA)	Develops and plans coordinated local, tribal, state, and federal efforts to deal with mass destruction in the United States. Assists in the coordination of long-term recovery programs.
U.S. Capitol Police Officer	Protects life and property; prevents, detects, and investigates criminal acts; and enforces traffic regulations throughout a large complex of congressional buildings and parks.
U.S. Park Police Officer	Prevents and detects criminal activity, conducts investigations, apprehends individuals suspected of committing offenses at designated areas within the National Park Service, primarily Washington, D.C., and provides protective services to some of the most recognizable monuments and memorials in the world.
Federal Police Officer	Maintains protection of employees and the property of designated federal agencies.
U.S. Postal Inspector	Protects postal employees and property. Investigates criminal activity involving the U.S. mail. Conducts investigations of postal crimes.

CHEMICAL, BIOLOGICAL, RADIOLOGICAL, AND NUCLEAR COUNTERMEASURES	
Positions	**Basic Mission**
Engineers	All specialties: chemical, mechanical, electronics, and systems.
Epidemiologists for Bioterrorism Preparedness	Research and establish methods for early recognition of chemical or biological threats.
Intelligence Officer	Gather and analyze intelligence. Covert and overt operations.
Scientists	All specialties: chemical, biological, radiological, nuclear, and physics.
FDA Inspector	Analyze food samples, protect the blood supply, investigate drug tampering, follow up on imported food enforcement inspections, and support domestic inspections.
NIH Scientific and Medical Personnel	Research bioterrorism and emerging infections to enhance our abilities to use vaccines, drugs, and therapies to protect against various infectious agents.

INFORMATION ANALYSIS AND INFRASTRUCTURE PROTECTION: THREAT ANALYSIS—INTELLIGENCE	
Positions	**Basic Mission**
Information Security Specialist	Responsible for recommending and maintaining security measures and policies for accessing critical information.
Counterterrorism Analysts	Monitor and assess the leadership, motivations, plans, and intentions of foreign terrorist groups and their sponsors.
Intelligence Officer	Gather intelligence and conduct analysis. Conduct covert and overt operations.
Cybercrime Technician	Protect U.S.-based cyberspace areas, and investigate criminal activities against the critical Internet infrastructure complex.

MILITARY HOMELAND CAREERS	
Positions	**Basic Mission**
Military Police Officer	Patrol and police assigned military facilities, ships, and bases.
Military Law Enforcement Officer	Administrative position. Supervises and conducts investigations involving military personnel.
Military Intelligence Officer	Gather intelligence and conduct analysis. Conduct covert and overt operations. Counterterrorism activities.

THE BEST OPPORTUNITIES: A FEW SELECTED AGENCIES

Some agencies cannot predict when and if they will be hiring due to budget factors. However, many agencies have received special funding and will be hiring in massive numbers in the near future. Throughout this book, a star (✪) will highlight agencies that have the best opportunity. These numbers are based on current recruitment activity with normal retirements cycle openings and are subject to sudden change due to budget issues. Below are a few selected agencies with outstanding career opportunities:

AGENCY	ANTICIPATED POSITIONS
Federal Bureau of Investigation	○ Over 1,000 special agents
Central Intelligence Agency	○ Over 2,000 various positions
Transportation Security Administration	○ Over 20,000 federal security screeners ○ Over 1,000 federal security supervisors
U.S. Coast Guard	○ Over 4,000 military positions
U.S. Customs Service	○ Over 800 inspectors
U.S. Capitol Police	○ Over 1,000 police officers
U.S. Border Patrol	○ Over 3,000 border patrol agents
Bureau of Diplomatic Security Special Agents	○ Over 700 agents

SPECIAL CONSIDERATIONS

Deciding what position is setting one part of your parameter. However, you should ask yourself several questions before you accept a position with a distant law enforcement agency.

1. *What level of first-hand encounter with terrorists can you handle?*
   Not everyone can confront terrorists face-to-face and deal with them. Doing so may mean taking their lives to stop an act of mass destruction and also putting your life at risk. Elite Delta forces, U.S. Coast Guard sea marshalls, and field agents of the FBI or CIA may find themselves in that very position.

2. *Where do you want to work?*
   Where are you willing to work? Not everyone can just pick up and move. If you have a family, then this must be a family decision. Anyone considering a position in a location they are not familiar with should conduct their own research on the prospective area before accepting the position.

3. *What about travel and reassignments?*
   Military and law enforcement personnel may be transferred several times during their careers throughout the world, which means the possibility of living on military bases until retirement or in remote locations. Unlike municipal and county law enforcement officers who basically work and live within their jurisdiction, federal law enforcement officers may have a position in which they have to conduct extensive travel for their duties. Like military personnel, they are subject to reassignment at various times in their careers.

4. Am I ready for the responsibility?

Being involved in homeland security is more than carrying some type of badge and gun. The duties and responsibilities, for the most part, are a significant burden that the individual must accept and that will affect his or her conduct both on and off duty, 24 hours a day. It is a job that changes people for better or worse. Some positions are going to be very difficult. That is why the decision to pursue a particular position must be well thought out and planned in advance.

Hint

Volunteer. Besides being patriotic, becoming a volunteer is the best way to obtain valuable experience and key contacts. Some established good homeland security organizations include the following:

- The American Red Cross (ARC) has over 1,000 local units that serve communities across the country and touch millions of people every year. ARC offers disaster and emergency relief, teachs lifesaving skills such as CPR and first aid, and collects and distributes half the nation's blood supply.
  http://www.redcross.org/services/volunteer/opportunities/vol.html

- The Civil Air Patrol (CAP) has 60,000 well-trained volunteers in 1,700 communities nationwide. Its members have excellent air/ground observation and communications assets at their disposal. CAP provides aerial reconnaissance, photography and transportation, disaster and damage assessment, and emergency service and operational missions.

- The United States Coast Guard Auxiliary has nearly 33,000 members who assist the Coast Guard in promoting boating safety. The Coast Guard Auxiliary assists the Coast Guard in non–law enforcement programs such as public education, vessel safety checks, safety patrols, and search and rescue.

"Republic. I like the sound of the word. It means people can live free, talk free. Go or come, buy or sell, be drunk or sober, however they choose. Some words give ya a feeling. Republic is one of those words that makes me tight in the throat. The same tightness a man gets when his baby takes his first step, or his first baby shaves, makes his first sound like a man. Some words can give ya a feeling that makes your heart warm. Republic is one of those words."

John Wayne in *The Alamo*

SECTION

BORDER AND TRANSPORTATION SECURITY CAREERS

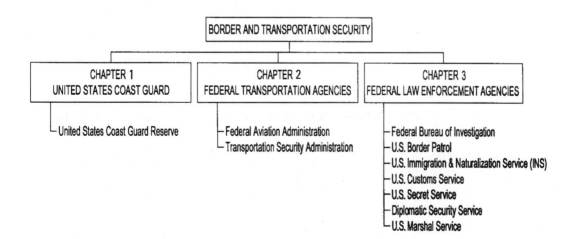

Chapter 1

UNITED STATES COAST GUARD OPPORTUNITIES

```
┌─────────────────────────┐
│ Homeland Security Level: │
│        Frontlines        │
└─────────────────────────┘
        │
        ├─ Port Security
        │
        ├─ Law Enforcement
        │
        ├─ Intelligence
        │
        └─ Sea Marshal's Program
```

UNITED STATES COAST GUARD

This chapter deals exclusively with the U.S. Coast Guard. Although its responsibilities have increased over the years, they always involve protecting the waterways.

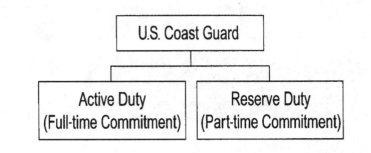

United States Coast Guard
United States Coast Guard Reserve
Civilian Employment
U.S. Coast Guard Recruiting
4200 Wilson Boulevard
Arlington, VA 22203
(800) GET-USCG
http://www.uscg.mil

OVERVIEW

Motto:	*Semper Paratus* (Always Ready)
Recruiting Slogans:	"The Lifesavers," "Jobs That Matter"

The United States Coast Guard, a historically poor cousin of the other military branches in both resources and support, suddenly finds itself in a critical need area of homeland security for the nation. As a side note, Don (one author of this book) served in the Coast Guard Reserve for 16 years in three occupational specialties—boatswain mate, port security, and investigator. All left Don with a sense of pride and accomplishment. Because the focus and responsibilities of the Coast Guard have dramatically changed, this whole chapter is dedicated to just Coast Guard Opportunities.

The Coast Guard has a proud history and good image with the public. A media outlet recently nicknamed the Coast Guard "The Swiss Army Knife of Federal Agencies" due to its wide and complex missions and can-do attitude with limited resources. Most people associate the Coast Guard not only with search and rescue but also with drug and illegal alien interdiction. Established in January 28, 1915, the Coast Guard became a component of the Department of Transportation on

April 1, 1967. The predecessor of the Coast Guard, the Revenue Cutter Service, was established in 1790 as a federal maritime law enforcement agency.

USCG HISTORY FACTOIDS

- In 1812, a "fleet of cutters" is ordered into action as arm of U.S. Navy in the war against the British.
- On April 12, 1861, the cutter *Harriet Lane* fires the first shot in the Civil War across the bow of the *Nashville,* which was ordered to heave to in attempting to enter Charleston Harbor.

Source: USCG History Office

The United States Coast Guard is a service of the armed forces at all times. In time of war or when the president directs, it becomes a part of the Department of Defense and comes under the command of the U.S. Navy. The Coast Guard consists of ships, aircraft, boats, and shore stations that conduct a variety of missions. Although one of the oldest services, it is also the smallest service.

The Coast Guard offers a wide variety of career and educational opportunities. The Coast Guard Reserve offers careers in the same fields as does the active Coast Guard. Additionally, civilian opportunities have increased in recent years.

"The Coast Guard's Deepwater [Program] will award a multiyear contract to replace aging ships and aircraft, and improve communications and information sharing. The whole purpose is to push out our maritime borders, giving us more time to identify threats and more time to respond."

President George W. Bush, June 24, 2002

The $17 billion Deepwater project will bring up to 91 ships, along with 35 fixed-wing aircraft, 34 helicopters, and 76 unmanned aerial vehicles, to the Coast Guard in the next 20 years.

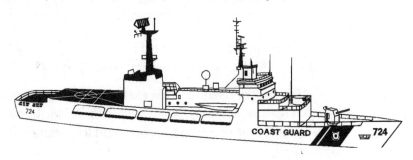

POSITIONS

Port Securityman
(Port Security)

The port security program is largely a reserve specialty; however, it is related to the port safety and security mission. Port security specialists enforce rules and regulations governing the safety and security of ports, vessels, and harbors. Furthermore, they conduct inspection of facilities and investigate pollution of U.S. waters. Civilian candidates can apply for this program directly through Coast Guard recruiting offices.

Special Agent/Investigator
(Office of Intelligence and Law Enforcement)

Coast Guard intelligence utilizes both regular and reserve members to act as internal and external law enforcement officers. Special agents investigate criminal matters including the interdiction of narcotics, and conduct background investigations of personnel. Special agents are primarily enlisted members of the Coast Guard. However, since September 11, that has changed to include civilian employees as well. Intelligence officers are commissioned officers in the Coast Guard. Coast Guard personnel interested in pursuing a career in the Office of Intelligence and Law Enforcement need to contact the district office they are assigned to directly.

Sea Marshal Program

This newly established program will assign USCG personnel as sea marshals. These special marshals will board, inspect, and search ships offshore and monitor the activity of commercial traffic in active shipping lanes. This program will develop in the future into a permanent career.

TERRORISM'S DARK HISTORY

October 7, 1985—Palestinian terrorists hijack the cruise liner *Achille Lauro* in response to the Israeli attack on PLO headquarters in Tunisia. Leon Klinghoffer, an elderly, wheelchair-bound American, is killed and thrown overboard.

Source: U.S. Department of State

MAIN MISSION

Because the U.S. Coast Guard has a larger variety of missions than the other services, it is necessary to provide a brief overview of each.

- *Aids to Navigation:* This establishes and maintains the U.S. aids to navigation system, which includes lights, buoys, day beacons, fog signals, marine radio beacons, and long-range radio navigation aids.

- *Bridge Administration:* This administers the statutes regulating the construction, maintenance, and operation of bridges and causeways across navigable waters.

- *Search and Rescue:* This maintains a system of rescue vessels, aircraft, and communications facilities to carry out its function of saving life and property in and over the high seas and the navigable waters of the United States.

- *Marine Inspection:* This is charged with formulating, administering, and enforcing various safety standards for the design, construction, equipment, and maintenance of commercial vessels.

- *Marine Licensing:* This administers a system for the evaluating and licensing of U.S. merchant marine personnel.

- *Marine Environmental Response:* This is responsible for enforcing the Federal Water Pollution Control Act and various other laws relating to the protection of the marine environment.

- *Waterways Management:* This is responsible for the safe and orderly passage of cargo, people, and vessels on the nation's waterways.

- *Ice Operations:* This operates the nation's ice-breaking vessels (icebreakers and ice-capable cutters), supported by aircraft, for ice reconnaissance, to facilitate maritime transportation, and to aid in the prevention of flooding in domestic waters.

- *Deepwater Ports:* This administers a licensing and regulatory program governing the construction, ownership (international aspects), and operation of deepwater ports on the high seas to transfer oil from tankers to shore.

- *Boating Safety:* This develops and directs a national boating safety program aimed at making the operation of small craft in U.S. waters both pleasurable and safe.

USCG HISTORY FACTOIDS

- April 12, 1902: Commissioned officers of the Revenue Cutter Service are granted the same pay and allowances "except forage" as are officers of corresponding rank in the army.
- January 28, 1915: The Coast Guard is formed by consolidating the Life-Saving Service and the Revenue Cutter Service.
- April 6, 1917: The Coast Guard becomes part of the navy with 200 officers, 5,000 enlisted personnel, and 15 cutters.
- December 1919: The Coast Guard begins a "war" against rum runners during Prohibition.

Source: USCG History Office

Special note: The Coast Guard recruits 8,000 new personnel each year.

HOMELAND
SECURITY
MISSION

Prevention
Deterrence
Crisis Management
Consequence Management

- *Port Safety and Security:* This is authorized to enforce rules and regulations governing the safety and security of ports and anchorages and the movement of vessels and prevention of pollution in U.S. waters.

- *Maritime Law Enforcement:* As the primary maritime law enforcement agency for the United State, the Coast Guard enforces or assists in the enforcement of applicable federal laws and treaties and other international agreements on the high seas and waters subject to the jurisdiction of the United States.

- *Military Readiness:* Coastal and harbor defense, including port security, are the most important military tasks assigned to the Coast Guard in times of national crisis.

A DAY IN THE U.S. COAST GUARD

Each day, the 35,000-plus active-duty, 8,000 reservists, and 32,000 auxiliary Coast Guard members provide services in over 3.4 million square miles of exclusive economic zones.

- Conduct 109 search and rescue cases.
- Save 10 lives.
- Assist 192 people in distress.
- Protect $2,791,841 in property.
- Pilot small boats for 396 sorties/missions.
- Fly aircraft in 164 missions, logging 324 hours, of which 19 hours are flown off of patrolling cutters.
- Law enforcement teams board 144 vessels.
- Seize 169 pounds of marijuana and 306 pounds of cocaine worth $9,589,000.
- Seize 1 drug-smuggling vessel every five days.
- Cutter and small boat crews interdict and rescue 14 illegal immigrants. ↓

- Marine safety personnel open eight new cases for marine violation of federal statutes.

- Process 238 seaman licenses and documents.

- Marine inspectors board 100 large vessels for port safety checks.

- Vessel examiners conduct 20 commercial fishing vessel safety exams and issue 11 fishing vessel compliance decals.

- Pollution investigators respond to 20 oil or hazardous chemical spills totaling 2,800 gallons.

- Investigate six vessel casualties involving collisions, allusions, or groundings.

- Buoy tenders and aids to navigational teams service 135 aids to navigation.

- Vessel traffic service controllers assist 2,509 commercial ships entering and leaving U.S. ports.

- Icebreakers and buoy tenders assist 196,938 tons of shipping daily during the Great Lakes ice season.

- International ice patrol sorties provide ice safety information to facilitate the 163,238 tons of shipping during the North Atlantic ice season.

- Auxiliary members conduct 377 vessel safety checks and teach boating safety courses to 550 boaters.

Source: U.S. Coast Guard

PROFILE OF USCG PERSONNEL

"There is a certain enthusiasm in liberty, that makes human nature rise above itself, in acts of bravery and heroism."

Alexander Hamilton, 1775; Forefather of the U.S. Cutter Revenue Service

OPPORTUNITIES FOR ENLISTED PERSONNEL

Enlisted Entrance Overview

Age: 17 to 28 years

Enlistments: 2 to 6 years (Regular Active Duty)

Recruit (Basic or Boot Camp) Training

Duration: 8 Weeks

Location: Cape May, N.J.

Instruction: Study seamanship, ordnance, damage control, Coast Guard history, and military and technical subjects.

Enlisted Promotion Path

Promotions occur through a series of written and practical exams that test your proficiency in your specialty. These are considered along with your time in each grade. It is possible to advance from seaman recruit to chief petty officer within 14 years. The stages are:

E1   *Recruit:* During (basic or boot camp) training.

E2   *Seaman* or *fireman apprentice:* Upon completion of basic training.

E3   *Seaman* or *fireman:* Possible after 6 months of active duty service, and with a commander's recommendation.

E4   *Petty officer third class:* Combination of active duty service, at least 6 months' time in grade, and a commander's recommendation.

E5–E6   *Petty officer second class* to *petty officer first class:* Possible after a test against your peers in job skill, and certain promotion criteria.

E7–E9   *Chief petty officer* and above must meet the criteria of a selection board.

CRITICAL NEED: ENLISTED CAREER FIELDS

- Operations Specialist (OS)
- Port Security (PS)
- Investigator (IV)
- Machinery Technicians (MK)
- Boatswain Mates (BM)

GENERAL ENLISTED CAREER FIELDS
Rates/Military Occupational Specialties

Administrative
- [ ] Storekeeper (SK)
- [ ] Yeoman (YN)

Aviation
- [ ] Aviation Electrician's Mate (AE)
- [ ] Aviation Electronics Technician (AT)
- [ ] Aviation Machinist Mate (AD)
- [ ] Aviation Structural Mechanic (AM)
- [ ] Aviation Survivalman (ASM)

Communications and Computer
- [ ] Telecommunications Specialist (TC)
- [ ] Formally Radioman (RM)
- [ ] Telephone Technician (TT)

Electrician and Electronics
- [ ] Electrician's Mate (EM)
- [ ] Electronics Technician (ET)

Engineering and Technical
- [ ] Radarman (RD)
- [ ] Damage Controlman (DC)

Mechanic
- [ ] Machinery Technician (MK)

Media and Public Affairs
- [ ] Public Affairs Specialist (PA)

Medical
- [ ] Health Services Technician (HS)

Ordnance
- [ ] Fire Control Technician (FT)
- [ ] Gunner's Mate (GM)

Scientific
- [ ] Marine Science Technician (MST)

Service (Cook)
- [ ] Subsistence Specialist (SS)

Ship and Boat Operations
- [ ] Boatswain Mate (BM)
- [ ] Quartermaster (QM)

Reservist-Only Ratings
- [ ] Port Securityman (PS)
- [ ] Data Processing Technician (DP)
- [ ] Investigator (IV)

FEATURED POSITION:

Warrant Officer (W1 to W3):

The rank of warrant officers in the Coast Guard is restricted to members who have demonstrated a potential for greater responsibility than normally expected of petty officers. This is not an entry-level position. The warrant officer is assigned responsibilities and has authority commensurate with his or her rank, including assignments as commanding officer and engineering officer aboard many types of units. Warrant officer examples include CWO3-Chief Warrant Officer Boatswain Mate.

USCG HISTORY FACTOIDS

- June 27, 1940: The president invokes the Espionage Act of 1917. The Coast Guard was given the port security mission.
- June 29, 1944: The Coast Guard cutter *Cobb* lands a helicopter on its deck. The Coast Guard was given the responsibility to develop helicopter operations as ASW (anti-submarine warfare) platform and search and rescue in 1942.
- January 1, 1946: The Coast Guard is again made a part of the Treasury Department.

Source: USCG History Office

OPPORTUNITIES FOR OFFICERS

STANDARD OFFICER COMMIS- SIONING PROGRAMS

U.S. Coast Guard Academy

○ Largest source of U.S. Coast Guard officers

The four-year academic program leads to a bachelor of science degree in a variety of majors. Upon graduation, the cadet is commissioned as an ensign in the Coast Guard.

U.S. Naval Academy Preparatory School

The U.S. Naval Academy Preparatory School (NAPS) accepts qualified civilian applicants and applicants from the regular and reserve components of the U.S. Navy, Marine Corps, and Coast Guard.

Officer Candidate School

Officer Candidate School (OCS) is a rigorous 17-week course of instruction that prepares candidates to serve effectively as officers in the United States Coast Guard. Candidates must have already earned a bachelor's degree and meet specific age and medical standards. Upon graduation, students are commissioned as ensigns in the United States Coast Guard.

Direct Commissions

There are several direct commissioning programs in the Coast Guard. There are programs for previously trained military officers, aviators, flight officers, lawyers, maritime academy graduates, engineers, and other critically needed specialists.

CRITICAL NEED: OFFICER CAREERS FIELDS

- Engineering
- Intelligence and Law Enforcement
- Marine Science
- Pilots

GENERAL OFFICER CAREER FIELDS
Military Occupational Specialties

Administration
- [ ] Personnel
- [ ] Communications
- [ ] Computers
- [ ] Finance and Accounting
- [ ] Instructor

Aviation
- [ ] Aircraft Pilots
- [ ] Helicopter Pilots
- [ ] Aviation Engineering
- [ ] Navigators

Combat
- [ ] Defense Operations

Engineering, Science, and Technical
- [ ] Chemists
- [ ] Civil Engineering
- [ ] Nuclear Engineering
- [ ] Naval Engineering
- [ ] Industrial Manager
- [ ] Ocean Engineering
- [ ] Environmental Protection
- [ ] Meteorologist

Human Services
- [ ] Religious

Intelligence
- [ ] Intelligence Services
- [ ] Attaché

Law Enforcement
- [ ] Maritime Law Enforcement
- [ ] Boating Safety
- [ ] Port Security and Safety
- [ ] Drug Interdiction

Legal
- [ ] Lawyer
- [ ] Judge

Marine Services
- [ ] Vessel Inspection
- [ ] Marine Inspection
- [ ] Marine Licensing

Media and Public Affairs
- [ ] Public Information

Medical
(U.S. Public Health Service Officers)
- [ ] Dental Officer
- [ ] Pharmacist
- [ ] Physician
- [ ] Registered Nurse
- [ ] Surgeon
- [ ] Therapist

Ship Operations
- [ ] Ship Officer
- [ ] Search and Rescue

USCG HISTORY FACTOIDS

- July 24, 1965: The navy requests Coast Guard cutters for Vietnam service. The Coast Guard provides cutters, aids to navigation and port security, and also supervises the handling of dangerous cargoes in Vietnam.
- April 1, 1967: The Coast Guard, after 177 years in the Treasury Department, is transferred to the newly formed Department of Transportation.
- August 1969: The icebreaker *Northwind* escorts the supertanker *Manhattan* across the top of North America. Very few vessels had ever made this northwest passage.
- July 1976: Women are admitted into the Coast Guard Academy, the first military academy to do this.

Source: USCG History Office

U.S. COAST GUARD RESERVE
(800) GET-USCG

A Special Opportunity

U.S. Coast Guard Reserve Skills Program

Allows first-time military enlistees with specialized professional skills to receive a petty officer rating (age 26–35 years). Prior service personnel up to age 42, who were E4 and above, may be able to enlist/reenlist.

MAJOR COAST GUARD COMMANDS

United States Coast Guard
Organization

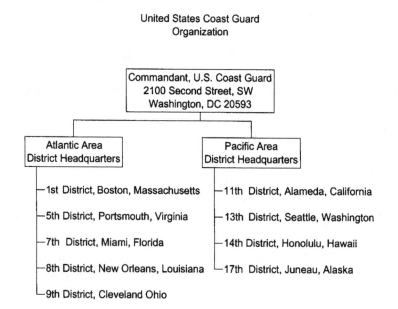

Commandant, U.S. Coast Guard
2100 Second Street, SW
Washington, DC 20593

Atlantic Area
District Headquarters

Pacific Area
District Headquarters

- 1st District, Boston, Massachusetts
- 5th District, Portsmouth, Virginia
- 7th District, Miami, Florida
- 8th District, New Orleans, Louisiana
- 9th District, Cleveland Ohio

- 11th District, Alameda, California
- 13th District, Seattle, Washington
- 14th District, Honolulu, Hawaii
- 17th District, Juneau, Alaska

Ships and Stations of the Coast Guard

Coast Guard Large Vessels: 242
Coast Guard Shore Stations: 1,234

Typical Shore Stations/Units

Tactical Law Enforcement Units
Sea Marshal Units
Aids to Navigation Teams
Air Stations
Bases/Support Centers
Electronic Shops
Small Boat Stations
Group Offices
Light Stations
LORAN (long-range aid to navigation) C Stations
Marine Safety Offices
Marine Inspection Offices
Communications Stations
Reserve Port Security Units
Vessel Traffic Services

INVENTORY OF AIRCRAFT, BOATS, AND SHIPS

OVERVIEW   The Coast Guard operates a variety of cutters for ocean missions and small boats for costal patrol and search and rescue. C-130 planes and helicopters assist in the missions of law enforcement, information gathering, and search and rescue. The polar icebreakers conduct scientific missions in the Arctic and Antarctic and perform ice-breaking duties for shipping.

Cutters

(Any Coast Guard vessel 65 feet in length or greater)

399-foot Polar Class Icebreaker
378-foot High-Endurance Cutter
295-foot Training Barque Eagle (Academy)
290-foot Inland Icebreaker
270-foot Medium Endurance Cutter
225-foot Seagoing Buoy Tender
210-foot Medium Endurance Cutter
180-foot Seagoing Buoy Tender
175-foot Coastal Buoy Tender
160-foot Inland Construction Tender
157-foot Coastal Buoy Tender
140-foot Icebreaking Tug
133-foot Coastal Buoy Tender
115-foot River Buoy Tender
110-foot Patrol Boat
100-foot Inland Buoy Tender
100-foot Inland Construction Tender
87-foot Coastal Patrol Boat
75-foot River Buoy Tender
65-foot River Buoy Tender
65-foot Inland Buoy Tender
65-foot Small Harbor Tug

SPECIAL CUTTER PROFILE: 378-FOOT HIGH-ENDURANCE CUTTER

Length:	378 feet
Beam:	43 feet
Displacement:	3,250 tons
Power Plant:	Two diesel engines/two gas turbine engines
Maximum Range:	14,000 miles
Maximum Speed:	29 knots
Primary Missions:	Law enforcement, defense, search and rescue
Typical Crew:	167 personnel (19 officers, 148 enlisted)

Planes

C-130	Hercules
HU-25	Falcon

Helicopters

H-60	Jayhawk
HH-65	Dolphin

Boats

(Sizes range from 64 feet in length down to 12 feet)

  52-foot Motor Lifeboat
  47-foot Motor Lifeboat
  44-foot Motor Lifeboat
  41-foot Utility Boat
  38-foot Deployable Pursuit Boat
  21-foot to 64-foot Aids to Navigation Boats
  Port Security Unit (PSU)
  Transportable Port Security Boat (TPSB)
  Rigid Inflatable Boat

SPECIAL BOAT PROFILE: TRANSPORTABLE PORT SECURITY BOAT (TPSB)

Length:	22 feet, 3 inches
Beam:	7 feet, 6 inches
Engines:	Twin 150-hp outboards
Speed:	40+ knots
Crew:	3–4 (including Coxswain)

USCG HISTORY FACTOIDS

- April 1980: The Cuban exodus of 1980 begins, the greatest Coast Guard rescue operation since WWII. Over 100,000 people are assisted by the Coast Guard.
- August 17, 1990: The Secretary of Transportation and commandant of the Coast Guard commit Coast Guard boarding teams to Operation Desert Shield.

Source: USCG History Office

Chapter 2

TRANSPORTATION AGENCY OPPORTUNITIES

☐ **Opportunities Within U.S. Transportation Agencies**

— **Federal Aviation Administration (FAA) Careers**

— **Transportation Security Administration (TSA) Careers**

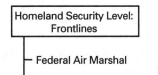

Homeland Security Level:
Frontlines

— Federal Air Marshal

— Federal Security Screener

— Federal Security Supervisor/Lead

— Federal Security Director/Assistant

OPPORTUNITIES WITHIN U.S. TRANSPORTATION AGENCIES

Federal transportation agencies are subdivided into two regulatory divisions: the Federal Aviation Administration (FAA) and the Transportation Security Administration (TSA). Both of these departments perform vital functions in the maintenance of homeland security.

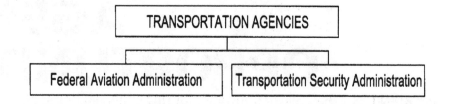

Federal Aviation Administration (FAA) Careers

Federal Aviation Administration
Human Resource Management Division
800 Independence Ave., S.W.
Washington, DC 20591
(405) 954-0250
www.jobs.faa.gov

POSITIONS   ***Civil Aviation Security Specialist*** $36,400 to $83,900
(Federal Air Marshal)

MAIN MISSION   Federal air marshals (FAMs) respond to criminal incidents aboard U.S. air carriers as well as other in-flight emergencies. FAMs are authorized to carry firearms and make arrests while preserving the safety of the aircraft, crew, and passengers. Regular and extended travel, both foreign and domestic, for several weeks at a time is required. Federal air marshal bases will be assigned throughout the country at major metropolitan areas.

HOMELAND SECURITY MISSION
Prevention
Deterrence
Crisis Management
Consequence Management

PROFILE OF AGENCY	Personnel:	Unknown (Currently staffing up)
REQUIREMENTS	Age:	Under 40 years of age
	Education:	Bachelor's degree or 3 years experience
	Vision:	20/20 corrected

Background Investigation

Top secret security clearance

Complete the federal air marshal training program conducted by the Federal Law Enforcement Training Center

OPPORTUNITIES Over 500 nationwide (*during staffing-up period)

COMMENTS You must like to fly, since the whole point of the position is to provide safety and security in-flight. After September 11, the call to reinstate the air marshal program was loud and clear. However, after the initial emergency hiring, the series will be closed and hiring will occur in a natural cycle of annual recruitment to fill positions vacated by retirements and turnover.

Air marshals must be willing to accept assignments anywhere in the United States, including possibly foreign assignments. The FAA/TSA has a rigorous application process. Candidates must complete a series of written tests and a formal interview. Candidates are rated on education/language ability and experience.

TERRORISM'S DARK HISTORY

June 14, 1985: A Trans World Airlines (TWA) flight was hijacked en route to Rome from Athens by two Lebanese Hizballah terrorists and forced to fly to Beirut. The eight crew members and 145 passengers were held for 17 days, during which one American hostage, U.S. Navy diver Robert Dean Stethem, was murdered. After being flown twice to Algiers, the aircraft was returned to Beirut after Israel released 435 Lebanese and Palestinian prisoners.

Source: U.S. Department of State

INTERNSHIP   No
PROGRAM

STUDENT   Unknown
PROGRAMS

WHERE TO   Applicants must complete the online application at **www.jobs.faa.gov**
APPLY   Contact Information: Aviation Careers Division (405) 954-4657

FAA Personnel Offices

Alaskan Region (Alaska)
Human Resource Management Division
Attn: AAL-14
222 West 7th Ave., #14
Anchorage, AK 99513-7587
(907) 271-5747

Western Pacific Region (California,
Nevada, Arizona, and the Pacific)
Human Resource Management Division
Attn: AWP-10
P.O. Box 92007
Los Angeles, CA 90009
(310) 725-7801 Voice
(310) 725-7848 TDD

Washington, DC Area
Human Resource Management Division
Attn: AHR-19
800 Independence Ave., S.W.
Washington, DC 20591
(202) 267-8007

Southern Region (Kentucky, Tennessee,
North Carolina, South Carolina,
Mississippi, Alabama, Georgia, and
Florida)
Human Resource Division, Attn: ASO-14
P.O. Box 20636
Atlanta, GA 30320
(404) 305-5330

Great Lakes Region (North Dakota,
South Dakota, Minnesota, Wisconsin,
Michigan, Illinois, Indiana, and Ohio)
Human Resource Management Division
Attn: AGL-18
2300 E. Devon Ave.
Des Plaines, IL 60018
(847) 294-7731

New England Region (Maine, New
Hampshire, Vermont, Massachusetts,
Connecticut, Rhode Island)
Human Resource Management Division
Attn: ANE-14
12 New England Executive Park
Burlington, MA 01803
(781) 238-7280 or
(781) 238-7254

Central Region (Missouri, Kansas, Iowa,
and Nebraska)
Human Resource Management Division
ACE-10
901 Locust St., Room 402
Kansas City, MO 64106
(816) 329-2650

FAA Technical Center (in Atlantic City, New Jersey)
Human Resource Management Branch
Attn: ACT-110
Atlantic City International Airport, NJ 08405
(609) 485-6620

Eastern Region (New York, Pennsylvania, West Virginia, Maryland, New Jersey, Delaware, and Virginia)
Human Resource Division, Attn: AEA-10
Federal Aviation Administration
One Aviation Plaza
Jamaica, NY 11434
(718) 553-3157 (air traffic jobs)
(718) 553-3137 (other jobs)

Aeronautical Center (Oklahoma City)
Personnel Operations Division
Attn: AMH-200
P.O. Box 25082
Oklahoma City, OK 73125
(405) 954-4508

Aviation Careers
Attn: AMH-300
P.O. Box 26650
Oklahoma City, OK 73126-4934
(405) 954-4657

Southwest Region (Texas, Arkansas, Louisiana, New Mexico, and Oklahoma)
Human Resource Management Division
Attn: ASW-10
Ft. Worth, TX 76193
(817) 222-5855 (recorded job information)
or
(817) 222-5850

Northwest Mountain Region (Washington, Oregon, Idaho, Wyoming, Colorado, Utah, and Montana)
Human Resource Division, Attn: ANM-14
1601 Lind Ave. S.W.
Renton, WA 98055-4056
(425) 227-2014

Major Airports (Base Locations)

Alaska
Ted Stevens Anchorage International Airport (ANC)

Arizona
Phoenix Sky Harbor International Airport (PHX)

California
Metropolitan Oakland International Airport (OAK)
Ontario International Airport (ONT)
Los Angeles International Airport (LAX)
Sacramento International Airport (SMF)
San Diego International Airport (SAN)

San Francisco International Airport (SFO)
John Wayne Airport (Orange County) (SNA)
San Jose International Airport (SJC)

Colorado
Denver International Airport (DEN)

Connecticut
Bradley International Airport (Hartford) (BDL)

Florida
Ft. Lauderdale-Hollywood International Airport (FLL)
Jacksonville International Airport (JAX)

Miami International Airport (MIA)
Orlando International Airport (MCO)
Tampa International Airport (TPA)
West Palm Beach International Airport
(PBI)

Georgia
Hartsfield Atlanta International Airport
(ATL)

Hawaii
Honolulu International Airport (HNL)

Illinois
Chicago Midway Airport (MDW)
Chicago O'Hare International Airport
(ORD)

Indiana
Indianapolis International Airport
(IND)

Louisiana
New Orleans International Airport (MSY)

Massachusetts
Logan International Airport (Boston)
(BOS)

Maryland
Baltimore-Washington International
Airport (BWI)

Michigan
Detroit Metro Wayne County Airport
(DTW)

Minnesota
Minneapolis-St. Paul International
Airport (MSP)

Missouri
Kansas City International Airport (MCI)
Lambert St. Louis International Airport
(STL)

North Carolina
Raleigh-Durham International Airport
(RDU)

New Jersey
Newark Liberty International Airport
(EWR)

Nevada
McCarran International Airport
(Las Vegas) (LAS)

New York
John F. Kennedy International Airport
(JFK)
LaGuardia Airport (LGA)

Ohio
Cleveland Hopkins International Airport
(CLE)
Port Columbus International Airport
(CMH)

Oregon
Portland International Airport (PDX)

Pennsylvania
Philadelphia International Airport
(PHL)
Pittsburgh International Airport (PIT)

Puerto Rico
Luis Muñoz Marín International Airport
(San Juan) (SJU)

Tennessee
Nashville International Airport (BNA)

Texas
Austin-Bergstrom International Airport
(AUS)
Dallas/Ft. Worth International Airport
(DFW)
George Bush Intercontinental Airport
(Houston) (IAH)

William P. Hobby Airport (Houston)
(HOU)
San Antonio International Airport
(SAT)

Utah
Salt Lake City International Airport
(SLC)

Virginia
Ronald Reagan Washington National
Airport (DCA)
Washington-Dulles International Airport
(IAD)

Washington
Seattle-Tacoma International Airport (SEA)

"Our flag means more than association and reward. It is the symbol of our national unity, our national endeavor, our national aspiration. It tells you of the struggle for independence, of union preserved, of liberty and union one and inseparable, of the sacrifice of brave men and women to whom the ideals and honors of this nation have been dearer than life. So many meanings from a single symbol—*e pluribus unum.*"

Admiral James Loy—former commandant of the U.S. Coast Guard, now the new Transportation Security Agency Administrator, 2002

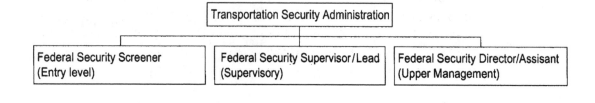

```
                    ┌─────────────────────────────────────────┐
                    │   Transportation Security Administration │
                    └─────────────────────────────────────────┘
        ┌────────────────────────┼────────────────────────────┐
┌──────────────────────┐ ┌──────────────────────────┐ ┌──────────────────────────┐
│ Federal Security      │ │ Federal Security         │ │ Federal Security         │
│ Screener              │ │ Supervisor/Lead          │ │ Director/Assisant        │
│ (Entry level)         │ │ (Supervisory)            │ │ (Upper Management)       │
└──────────────────────┘ └──────────────────────────┘ └──────────────────────────┘
```

Transportation Security Administration (TSA) Careers —

Transportation Security Administration
400 Seventh Street Southwest
Washington, DC 20590
(888) 328-6172
www.tsa.dot.gov

**MAIN
MISSION**

✪ *A great entry-level opportunity for a potential federal employee is with the new federal security screeners series.*

The TSA is responsible for security relating to civil aviation, maritime situations, and all other modes of transportation, including transportation facilities. It is the lead agency for security at airports, at ports, and on the nation's railroads, highways, and public transit systems. The TSA is responsible for federal security screening operations for passenger air transportation and intelligence information related to transportation security; managing and carrying out program and regulatory activities; and discovering, preventing, and dealing with threats to transportation security.

POSITIONS

Federal Security Screener (Entry Level) $23,600 to $35,400

These entry-level screeners identify dangerous or deadly objects in baggage, in cargo, and on passengers. They prevent those objects from being transported onto the aircraft. They may use various types of electronic detection and imaging machines for this purpose, such as X-ray machines, trace detection machines, walk-through metal detectors, and handheld metal detectors. They also perform physical searches of baggage or cargo and pat-down searches of airline passengers.

Federal Security Supervisor/Lead (Supervisory)
$36,400–$56,400

Individuals in this supervisory position manage the performance and training of personnel who provide the frontline security and protection of air travelers, airplanes, and airports. They identify dangerous or deadly objects in baggage, cargo, and on passengers, and they prevent those objects from being transported onto the aircraft. They perform the full range of supervisory duties, including approving leave, scheduling work, and managing performance.

Federal Security Director/Assistant (Upper Management)
$104,800 to $150,000

These upper-management employees have direct responsibility and oversight for passenger, baggage, and air cargo security screening and for all TSA personnel. They coordinate with airport and airline management and also other federal, state, and local government and law enforcement organizations. They implement security technology and manage all TSA resources associated with the airport, including personnel, funds, equipment, and information. These employees are responsible for crisis management, data and communications network protection, and airport security risk assessments. They have responsibility for the security and screening standards for airport employees and passengers as well as employee security awareness training. They also supervise federal law enforcement activity.

HOMELAND SECURITY MISSION

Prevention
Deterrence
Crisis Management
Consequence Management

TERRORISM'S DARK HISTORY

"The brothers, who conducted the operation, all they knew was that they have a martyrdom operation and we asked each of them to go to America but they didn't know anything about the operation, not even one letter. But they were trained and we did not reveal the operation to them until they are there and just before they boarded the planes . . . ."

Osama bin Laden, December 13, 2001—transcript of video tape

PROFILE OF AGENCY

Personnel: 50,000+

REQUIREMENTS   **Federal Security Screener   (Entry Level)**
High school diploma, GED, or equivalent.

Federal Security Supervisor/Lead   (Supervisory)
High school diploma, GED, or equivalent or at least one year of full-time work experience in security work, aviation screener work, or

X-ray technician work. Specialized experience in identifying dangerous or deadly objects in baggage, cargo, or on passengers is necessary.

Federal Security Director/Assisant   (Upper Management)
Advanced degree and management training. Need extensive field and executive experience in security and crisis prevention positions. Experience in at least one of the following areas is required for consideration: law enforcement, operational field intelligence, federal protective services, and aviation security. Field experience in professional asset protection, risk detection and classification, risk avoidance, and event recovery is needed. Senior-level experience in management of highly measured and complex field operations is required.

All positions require background investigations as well as drug and alcohol testing. Some require top-secret clearance.

"Are you guys ready? Let's roll. . . ."
> Todd Beamer, September 11, 2001 airline
> passenger, victim, and American hero

OPPORTUNITIES

Federal Security Screener	Over 20,000
Federal Security Supervisor/Lead	Over 1,000
Federal Security Director/Assistant	Over 100

COMMENTS   After the initial emergency hiring, additional hiring will occur in a natural cycle of annual recruitment to fill retirements and turnover. Candidates must complete a series of written tests and a formal interview. Candidates are rated on education, ability, and experience.

INTERNSHIP PROGRAM   Yes

STUDENT PROGRAMS   Unknown

WHERE TO APPLY   Call (888) 328-6172 or apply online at **www.tsa.dot.gov** or directly at any of the following airports.

Major U.S. Airport Locations

Alaska
Ted Stevens Anchorage International
Airport (ANC)

Arizona
Phoenix Sky Harbor International
Airport (PHX)

California
Metropolitan Oakland International
Airport (OAK)
Ontario International Airport (ONT)
Los Angeles International Airport (LAX)
Sacramento International Airport (SMF)
San Diego International Airport (SAN)
San Francisco International Airport (SFO)
John Wayne Airport (Orange County)
(SNA)
San Jose International Airport (SJC)

Colorado
Denver International Airport (DEN)

Connecticut
Bradley International Airport (Hartford)
(BDL)

Florida
Ft. Lauderdale-Hollywood International
Airport (FLL)
Jacksonville International Airport (JAX)
Miami International Airport (MIA)
Orlando International Airport (MCO)
Tampa International Airport (TPA)
West Palm Beach International Airport
(PBI)

Georgia
Hartsfield Atlanta International Airport
(ATL)

Hawaii
Honolulu International Airport (HNL)

Illinois
Chicago Midway Airport (MDW)
Chicago O'Hare International Airport
(ORD)

Indiana
Indianapolis International Airport (IND)

Louisiana
New Orleans International Airport (MSY)

Massachusetts
Logan International Airport (Boston)
(BOS)

Maryland
Baltimore-Washington International
Airport (BWI)

Michigan
Detroit Metro Wayne County Airport
(DTW)

Minnesota
Minneapolis-St. Paul International
Airport (MSP)

Missouri
Kansas City International Airport (MCI)
Lambert St. Louis International Airport
(STL)

North Carolina
Raleigh-Durham International Airport
(RDU)

New Jersey
Newark Liberty International Airport
(EWR)

Nevada
McCarran International Airport
(Las Vegas) (LAS)

New York
John F. Kennedy International Airport
  (JFK)
LaGuardia Airport (LGA)

Ohio
Cleveland Hopkins International Airport
  (CLE)
Port Columbus International Airport
  (CMH)

Oregon
Portland International Airport (PDX)

Pennsylvania
Philadelphia International Airport (PHL)
Pittsburgh International Airport (PIT)

Puerto Rico
Luis Muñoz Marín International Airport
  (San Juan) (SJU)

Tennessee
Nashville International Airport (BNA)

Texas
Austin-Bergstrom International Airport
  (AUS)
Dallas/Ft. Worth International Airport
  (DFW)
George Bush Intercontinental Airport
  (Houston) (IAH)
William P. Hobby Airport (Houston)
  (HOU)
San Antonio International Airport (SAT)

Utah
Salt Lake City International Airport
  (SLC)

Virginia
Ronald Reagan Washington National
  Airport (DCA)
Washington-Dulles International Airport
  (IAD)

Washington
Seattle-Tacoma International Airport
  (SEA)

"Sure I wave the American flag. Do you know a better flag to wave? Sure I love my country with all her faults. I'm not ashamed of that, never have been, never will be. . . ."

". . . The total divisiveness that has burdened many other nations hasn't caught on here. We have our disagreements, but let some other country step on our tail and they'll find out how quickly Americans become united."

John Wayne, *America, Why I Love Her*

Chapter 3

HOMELAND SECURITY FEDERAL LAW ENFORCEMENT OPPORTUNITIES

☐ **U.S. Department of Homeland Security/Department of Justice Opportunities**

☐ **U.S. Department of Homeland Security/Department of Treasury Opportunities**

☐ **U.S. Department of State Opportunities**

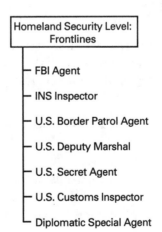

Homeland Security Level: Frontlines
- FBI Agent
- INS Inspector
- U.S. Border Patrol Agent
- U.S. Deputy Marshal
- U.S. Secret Agent
- U.S. Customs Inspector
- Diplomatic Special Agent

U.S. DEPARTMENT OF HOMELAND SECURITY/
DEPARTMENT OF JUSTICE OPPORTUNITIES

*Important Update Information:

On March 1, 2003, services provided by the Immigration and Naturalization Service (INS), U.S. Border Patrol, and U.S. Customs Service were transitioned into the Department of Homeland Security (D.H.S.), under various bureaus.

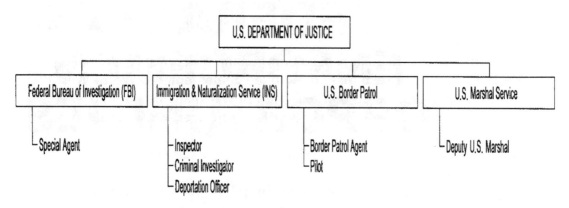

Federal Bureau of Investigation (FBI) Careers

Federal Bureau of Investigation
Headquarters
Ninth Street and
Pennsylvania Avenue, N.W.
Washington, DC 20535
(202) 324-3000
www.fbi.gov

POSITION	***Special Agent GS-10***	$37,939–$49,324

MAIN MISSION   The FBI functions only within the United States. It investigates civil rights and applicant matters with additional national priority given to organized crime/drugs, counterterrorism, foreign counterintelligence, violent crimes, and white-collar crime. The FBI is a unique institution in the federal government in that it is responsible for sensitive foreign counterintelligence matters, important civil investigations, background inquiries on persons nominated for high public office, and criminal investigations that may involve prominent figures in both the public and private sectors.

HOMELAND
SECURITY
MISSION

Prevention
Deterrence
Crisis Management
Consequence Management
Attribution

FBI HISTORICAL FACTOIDS

- January 1, 1941: The FBI created a disaster squad to assist civilian authorities in identifying persons who died in a Virginia plane crash. FBI personnel were among the victims.
- December 7, 1941: The Japanese bombed the U.S. naval facility at Pearl Harbor, Hawaii. In response, the United States entered World War II. J. Edgar Hoover ordered that existing FBI war plans be put into effect, and Attorney General Francis Biddle authorized the bureau to act against dangerous enemy aliens. Within 72 hours, the FBI was working on a twenty-four hour a day basis and had taken 3,846 enemy aliens into custody. Agents seized contraband, including short-wave radios, dynamite, weapons, and ammunition.

Source: FBI

PROFILE OF
AGENCY

Law Enforcement Personnel:	Special Agents 10,000+
Support Personnel:	13,500
Major States of Assignment:	CA, DC, NY, FL, IL, PA, VA, TX

REQUIREMENTS

Age:	23 to 37 years
Education:	Bachelor's degree (minimum)
Vision:	20/20 corrected
	20/40 uncorrected

Background Investigation

OPPORTUNITIES   Over 1,000 nationwide

COMMENTS

FBI Degree Entry Programs:	Accounting, Engineering, Science, Law, Language, Diversified

Agents must be willing to accept assignments anywhere in the United States and possibly in foreign countries. The FBI has a rigorous application process. Candidates must complete a series of written tests and a formal interview. Candidates are rated on their education, language ability, and experience. Radial keratotomy is a disqualifying factor. Training is held at the FBI academy in Quantico, Virginia.

Currently, the FBI is particularly interested in hiring candidates with backgrounds in Central Eurasian, East Asian, and Middle Eastern languages.

TERRORISM'S DARK HISTORY

December 21, 1988: A bomb destroyed Pan Am flight 103 over Lockerbie, Scotland. All 259 people aboard the Boeing 747 were killed, including 189 Americans, as were 11 people on the ground. An extensive investigation by the FBI, U.S., and foreign police authorities followed. As a result, two Libyan intelligence officers were charged with planting the bomb. They were eventually turned over by the Libyan government and tried. The trial, conducted in the Netherlands under Scottish law, began in May 2000 and ended in February 2001. Abdelbaset Al Mohmed al-Megrahi was convicted and received a life sentence. The other defendant, Al-Amin Khalifah Fhimah, was acquitted.

Source: U.S. Department of State

INTERNSHIP PROGRAM   Yes

STUDENT PROGRAMS   Undergraduate Programs
Graduate Studies Programs

WHERE TO APPLY   The FBI is authorized to hire its own personnel directly. Unlike most federal agencies, it does not hire through the Office of Personnel Management. The FBI recruits candidates through its 56 field offices; FBI headquarters finalizes all appointments. Contact the FBI office nearest you for an application.

Field Offices

Federal Bureau of Investigation
Room 1400
2121 8th Avenue N.
Birmingham, AL 35203-2396
(205) 326-6166

Federal Bureau of Investigation
One St. Louis Centre
1 St. Louis Street, 3rd Floor
Mobile, AL 36602-3930
(334) 438-3674

Federal Bureau of Investigation
101 East Sixth Avenue
Anchorage, AK 99501-2524
(907) 258-5322

Federal Bureau of Investigation
Suite 400
201 East Indianola Avenue
Phoenix, AZ 85012-2080
(602) 279-5511

Federal Bureau of Investigation
Suite 200
Two Financial Centre
10825 Financial Centre Parkway
Little Rock, AR 72211-3552
(501) 221-9100

Federal Bureau of Investigation
Suite 1700, FOB
11000 Wilshire Boulevard
Los Angeles, CA 90024-3672
(310) 477-6565

Federal Bureau of Investigation
4500 Orange Grove Avenue
Sacramento, CA 95841-4205
(916) 481-9110

Federal Bureau of Investigation
Federal Office Building
9797 Aero Drive
San Diego, CA 92123-1800
(858) 565-1255

Federal Bureau of Investigation
450 Golden Gate Avenue, 13th Floor
San Francisco, CA 94102-9523
(415) 553-7400

Federal Bureau of Investigation
Federal Office Building, Room 1823
1961 Stout Street, 18th Floor
Denver, CO 80294-1823
(303) 629-7171

Federal Bureau of Investigation
Room 535, FOB
150 Court Street
New Haven, CT 06510-2020
(203) 777-6311

Federal Bureau of Investigation
Washington Metropolitan Field Office
601 4th Street, N.W.
Washington, DC 20535-0002
(202) 278-2000

Federal Bureau of Investigation
Suite 200
7820 Arlington Expressway
Jacksonville, FL 32211-7499
(904) 721-1211

Federal Bureau of Investigation
16320 Northwest Second Avenue
North Miami Beach, FL 33169-6508
(305) 944-9101

Federal Bureau of Investigation
Room 610, FOB
500 Zack Street
Tampa, FL 33602-3917
(813) 273-4566

Federal Bureau of Investigation
Suite 400
2635 Century Parkway, Northeast
Atlanta, GA 30345-3112
(404) 679-9000

Federal Bureau of Investigation
Room 4-230, Kalanianaole FOB
300 Ala Moana Boulevard
Honolulu, HI 96850-0053
(808) 521-1411

Federal Bureau of Investigation
Room 905
E. M. Dirksen Federal Office Building
219 South Dearborn Street
Chicago, IL 60604-1702
(312) 431-1333

Federal Bureau of Investigation
Suite 400
400 West Monroe Street
Springfield, IL 62704-1800
(217) 522-9675

Federal Bureau of Investigation
Room 679, FOB
575 North Pennsylvania Street
Indianapolis, IN 46204-1585
(317) 639-3301

Federal Bureau of Investigation
Room 500
600 Martin Luther King Jr. Place
Louisville, KY 40202-2231
(502) 583-3941

Federal Bureau of Investigation
2901 Leon C. Simon Dr.
New Orleans, LA 70126
(504) 816-3000

Federal Bureau of Investigation
7142 Ambassador Road
Baltimore, MD 21244-2754
(410) 265-8080

Federal Bureau of Investigation
Suite 600
One Center Plaza
Boston, MA 02108
(617) 742-5533

Federal Bureau of Investigation
26th Floor, P. V. McNamara FOB
477 Michigan Avenue
Detroit, MI 48226
(313) 965-2323

Federal Bureau of Investigation
Suite 1100
111 Washington Avenue, South
Minneapolis, MN 55401-2176
(612) 376-3200

Federal Bureau of Investigation
Room 1553, FOB
100 West Capitol Street
Jackson, MS 39269-1601
(601) 948-5000

Federal Bureau of Investigation
1300 Summit
Kansas City, MO 64105-1362
(816) 512-8200

Federal Bureau of Investigation
2222 Market Street
St. Louis, MO 63103-2516
(314) 231-4324

Federal Bureau of Investigation
10755 Burt Street
Omaha, NE 68114-2000
(402) 493-8688

Federal Bureau of Investigation
John Lawrence Bailey Building
700 East Charleston Boulevard
Las Vegas, NV 89104-1545
(702) 385-1281

Federal Bureau of Investigation
1 Gateway Center, 22nd Floor
Newark, NJ 07102-9889
(973) 792-3000

Federal Bureau of Investigation
Suite 300
415 Silver Avenue, Southwest
Albuquerque, NM 87102
(505) 224-2000

Federal Bureau of Investigation
200 McCarty Avenue
Albany, NY 12209
(518) 465-7551

Federal Bureau of Investigation
One FBI Plaza
Buffalo, NY 14202-2698
(716) 856-7800

Federal Bureau of Investigation
26 Federal Plaza, 23rd Floor
New York, NY 10278-0004
(212) 384-1000

Federal Bureau of Investigation
Suite 900, Wachovia Building
400 South Tyron Street
Charlotte, NC 28285-0001
(704) 377-9200

Federal Bureau of Investigation
Room 9000
550 Main Street
Cincinnati, OH 45202-8501
(513) 421-4310

Federal Bureau of Investigation
Room 3005
Federal Office Building
1240 East 9th Street
Cleveland, OH 44199-9912
(216) 522-1400

Federal Bureau of Investigation
3301 West Memorial Drive
Oklahoma City, OK 73134
(405) 290-7770

Federal Bureau of Investigation
Suite 400, Crown Plaza Building
1500 Southwest 1st Avenue
Portland, OR 97201-5828
(503) 224-4181

Federal Bureau of Investigation
8th Floor
William J. Green Jr. FOB
600 Arch Street
Philadelphia, PA 19106
(215) 418-4000

Federal Bureau of Investigation
Suite 300
U.S. Post Office Building
700 Grant Street
Pittsburgh, PA 15219-1906
(412) 471-2000

Federal Bureau of Investigation
Room 526, U.S. Federal Bldg.
150 Carlos Chardon Avenue
Hato Rey
San Juan, PR 00918-1716
(787) 754-6000

Federal Bureau of Investigation
151 Westpark Blvd.
Columbia, SC 29210-3857
(803) 551-4200

Federal Bureau of Investigation
Suite 600, John J. Duncan FOB
710 Locust Street
Knoxville, TN 37902-2537
(865) 544-0751

Federal Bureau of Investigation
Suite 3000, Eagle Crest Bldg.
225 North Humphreys Blvd.
Memphis, TN 38120-2107
(901) 747-4300

Federal Bureau of Investigation
Suite 300
1801 North Lamar
Dallas, TX 75202-1795
(214) 720-2200

Federal Bureau of Investigation
660 S. Mesa Hills Drive
El Paso, TX 79912-5533
(915) 832-5000

Federal Bureau of Investigation
2500 East TC Jester
Houston, TX 77008-1300
(713) 693-5000

Federal Bureau of Investigation
Suite 200
U.S. Post Office Courthouse Bldg.
615 East Houston Street
San Antonio, TX 78205-9998
(210) 225-6741

Federal Bureau of Investigation
Suite 1200, 257 Towers Bldg.
257 East, 200 South
Salt Lake City, UT 84111-2048
(801) 579-1400

Federal Bureau of Investigation
150 Corporate Boulevard
Norfolk, VA 23502-4999
(757) 455-0100

Federal Bureau of Investigation
1970 E. Parham Road
Richmond, VA 23228
(804) 261-1044

Federal Bureau of Investigation
Suite 600
330 East Kilbourn Avenue
Milwaukee, WI 53202-6627
(414) 276-4684

Federal Bureau of Investigation
1110 Third Avenue
Seattle, WA 98101-2904
(206) 622-0460

According to the U.S. Department of Justice, there are over 12,500 general purpose local police departments, 3,086 sheriff's departments, 49 primary state police departments, and 1,721 special police agencies. In addition, there are over 70 federal law enforcement agencies.

Source: U.S. Department of Justice

U.S. Immigration and Naturalization Service (INS) Careers

*Important Update Information:
On March 1, 2003, services formerly provided by the Immigration and Naturalization Service (INS) were transitioned into the Department of Homeland Security (DHS), under the Bureau of Citizenship and Immigration Services (BCIS). For the purposes of this book, we will continue to refer to the department as INS, since it will take some time for these departmental changes to be fully realized.

U.S. Immigration and Naturalization Service
425 I Street, NW
Washington, DC 20536
(202) 514-2690
www.immigration.gov

POSITIONS

Deportation Officer GS-5/7		$25,822–$41,585
Inspector GS-5/7		$25,822–$41,585
Special Agent GS-5/7		$25,822–$41,585

MAIN MISSION

The Immigration and Naturalization Service (INS) mission involves inspections, investigations, detention and deportation, as well as U.S. border patrol. INS is charged with preventing unlawful entry, employment, or receipt of benefits by those not entitled to receive them and with apprehending those aliens who enter and remain illegally in the United States. Special agents investigate illegal entry activities and other criminal matters relating to immigration and naturalization laws. Immigration inspectors are stationed anywhere that people enter the United States, primarily at land ports, seaports, and airports. They prevent ineligible persons from entering the United States. Deportation officers provide control and removal of persons who have been ordered deported from or otherwise required to depart the United States.

"We can never eliminate the threat completely. We can never eliminate the notion of surprise, of terrorist attack, particularly in a society that's as open and as free and as diverse and as large as we are in the United States of America . . . [but] I believe we can significantly, significantly reduce the vulnerability to terrorism and terrorist attack over time. We can give Americans greater peace of mind, convenience, and commerce."

President George W. Bush, June 10, 2002

HOMELAND SECURITY MISSION	Prevention		
	Deterrence		
	Crisis Management		
PROFILE OF AGENCY	Law Enforcement Personnel:	9,466	
REQUIREMENTS	Age:	21 to 37 years	
	Education:	Bachelor's degree	and/ or
	Experience:	3 years general	GS-5
		1 year specialized	GS-7
	Vision:	20/20 corrected	
		20/200 uncorrected	
	Background Investigation		
OPPORTUNITIES	Up to 1,000 Nationwide		
COMMENTS	Candidates must complete a series of written tests and a formal interview. Candidates are rated on education/language ability and experience. Training is held at the Federal Law Enforcement Training Center, Glynco, GA.		
INTERNSHIP PROGRAM	Yes		

WHERE TO   Above Address or Regional Office
APPLY

Regional Offices

Immigration and Naturalization Service
Eastern Region
Federal Building, Elmwood Avenue
Burlington, VT 05401

Southern Region
Skyline Center, Building C
311 North Stemmons Freeway
Dallas, TX 75207

Northern Region
Federal Building
Fort Snelling
Twin Cities, MN 55111

Western Region
Terminal Island
San Pedro, CA 90731

U.S. Border Patrol (USBP) Careers

*Important Update Information:
On March 1, 2003, the border inspection functions formerly carried out by the U.S. Border Patrol were transferred to the Bureau of Customs and Border Protection.

U.S. Border Patrol
Bureau of Customs and Border Protection
425 I Street, N.W.
Washington, DC 20536
(800) 238-1945
www.usborderpatrol.gov
www.immigration.gov

POSITIONS	***Border Patrol Agent GS-5***	$25,822–$41,585
	Pilot GS-9	$34,451–$44,783

MAIN   Interdicts aliens and narcotics or other contraband between ports of
MISSION   entry, detains and deports illegal aliens, and performs intelligence
                  functions related to INS responsibilities. Historically, the border patrol
                  is responsible for the "linewatch." Linewatch involves the detection
                  and apprehension of illegal aliens and smugglers on the U.S. borders.

HOMELAND   Prevention
SECURITY   Deterrence
MISSION   Crisis Management

PROFILE OF   Law Enforcement Personnel: 3,900 Border Patrol Agents
AGENCY   Major States of Assignment: AZ, CA, NM, TX

REQUIREMENTS Age: 21 to 37 years

Education: Bachelor's degree   and/or
Experience: 3 years general   GS-5
                                1 year specialized   GS-7

Language: Spanish
Vision: 20/20 corrected
                                20/70 uncorrected

Background Investigation

OPPORTUNITIES Over 3,000 Border Patrol Agents

COMMENTS Must learn the Spanish language. A border patrol agent's first duty station is on the United States–Mexico border. Agents may be stationed in small, isolated communities that may not have adequate schools or medical facilities. Agents routinely work overtime. Training: 8 weeks of U.S. Border Patrol Agent School at the Federal Law Enforcement Training Center in Glynco, GA.

Military folks have an advantage—and may retain leave and retirement benefits earned on active duty.

INTERNSHIP PROGRAM Unknown

WHERE TO APPLY Above Address or Regional Office or Border Patrol Agent Online Application: **www.staffing.opm.gov/BPA/**
(800) 238-1945

"The battle, sir, is not to the strong alone; it is to the vigilant, the active, the brave."

Patrick Henry, March 23, 1775

Regional Offices

Western Region
Terminal Island
San Pedro, CA 90731

Northern Region
Federal Building
Fort Snelling
Twin Cities, MN 55111

Southern Region
Skyline Center, Building C
311 North Stemmons Freeway
Dallas, TX 75207

Eastern Region
Federal Building, Elmwood Avenue
Burlington, VT 05401

U.S. Marshal Service Careers

U.S. Marshal Service
600 Army Navy Drive
Arlington, VA 22202
(202) 307-9065
www.usdoj.gov/marshals

POSITION	*Deputy U.S. Marshal GS-5*	$25,822–$41,585

MAIN MISSION

The United States Marshal Service is the nation's oldest federal law enforcement agency, having served as a vital link between the executive and judicial branches of the government since 1789. The Marshal Service performs tasks that are essential to the operation of virutally every aspect of the federal justice system. The service is responsible for providing support and protection for the federal courts, including security for over 700 judicial facilities and nearly 2,000 judges and magistrates, as well as countless other trial participants such as jurors and attorneys. In addition, deputy U.S. marshals apprehend federal fugitives; operate the Federal Witness Security program, ensuring the safety of endangered government witnesses; maintain the custody of and transport thousands of federal prisoners annually; execute court orders and arrest warrants; seize, manage, and sell property forfeited to the government by drug traffickers and other criminals; assist the Justice Department's seizure and forfeiture program; respond to emergency circumstances, including civil disturbances, terrorist incidents, and other crisis situations through its Special Operations Group; and restore order in riot and mob violence situations.

HOMELAND SECURITY MISSION

Prevention
Deterrence
Crisis Management
Consequence Management
Attribution

PROFILE OF AGENCY

Law Enforcement Personnel: 3,500 Deputy Marshals/
                                                              Administrative personnel
Major States of Assignment: 427 Office Locations

REQUIREMENTS

Age:	21 to 37 years
Education:	Bachelor's degree and/ or
Experience:	3 years general GS-5
	1 year specialized GS-7
Vision:	20/20 corrected
	20/40 uncorrected

Background Investigation

OPPORTUNITIES Over 500 nationwide

COMMENTS Deputy U.S. marshals travel frequently for extended periods of time and must be available for reassignment to other duty stations. Recently the U.S. Marshal Service had a special hiring period of active duty military personnel—active service personnel should monitor for further special hiring:

Operation Shining Star IV (OSS4) was/is an accelerated recruitment drive for active duty military personnel, on selected military installations, that targeted individuals who meet the qualifications and/or education requirements of the deputy U.S. marshal position. You had to be on active duty as of a set time period and also be separating from the military (or on terminal leave) within a set time to be eligible to take the test.

To be eligible to participate in Operation Shining Star as a reservist or national guard, you must be on active duty for a minimum of 179 days; a copy of your orders is required.

In order to qualify, you must:
- BE ON ACTIVE DUTY;
- be between the ages of 21 and 36—NO WAIVERS;
- have a Bachelor's degree or three years of responsible experience;
- not be in the National Guard or reserves (see above explanation);
- pass a written test;
- pass an oral interview;
- be in excellent physical condition;
- pass a medical examination and fitness test;
- have no conviction for domestic violence;
- pass a background investigation; and
- complete a rigorous 10-week basic training program at the U.S. Marshals Service Training Academy.

Registration packets are available at (202) 307-8678, or call for questions.

Source: U.S. Marshal Service

Training is held at the Federal Law Enforcement Training Center, Glynco, GA.

INTERNSHIP   Unknown
PROGRAM

WHERE TO   Address Above
APPLY

Field Offices

Northern District of Alabama (N/AL)
U.S. Marshal
1729 N. 5th Avenue
Room 240
Birmingham, AL 35203
(205) 731-1712

Middle District of Alabama (M/AL)
U.S. Marshal
Frank M. Johnson Federal Building
15 Lee Street
Room 224
Montgomery, AL 36104
(334) 223-7401

Southern District of Alabama (S/AL)
U.S. Marshal
U.S. Courthouse
113 St. Joseph Street
Room 413
Mobile, AL 36602
(205) 690-2841

District of Alaska (D/AK)
U.S. Marshal
U.S. Courthouse
222 W. 7th Avenue
Room 189
Anchorage, AK 99513
(907) 271-5154

District of Arizona (D/AZ)
U.S. Marshal
Sandra Day O'Connor U.S. Courthouse
401 W. Washington Street, SPC 64
Suite 270
Phoenix, AZ 85003-2159
(602) 382-8767

Eastern District of Arkansas (E/AR)
U.S. Marshal
U.S. Courthouse
600 W. Capitol Avenue
Room 445
Little Rock, AR 72201
(501) 324-6256

Western District of Arkansas (W/AR)
U.S. Marshal
Judge Isaac C. Parker Federal Building
30 S. 6th Street
Room 243
Fort Smith, AR 72901
(501) 783-5215

Northern District of California (N/CA)
U.S. Marshal
U.S. Courthouse/Phillip Burton Building
450 Golden Gate Avenue
Room 20-6888
San Francisco, CA 94102
(415) 436-7677

Eastern District of California (E/CA)
U.S. Marshal
U.S. Courthouse
501 I Street
Sacramento, CA 95814
(916) 930-2030

Central District of California (C/CA)
U.S. Marshal
U.S. Courthouse 312 N. Spring Street
Room G-23
Los Angeles, CA 90012
(213) 894-6820

Southern District of California (S/CA)
U.S. Marshal
U.S. Courthouse
940 Front Street
Room LL B-71
San Diego, CA 92189
(619) 557-6620

District of Colorado (D/CO)
U.S. Marshal
U.S. Courthouse
1929 Stout Street
Room C-324
Denver, CO 80294
(303) 844-2801

District of Connecticut (D/CT)
U.S. Marshal
U.S. Courthouse
141 Church Street
Room 323
New Haven, CT 06510
(203) 773-2107

District of Columbia (DC/DC)
U.S. Marshal
U.S. Courthouse
3rd & Constitution Avenue, N.W.
Room 1103
Washington, DC 20001
(202) 353-0600

District of Columbia (Superior Court)
U.S. Marshal
H. Carl Moultrie Courthouse
500 Indiana Avenue, N.W.
Room C-250
Washington, DC 20001
(202) 616-8600

District of Delaware (D/DE)
U.S. Marshal
U.S. Courthouse
844 King Street
Room 4311
Wilmington, DE 19801
(302) 573-6176

Northern District of Florida (N/FL)
U.S. Marshal
U.S. Courthouse
110 E. Park Avenue
Room 100
Tallahassee, FL 32302
(904) 942-8400

Middle District of Florida (M/FL)
U.S. Marshal
U.S. Courthouse
801 N. Florida Avenue, 4th Floor
Tampa, FL 33602-4519
(813) 274-6401

Southern District of Florida (S/FL)
U.S. Marshal
Federal Courthouse Square
301 N. Miami Avenue
Room 205
Miami, FL 33128
(305) 536-5346

Northern District of Georgia (N/GA)
U.S. Marshal
Federal Building
75 Spring Street, S.W.
Room 1669
Atlanta, GA 30303
(404) 331-6833

Middle District of Georgia (M/GA)
U.S. Marshal
U.S. Courthouse
3rd and Mulberry Street
Room 101
Macon, GA 31201
(912) 752-8280

Southern District of Georgia (S/GA)
U.S. Marshal
U.S. Courthouse
125 Bull Street
Room 333
Savannah, GA 31401
(912) 652-4212

District of Guam (D/GU)
U.S. Marshal
344 U.S. Courthouse
520 West Soledad Avenue
Hagatna, Guam 96910
011-671-477-7827

District of Hawaii (D/HI)
U.S. Marshal
U.S. Courthouse
300 Ala Moana Boulevard
Room C-103
Honolulu, HI 96850
(808) 541-3000

District of Idaho (D/ID)
U.S. Marshal
U.S. Courthouse
550 W. Fort Street, MSC-10
Room 777
Boise, ID 83724
(208) 334-1298

Northern District of Illinois (N/IL)
U.S. Marshal
219 S. Dearborn Street
Room 2444
Chicago, IL 60604
(312) 353-5290

Central District of Illinois (C/IL)
U.S. Marshal
600 E. Monroe Street
Room 333
Springfield, IL 62701
(217) 492-4430

Southern District of Illinois (S/IL)
U.S. Marshal
U.S. Courthouse
750 Missouri Avenue
Room 127
East St. Louis, IL 62201
(618) 482-9336

Northern District of Indiana (N/IN)
U.S. Marshal
Federal Building
204 S. Main Street
Room 233
South Bend, IN 46601
(219) 236-8291

Southern District of Indiana (S/IN)
U.S. Marshal
U.S. Courthouse
46 E. Ohio Street
Room 227
Indianapolis, IN 46204
(317) 226-6566

Northern District of Iowa (N/IA)
U.S. Marshal
Federal Building
101 First Street, S.E.
Room 320
Cedar Rapids, IA 52401
(319) 362-4411

Southern District of Iowa (S/IA)
U.S. Marshal
U.S. Courthouse
123 E. Walnut Street
Room 208
Des Moines, IA 50309
(515) 284-6240

District of Kansas (D/KS)
U.S. Marshal
Federal Building
444 S.E. Quincy
Room 456
Topeka, KS 66683
(785) 295-2775

Eastern District of Kentucky (E/KY)
U.S. Marshal
Federal Building
Barr and Limestone Streets
Room 162
Lexington, KY 40507
(606) 233-2601

Western District of Kentucky (W/KY)
U.S. Marshal
U.S. Courthouse
601 W. Broadway
Room 162
Louisville, KY 40202
(502) 582-5141

Eastern District of Louisiana (E/LA)
U.S. Marshal
U.S. Courthouse
500 Camp Street
Room C-600
New Orleans, LA 70130
(504) 589-6079

Middle District of Louisiana (M/LA)
U.S. Marshal
U.S. Courthouse
777 Florida Street
Room G-48
Baton Rouge, LA 70801
(225) 389-0364

Western District of Louisiana (W/LA)
U.S. Marshal
U.S. Courthouse
300 Fannin Street
Suite 1202
Shreveport, LA 71101
(318) 676-4200

District of Maine (D/ME)
U.S. Marshal
156 Federal Street
1st Floor
Portland, ME 04101
(207) 780-3355

District of Maryland (D/MD)
U.S. Marshal
U.S. Courthouse
101 W. Lombard Street
Room 605
Baltimore, MD 21201
(410) 962-2220

District of Massachusetts (D/MA)
U.S. Marshal
John Joseph Moakley Courthouse
1 Courthouse Way
Suite 1-500
Boston, MA 02210
(617) 748-2500

Eastern District of Michigan (E/MI)
U.S. Marshal
Federal Building
231 W. Lafayette Street
Room 120
Detroit, MI 48226
(313) 226-4922

Western District of Michigan (W/MI)
U.S. Marshal
Federal Building
110 Michigan Avenue, N.W.
Room 544
Grand Rapids, MI 49503
(616) 456-2438

District of Minnesota (D/MN)
U.S. Marshal
U.S. Courthouse
110 S. 4th Street
Room 523
Minneapolis, MN 55401
(612) 664-5900

Northern District of Mississippi (D/MS)
U.S. Marshal
Federal Building
911 Jackson Avenue
Room 348
Oxford, MS 38655
(601) 234-6661

Southern District of Mississippi (D/MS)
U.S. Marshal: Nehemiah Flowers
James O. Eastland Courthouse Building
245 E. Capitol Street
Suite 305
Jackson, MS 39201
(601) 965-4444

Eastern District of Missouri (E/MO)
U.S. Marshal
Thomas Eagleton Courthouse
111 S. 10th Street
Room 2319
St. Louis, MO 63102-1116
(314) 539-2212

Western District of Missouri (W/MO)
U.S. Marshal
U.S. Courthouse
400 E. 9th Street
Room 3740
Kansas City, MO 64106
(816) 512-2000

District of Montana (D/MT)
U.S. Marshal
Federal Building
215 1st Avenue N.
Room 307
Great Falls, MT 59401
(406) 453-7597

District of Nebraska (D/NE)
U.S. Marshal
Zorinsky Federal Building
215 N. 17th Street
Room 8121
Omaha, NE 68102
(402) 221-4781

District of Nevada (D/NV)
U.S. Marshal
U.S. Courthouse
300 Las Vegas Boulevard S.
Room 448
Las Vegas, NV 89101
(702) 388-6355

District of New Hampshire (D/NH)
U.S. Marshal
Federal Building
55 Pleasant Street
Room 409
Concord, NH 03301
(603) 225-1632

District of New Jersey (D/NJ)
U.S. Marshal
U.S. Courthouse/Post Office
Federal Square
Room 500
Newark, NJ 07101
(973) 645-2404

District of New Mexico (D/NM)
U.S. Marshal
U.S. Courthouse
500 Gold Avenue S.W.
Room 12403
Albuquerque, NM 87102
(505) 346-6400

Northern District of New York (N/NY)
U.S. Marshal
227 Federal Building
Federal Station
Syracuse, NY 13261
(315) 448-0341

Eastern District of New York (E/NY)
U.S. Marshal
U.S. Courthouse
225 Cadman Plaza E.
Room 172
Brooklyn, NY 11201
(718) 254-6700

Southern District of New York (S/NY)
U.S. Marshal
500 Pearl Street
Suite 400
New York, NY 10007
(212) 637-6000

Western District of New York (W/NY)
U.S. Marshal
U.S. Courthouse
68 Court Street
Room 129
Buffalo, NY 14202
(716) 551-4851

Eastern District of North Carolina (E/NC)
U.S. Marshal
Federal Building
310 New Bern Avenue
Room 744
Raleigh, NC 27611
(919) 856-4153

Middle District of North Carolina (M/NC)
U.S. Marshal
U.S. Courthouse
324 W. Market Street
Room 234
Greensboro, NC 27402
(336) 333-5354

Western District of North Carolina (W/NC)
U.S. Marshal
U.S. Courthouse
100 Otis Street
Room 315
Asheville, NC 28801
(828) 771-7400

District of North Dakota (D/ND)
U.S. Marshal
Old Federal Building
655 1st Avenue N.
Rom 317
Fargo, ND 58108
(701) 297-7300

District of the Northern Mariana Islands (D/MP)
U.S. Marshal
Horiguchi Building, 1st Floor
Garpan, Saipan, MP 96950
011-670-234-6563

Northern District of Ohio (N/OH)
U.S. Marshal
U.S. Courthouse
201 Superior Avenue
Room B-1
Cleveland, OH 44114
(216) 522-2154

Southern District of Ohio (S/OH)
U.S. Marshal
U.S. Courthouse
85 Marconi Boulevard
Room 460
Columbus, OH 43215
(614) 469-5540

Northern District of Oklahoma (N/OK)
U.S. Marshal
U.S. Courthouse
333. W. 4th Street
Room 4557
Tulsa, OK 74103
(918) 581-7738

Eastern District of Oklahoma (E/OK)
U.S. Marshal
U.S. Courthouse
111 N. 5th Street
Room 136
Muskogee, OK 74401
(918) 687-2523

Western District of Oklahoma (W/OK)
U.S. Marshal
U.S. Courthouse
200 N.W. 4th Street
Room 2418
Oklahoma City, OK 73102
(405) 231-4206

District of Oregon (D/OR)
U.S. Marshal
U.S. Courthouse
1000 S.W. 3rd Avenue
Room 401
Portland, OR 97204
(503) 326-2209

Eastern District of Pennsylvania (E/PA)
U.S. Marshal
U.S. Courthouse
601 Market Street
Room 2110
Philadelphia, PA 19106
(215) 597-7273

Middle District of Pennsylvania (M/PA)
U.S. Marshal
Federal Building
Washington Avenue and Linden Street
Room 231
Scranton, PA 18501
(570) 346-7277

Western District of Pennsylvania (W/PA)
U.S. Marshal
U.S. Courthouse
7th Avenue and Grant Street
Room 539
Pittsburgh, PA 15219
(412) 644-3351

District of Puerto Rico (D/PR)
U.S. Marshal
Federal Building
150 Carlos Chardon Avenue
Room 200
Hato Rey, PR 00918
(787) 766-6000

District of Rhode Island (D/RI)
U.S. Marshal
Kennedy Plaza
Fleet Center
Suite 300
Providence, RI 02901
(401) 528-5302

District of South Carolina (D/SC)
U.S. Marshal
U.S. Courthouse
1845 Assembly Street
Room B-31
Columbia, SC 29202
(803) 765-5821

District of South Dakota (D/SD)
U.S. Marshal
Federal Building
400 S. Phillips Avenue
Room 216
Sioux Falls, SD 57104
(605) 330-4351

Eastern District of Tennessee (E/TN)
U.S. Marshal
Federal Building
800 Market Street
Suite 2-3107
Knoxville, TN 37902
(615) 545-4182

Middle District of Tennessee (M/TN)
U.S. Marshal
Estes Kefauver Federal Building
110 9th Avenue S.
Room A750
Nashville, TN 37203
(615) 736-5417

Western District of Tennessee (W/TN)
U.S. Marshal
Federal Building
167 N. Main Street
Room 1029
Memphis, TN 38103
(901) 544-3304

Northern District of Texas (N/TX)
U.S. Marshal
Federal Building
1100 Commerce Street
Room 16F47
Dallas, TX 75242
(214) 767-0836

Eastern District of Texas (E/TX)
U.S. Marshal
Federal Building
300 Willow Street
Room 329
Beaumont, TX 75702
(409) 839-2581

Southern District of Texas (S/TX)
U.S. Marshal
U.S. Courthouse
515 Rusk Avenue
Room 10130
Houston, TX 77002
(713) 718-4800

Western District of Texas (W/TX)
U.S. Marshal
U.S. Courthouse
655 E. Durango Boulevard
Room 235
San Antonio, TX 78206
(210) 472-6540

District of Utah (D/UT)
U.S. Marshal
U.S. Post Office and Courthouse
350 S. Main Street
Room B-20
Salt Lake City, UT 84101
(801) 524-5693

District of Vermont (D/VT)
U.S. Marshal
11 Elmwood Avenue
Suite 601
Burlington, VT 05401
(802) 951-6271

District of the Virgin Islands (D/VI)
U.S. Marshal
U.S. Courthouse
Veteran's Drive
Room 371
St. Thomas, VI 00801
(340) 774-2743

Eastern District of Virginia (E/VA)
U.S. Marshal
401 Courthouse Square
Alexandria, VA 22314
(703) 274-2013

Western District of Virginia (W/VA)
U.S. Marshal
Federal Building
210 Franklin Road SW
Room 247
Roanoke, VA 24009
(703) 857-2230

Eastern District of Washington (E/WA)
U.S. Marshal
U.S. Courthouse
920 W. Riverside Avenue
Room 888
Spokane, WA 99201
(509) 353-2781

Western District of Washington (W/WA)
U.S. Marshal
U.S. Courthouse
1010 5th Avenue
Room 300
Seattle, WA 98104
(206) 553-5500

Northern District of West Virginia (N/WV)
U.S. Marshal
U.S. Courthouse
500 W. Pike Street
P.O. Box 2807
Clarksburg, WV 26302
(304) 623-0486

Southern District of West Virginia (S/WV)
U.S. Marshal
300 Virginia Street East
Suite 3602
Charleston, WV 25301
(304) 347-5136

Eastern District of Wisconsin (E/WI)
U.S. Marshal
U.S. Courthouse
517 E. Wisconsin Avenue
Suite 38
Milwaukee, WI 53202
(414) 297-3707

Western District of Wisconsin (W/WI)
U.S. Marshal
U.S. Courthouse
120 N. Henry Street
Room 440
Madison, WI 53703
(608) 264-5161

District of Wyoming (D/WY)
U.S. Marshal: James Rose
Joseph C. O'Mahoney Federal Center
2120 Capitol Avenue
Room 2124
Cheyenne, WY 82001
(307) 772-2196

"God grants liberty only to those who love it, and are always ready to guard and defend it."

Daniel Webster

U.S. DEPARTMENT OF HOMELAND SECURITY/ DEPARTMENT OF TREASURY OPPORTUNITIES

Important Update Information:

On March 1, 2003, functions of several border and security agencies (including the U.S. Customs Service) were transferred into the Directorate of Border and Transportation Security, within the Department of Homeland Security. In the future, the department will be known as the Bureau of Immigration and Customs Enforcement (BICE). The U.S. Secret Service was also transferred into the DHS, remaining intact and reporting directly to the secretary.

U.S. Customs Service (USCS) Careers

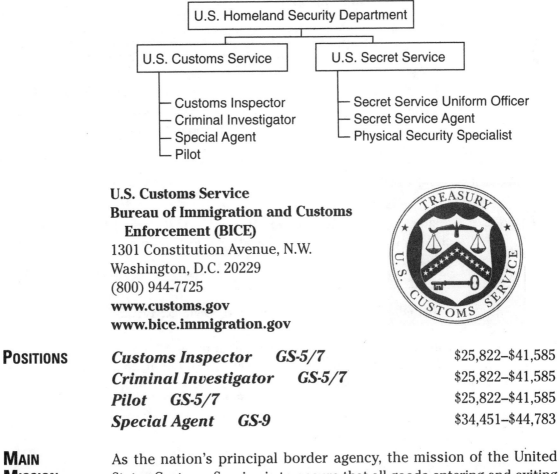

U.S. Customs Service
Bureau of Immigration and Customs Enforcement (BICE)
1301 Constitution Avenue, N.W.
Washington, D.C. 20229
(800) 944-7725
www.customs.gov
www.bice.immigration.gov

POSITIONS			
Customs Inspector	*GS-5/7*		$25,822–$41,585
Criminal Investigator		*GS-5/7*	$25,822–$41,585
Pilot	*GS-5/7*		$25,822–$41,585
Special Agent		*GS-9*	$34,451–$44,783

MAIN MISSION

As the nation's principal border agency, the mission of the United States Customs Service is to ensure that all goods entering and exiting the United States do so in accordance with all United States laws and regulations. This mission includes enforcing U.S. laws intended to prevent illegal trade practices; protecting the American public and environment from the introduction of prohibited hazardous and noxious products; assessing and collecting revenues in the forms of duties, taxes, and fees on imported merchandise; regulating the movement of persons, carriers, merchandise, and commodities between the United States and other nations while facilitating the movement of all legitimate cargo, carriers, travelers, and mail; interdicting narcotics and other contraband; and enforcing certain provisions of the export control laws of the United States. Customs inspectors enforce the laws governing the importation or exportation of merchandise, including the inspection of persons and carriers entering or leaving the United States.

HOMELAND SECURITY MISSION

Prevention
Deterrence
Crisis Management

PROFILE OF AGENCY

Law Enforcement Personnel:	10,120
Major States of Assignment:	AZ, CA, FL, NJ, NY, TX

REQUIREMENTS

Age:	21 to 37 years	
Education:	Bachelor's degree	and/or
Experience:	3 years general	GS-5
	1 year specialized	GS-7
Vision:	20/20 corrected	
	20/200 uncorrected	

Background Investigation

OPPORTUNITIES Over 1,000 nationwide

COMMENTS Major degree fields—Accounting, Aviation, Criminal Justice, Law. Training is held at the Federal Law Enforcement Training Center, Glynco, GA.

A TYPICAL DAY IN THE U.S. CUSTOMS SERVICE

Processes:
• Over 1.3 million passengers
• Over 50,889 trucks/containers
• 588 vessels
• 2,642 aircraft
• 355,004 vehicles

Executes over:
• 64 arrests
• 107 narcotics seizures
• 9 currency seizures
• 223 other seizures*

Seizes:
• 5,059 pounds of narcotics
• Over $15,800 in arms and ammunition
• $525,791 in merchandise
• $443,907 in currency

*Conveyances, ammunition, commercial merchandise, real estate, firearms and weapons, child pornography

Source: U.S. Customs

WHERE TO APPLY   (800) 944-7725 or **www.customs.gov** or directly at the regional office nearest you.

Regional Offices

U.S. Customs Service
150 N. Royal
Mobile, AL 36602
(334) 441-6061

U.S. Customs Service
605 W. 4th Avenue
Anchorage, AK 99501
(907) 271-2675

U.S. Customs Service
International and Terrace Streets
Nogales, AZ 85621
(520) 287-1410

U.S. Customs Service
Suite 705, 1 World Trade Center
Long Beach, CA 90831
(310) 980-3100

U.S. Customs Service
880 Front Street
San Diego, CA 92188
(619) 557-5455

U.S. Customs Service
555 Battery Street
San Francisco, CA 94718
(415) 744-7700

U.S. Customs Service
300 S. Ferry Street
San Pedro, CA 90731
(310) 514-6001

U.S. Customs Service
1301 Constitution Avenue, N.W.
Washington, DC 20229
(202) 927-1000

U.S. Customs Service
P.O. Box 17423
Washington, DC 20041
(703) 318-5900

U.S. Customs Service
909 S.E. 1st Avenue
Miami, FL 33131
(305) 536-5952

U.S. Customs Service
77 S.E. 5th Street
Miami, FL 33131
(305) 869-2800

U.S. Customs Service
4430 E. Adams Drive
Tampa, FL 33605
(813) 228-2381

U.S. Customs Service
1 E. Bay Street
Savannah, GA 31401
(912) 652-4256

U.S. Customs Service
335 Merchant Street
Honolulu, HI 96806
(808) 522-8060

U.S. Customs Service
55 E. Monroe Street
Chicago, IL 60603
(312) 353-4733

U.S. Customs Service
610 S. Canal Street
Chicago, IL 60607
(312) 353-6100

U.S. Customs Service
423 Canal Street
New Orleans, LA 70130
(504) 670-2391

U.S. Customs Service
312 Fore Street
Portland, ME 04112
(207) 780-3326

U.S. Customs Service
40 S. Gray Street
Baltimore, MD 21202
(410) 962-2666

U.S. Customs Service
10 Causeway Street
Boston, MA 02222
(617) 898-6210

U.S. Customs Service
477 Michigan Avenue
Detroit, MI 48226
(313) 226-3177

U.S. Customs Service
209 Federal Building
Duluth, MN 55802
(218) 720-5201

U.S. Customs Service
110 S. 4th Street
Minneapolis, MN 55401
(612) 348-1690

U.S. Customs Service
7911 Forsyth Building
St. Louis, MO 63105
(314) 428-2662

U.S. Customs Service
300 2nd Avenue S.
Great Falls, MT 59401
(406) 453-7631

U.S. Customs Service
111 W. Huron Street
Buffalo, NY 14202
(716) 846-4373

U.S. Customs Service
Kennedy Airport
New York, NY 11430
(718) 553-1542

U.S. Customs Service
127 N. Water Street
Ogdensburg, NY 13669
(315) 393-0660

U.S. Customs Service
1801-R Crossbeam Drive
Charlotte, NC 28217
(704) 329-6100

U.S. Customs Service
Post Office Building
Pembina, ND 58271
(701) 825-6201

U.S. Customs Service
6747 Engle Road
Middleburg Heights, OH 44130
(440) 891-3800

U.S. Customs Service
511 N.W. Broadway
Columbia Snake, OR 97209
(503) 326-2865

U.S. Customs Service
2nd and Chestnut Streets
Philadelphia, PA 19106
(215) 597-4606

U.S. Customhouse
P.O. Box 2112
San Juan, PR 00903
(809) 729-6950

U.S. Customs Service
49 Pavillon Avenue
Providence, RI 02905
(401) 528-5081

U.S. Customs Service
200 E. Bay Street
Charleston, SC 29401
(803) 727-4312

U.S. Customs Service
P.O. Box 619050
DFW Airport, TX 75261
(972) 574-2170

U.S. Customs Service
Bridge of the Americas
P.O. Box 9516
El Paso, TX 79985
(915) 540-5800

U.S. Customs Service
1717 E. Loep
Houston, TX 77019
(713) 671-1000

U.S. Customs Service
5850 San Felipe Street
Houston, TX 77057
(713) 942-6843

U.S. Customs Service
Lincoln-Juarez Bridge
Laredo, TX 78044
(210) 726-2267

U.S. Customs Service
4550 75th Avenue
Port Arthur, TX 77642
(409) 724-0087

U.S. Customs Service
50 S. Main Street
St. Albans, VT 05478
(802) 524-7352

U.S. Customs Service
U.S. Federal Building, Veterans Drive
St. Thomas, VI 60801
(809) 774-2510

U.S. Customs Service
101 E. Main Street
Norfolk, VA 23510
(757) 533-4200

U.S. Customs Service
1000 2nd Avenue, Suite 2100
Seattle, WA 98104
(206) 553-0770

U.S. Customs Service
6269 Ace Industrial Drive
Cudahy, WI 53110
(414) 571-2860

U.S. Secret Service (USSS) Careers ———————————

U.S. Secret Service
Personnel Division
950 H Street, N.W., Suite 920
Washington, DC 20223
(202) 406-5800
www.secretservice.gov

POSITIONS

Secret Service Agent	*GS-5/7/9*	$34,451–$44,783
Secret Service Uniform Officer	*GS-5/7*	$25,822–$41,585
Physical Security Specialists	*GS-5/7*	$25,822–$41,585

MAIN MISSION

The Secret Service is charged with protecting the life of the president and vice president of the United States and their immediate families, the president-elect and vice president-elect and their immediate families, former presidents and their wives, the widows of former presidents until death or remarriage, minor children of a former president until they reach 16 years of age, heads of a foreign state or foreign government (when in the U.S.), and, at the direction of the president, official representatives of the United States performing special missions abroad. Furthermore, the Secret Service provides security at the White House complex, the Treasury Building and Treasury Annex, buildings that house presidential offices, the vice president's residence, and various foreign diplomatic missions in the Washington, DC metropolitan area or in other areas as designated by the president. The mission of the Secret Service includes investigations related to certain criminal violation of the Federal Deposit Insurance Act, the Federal Land Bank Act, and the Government Losses in Shipment Act. The Secret Service is also charged with the detection and arrest of any person committing any offense against the laws of the United States relating to coins, currency, stamps, government bonds, checks, credit/debt card fraud, computer fraud, false identification crime, and other obligations or securities of the United States. The Secret Service protects visiting dignitaries and investigates threats against them. It investigates counterfeiting and computer fraud, including mobile phone cloning. It also provides physical security for treasury buildings in Washington, DC.

HOMELAND SECURITY MISSION	Prevention
	Deterrence
	Crisis Management
	Consequence Management
	Attribution

PROFILE

Law Enforcement Personnel: 2,100 special agents
1,200 uniformed division officers
1,700 other support personnel

Major States of Assignment: CA, DC, NY, TX

REQUIREMENTS

Age:	21 to 37 years	
Education:	Bachelor's degree	and/ or
Experience:	3 years general	GS-5
	1 year specialized	GS-7
Vision:	20/20 corrected	
	20/60 uncorrected	

Background Investigation

OPPORTUNITIES   Over 800 Agents (in the next four years)

COMMENTS   Major degree fields—Accounting, Criminal Justice, Law.
Agents train at the Federal Law Enforcement Training Center, Glynco, GA.

U.S. SECRET SERVICE HISTORY FACTOIDS

- 1865: The U.S. Secret Service was founded as a branch of the U.S. Treasury Department and is one of the nation's oldest federal investigative law enforcement agencies. The original mission was to investigate counterfeiting of U.S. currency. It was estimated that one-third to one-half of the currency in circulation at that time was counterfeit.
- After the 1901 assassination of President William McKinley in Buffalo, New York, the Secret Service was assigned the responsibility of protecting the president.

Source: U.S. Secret Service

WHERE TO APPLY   (202) 406-5800 or **www.secretservice.gov** or any of the field offices listed below.

Field Offices

U.S. Secret Service
Suite 1125, Daniel Building
15 South 20th Street
Birmingham, AL 35233
(205) 731-1144

U.S. Secret Service
182 St. Francis Street
Mobile, AL 32501
(334) 441-5851

U.S. Secret Service
1 Commerce Street, Suite 605
Montgomery, AL 36104
(334) 223-7601

U.S. Secret Service
Federal Building and U.S. Courthouse
222 West 7th Avenue, Room 559
Anchorage, AK 99513-7592
(907) 271-5148

U.S. Secret Service
3200 North Central Avenue
Phoenix, AZ 85012
(602) 640-5580

U.S. Secret Service
300 W. Congress Street
Box FB-56, Room 4-V
Tucson, AZ 85701
(520) 670-4730

U.S. Secret Service
111 Center Street
Little Rock, AR 72201-4419
(501) 324-6241

U.S. Secret Service
5200 North Palm Avenue, Suite 207
Fresno, CA 93704
(209) 487-5204

U.S. Secret Service
255 E. Temple Street, 17th Floor
Los Angeles, CA 90012
(213) 894-4830

U.S. Secret Service
4371 Latham Street, Suite 203
Riverside, CA 92501
(909) 276-6781

U.S. Secret Service
501 I Street, Suite 9-500
Sacramento, CA 95814-2322
(916) 930-2130

U.S. Secret Service
550 West C Street, Suite 660
San Diego, CA 92101
(619) 557-5640

U.S. Secret Service
345 Spear Street, Suite 530,
San Francisco, CA 94105
(415) 744-9026

U.S. Secret Service
280 S. First Street, Suite 2050
San Jose, CA 95113
(408) 535-5288

U.S. Secret Service
200 W. Santa Ana Boulevard
Santa Ana, CA 92701-4164
(714) 246-8257

U.S. Secret Service
P.O. Box 3969,
Ventura, CA 93006-3969
(805) 339-9180

U.S. Secret Service
212 N. Wahsatch, Room 204
Colorado Springs, CO 80903
(719) 632-3325

U.S. Secret Service
1660 Lincoln Street
Denver, CO 80264
(303) 866-1010

U.S. Secret Service
265 Church Street, Suite 1201
New Haven, CT 06510
(203) 865-2449

U.S. Secret Service
920 King Street
Wilmington, DE 19801
(302) 573-6188

U.S. Secret Service
1100 L Street N.W., Suite 6000
Washington, DC 20005
(202) 406-8000

U.S. Secret Service
5200 Belfort Road, Suite 200
Jacksonville, FL 32256-6012
(904) 724-6711

U.S. Secret Service
8375 N.W. 53rd Street
Miami, FL 33166
(305) 629-1800

U.S. Secret Service
135 West Central Boulevard
Orlando, FL 32801
(407) 648-6333

U.S. Secret Service
325 John Knox Road
Tallahassee, FL 32303
(850) 942-9523

U.S. Secret Service
501 East Polk Street
Tampa, FL 33602
(813) 228-2636

U.S. Secret Service
505 South Flagler Drive
West Palm Beach, FL 33401
(561) 659-0184

U.S. Secret Service
P.O. Box 1093
Albany, GA 31701
(912) 430-8442

U.S. Secret Service
P.O. Box 54407
Atlanta, GA 30308-0407
(404) 331-6111

U.S. Secret Service
33 Bull Street
Savannah, GA 31401-3334
(912) 652-4401

U.S. Secret Service
300 Ala Mdana Boulevard, Room 6-210
Honolulu, HI 96850
(808) 541-1912

U.S. Secret Service
550 Fort Street, Box 001
Boise, ID 83724-0001
(208) 334-1403

U.S. Secret Service
300 S. Riverside Plaza
Suite 1200 North
Chicago, IL 60606
(312) 353-5431

U.S. Secret Service
400 West Monroe Street, Suite 301
Springfield, IL 62704
(217) 492-4033

U.S. Secret Service
P.O. Box 530
Newburgh, IN 47629
(812) 858-7365

U.S. Secret Service
575 N. Pennsylvania Street, Suite 211
Inidanapolis, IN 46204
(317) 226-6444

U.S. Secret Service
P.O. Box 477
South Bend, IN 46624
(219) 273-3140

U.S. Secret Service
210 Walnut Street, Suite 637
Des Moines, IA 50309-2107
(515) 284-4565

U.S. Secret Service
301 N. Main, Suite 275
Wichita, KS 67202
(316) 269-6694

U.S. Secret Service
P.O. Box 910570,
Lexington, KY 40591-0570
(859) 223-2358

U.S. Secret Service
600 Dr. M. L. K. Jr. Place
Louisville, KY 40202
(502) 582-5171

U.S. Secret Service
One American Place
Baton Rouge, LA 70825
(225) 389-0763

U.S. Secret Service
501 Magazine Street
New Orleans, LA 70130
(504) 589-4041

U.S. Secret Service
401 Edwards Street
Shreveport, LA 71101
(318) 676-3500

U.S. Secret Service
100 Middle Street
West Tower, 2nd Floor
Portland, ME 04101
(207) 780-3493

U.S. Secret Service
100 S. Charles Street, 11th Floor
Baltimore, MD 21201
(410) 962-2200

U.S. Secret Service
U.S. Naval Academy Room 105
Police Dept. H.Q. Bldg. #257
Annapolis, MD 21402
(410) 268-7286

U.S. Secret Service
Rowley Training Center
9200 Powder Mill Road, Rte. 2
Laurel, MD 20708
(301) 344-8530

U.S. Secret Service
10 Causeway Street, Suite 791
Boston, MA 02222-1080
(617) 565-5640

U.S. Secret Service
477 Michigan Avenue, Suite 1000
Detroit, MI 48226
(313) 226-6400

U.S. Secret Service
330 Ionia Avenue, N.W., Suite 302
Grand Rapids, MI 49503-2350
(616) 454-4671

U.S. Secret Service
301 E. Genesee
Saginaw, MI 48607
(989) 752-8076

U.S. Secret Service
300 South 4th Street, Suite 750
Minneapolis, MN 55415
(612) 348-1800

U.S. Secret Service
100 West Capitol Street
Jackson, MS 39269
(601) 965-4436

U.S. Secret Service
1150 Grand Avenue
Kansis City, MO 64106
(816) 460-0600

U.S. Secret Service
901 St. Louis Street
Springfield, MO 65806
(417) 864-8340

U.S. Secret Service
111 S. 10th Street, Suite 11.346
St. Louis, MO 63102
(314) 539-2238

U.S. Secret Service
11 Third Street North
Great Falls, MT 59401
(406) 452-8515

U.S. Secret Service
2707 North 108 Street, Suite 301
Omaha, NE 68164
(402) 965-9670

U.S. Secret Service
600 Las Vegas Boulevard South, Suite 700
Las Vegas, NV 89101
(702) 388-6571

U.S. Secret Service
100 West Liberty Street
Reno, NV 89501
(775) 784-5354

U.S. Secret Service
1750 Elm Street, Suite 802
Manchester, NH 03104
(603) 626-5631

U.S. Secret Service
6601 Ventnor Avenue
Ventnor City, NJ 08406
(609) 487-1300

U.S. Secret Service
34 Headquarters Plaza
Morristown, NJ 07960-3990
(973) 656-4500

U.S. Secret Service
402 East State Street
Trenton, NJ 08608
(609) 989-2008

U.S. Secret Service
505 Marquette Street, N.W.
Albuquerque, NM 87102
(505) 248-5290

U.S. Secret Service
39 North Pearl Street, 2nd Floor
Albany, NY 12207
(518) 436-9600

U.S. Secret Service
610 Main Street
Buffalo, NY 14202
(716) 551-4401

U.S. Secret Service
John F. Kennedy International Airport
Jamaica, NY 11430
(718) 553-0911

U.S. Secret Service
35 Pinelawn Road
Melville, NY 11747
(631) 249-0404

U.S. Secret Service
335 Adams Street, 32nd Floor
Brooklyn, NY 11201
(718) 722-0712

U.S. Secret Service
100 State Street
Rochester, NY 14614
(716) 263-6830

U.S. Secret Service
100 S. Clinton Street, Room 1371
Syracuse, NY 13261
(315) 448-0304

U.S. Secret Service
140 Grand Street
White Plains, NY 10601
(914) 682-6300

U.S. Secret Service
6302 Fairview Road
Charlotte, NC 28210
(704) 442-8370

U.S. Secret Service
4905 Kogger Boulevard, Suite 220
Greensboro, NC 27407
(336) 547-4180

U.S. Secret Service
4700 Falls of Neuse Road, Suite 295
Raleigh, NC 27609
(919) 790-2834

U.S. Secret Service
1717 Shipyard Boulevard, Suite 340
Wilmington, NC 28403
(910) 815-4511

U.S. Secret Service
657 2nd Avenue North, Suite 302A
Fargo, ND 58102
(701) 239-5070

U.S. Secret Service
550 Main Street
Cincinnati, OH 45202
(513) 684-3585

U.S. Secret Service
6100 Rockside Woods Boulevard
Cleveland, OH 44131-2334
(216) 706-4365

U.S. Secret Service
500 South Front Street
Columbus, OH 43215
(614) 469-7370

U.S. Secret Service
200 West Second Street, Room 811
Dayton, OH 45402
(937) 225-2900

U.S. Secret Service
4 Seagate Center, Suite 702
Toledo, Ohio 43604
(419) 259-6434

U.S. Secret Service
4013 N.W. Expressway, Suite 650
Lakepoint Towers
Oklahoma City, OK 73116
(405) 810-3000

U.S. Secret Service
125 W. 15th Street
Tulsa, OK 74119-3824
(918) 581-7272

U.S. Secret Service
1001 S.W. 5th Avenue, Suite 1020
Portland, OR 97204
(503) 326-2162

U.S. Secret Service
600 Arch Street
Philadelphia, PA 19106
(215) 861-3300

U.S. Secret Service
1000 Liberty Avenue
Pittsburgh, PA 15222
(412) 395-6484

U.S. Secret Service
P.O. Box 247
Scranton, PA 18501
(717) 346-5781

U.S. Secret Service
1510 F. D. Roosevelt Avenue, Suite 3B
Guaynabo, PR 00968
(787) 277-1515

U.S. Secret Service
380 Westminster Street, Suite 343
Providence, RI 02903
(401) 331-6456

U.S. Secret Service
5900 Core Avenue
North Charleston, SC 29406
(843) 747-7242

U.S. Secret Service
1835 Assembly Street
Columbia, SC 29201
(803) 765-5446

U.S. Secret Service
7 Laurens Street, Suite 508
NCNB Plaza
Greenville, SC 29601
(864) 233-1490

U.S. Secret Service
P.O. Box #2240
Sioux Falls, SD 57101
(605) 330-4565

U.S. Secret Service
P.O. Box 6279
Chattanooga, TN 37401
(423) 752-5125

U.S. Secret Service
710 Locust Street
Knoxville, TN 37902
(423) 545-4627

U.S. Secret Service
5350 Poplar Avenue
Memphis, TN 38119
(901) 544-0333

U.S. Secret Service
801 Broadway Street
Nashville, TN 37203
(615) 736-5841

U.S. Secret Service
300 E. 8th Street
Austin, TX 78701
(512) 916-5103

U.S. Secret Service
125 E. John W. Carpenter, Suite 300
Irving, TX 75062-2752
(972) 868-3200

U.S. Secret Service
4849 North Mesa
El Paso, TX 79912
(915) 533-6950

U.S. Secret Service
602 Sawyer Street
Houston, TX 77007
(713) 868-2299

U.S. Secret Service
1205 Texas Avenue, Room 813
Lubbock, TX 79401
(806) 472-7347

U.S. Secret Service
200 S. 10th Street
McAllen, TX 78501
(210) 630-5811

U.S. Secret Service
727 E. Durango Boulevard
San Antonio, TX 78206-1265
(361) 308-6220

U.S. Secret Service
6101 South Broadway
Tyler, TX 75703
(903) 534-2933

U.S. Secret Service
57 W. 200 South Street, Suite 450
Salt Lake City, UT 84101-1610
(801) 524-5910

U.S. Secret Service
200 Granby Street, Suite 640
Norfolk, VA 23510
(757) 441-3200

U.S. Secret Service
600 E. Main Street
Richmond, VA 23219
(804) 771-2274

U.S. Secret Service
105 Franklin Road, S.W., Suite 2
Roanoke, VA 24011
(540) 345-4301

U.S. Secret Service
915 2nd Avenue
Seattle, WA 98174
(206) 220-6800

U.S. Secret Service
601 W. Riverside Avenue
Spokane, WA 99201-0611
(509) 353-2532

U.S. Secret Service
Summers and Lee Streets
Charleston, WV 25301
(304) 347-5188

U.S. Secret Service
660 W. Washington Avenue, Suite 305
Madison, WI 53703
(608) 264-5191

U.S. Secret Service
517 E. Wisconsin Avenue
Milwaukee, WI 53202
(414) 297-3587

U.S. Secret Service
2120 Capitol Avenue, Suite 3026
Cheyenne, WY 82001
(307) 772-2380

Overseas Offices

U.S. Secret Service
Bangkok
P.O. Box 64
American Embassy—BANGKOK
APO AP, 96546
011-662-255-1959

U.S. Secret Service
Berlin
PSC 120, BOX 3000
APO AE 09265
011-49-30-8305-1450

U.S. Secret Service
Bogota
American Embassy—Bogata
USSS Unit 5146
APO AA 34038
011-571-315-1319

U.S. Secret Service
Bonn
USSS—American Embassy BONN
PCS 117, BOX 300
APO AE 09265
011-49-228-339-2587

U.S. Secret Service
Hong Kong
25 Garden Road
Central Hong Kong
011-852-2841-2524

U.S. Secret Service
London
PSC 801, Box 28
FPO AE 09498-4064
011-44-171-499-9000

U.S. Secret Service
Manila
American Embassy/USSS
FPO AP 96515
011-632-523-1167

U.S. Secret Service
Milan
USSS PSC 59
Milan APO AE 09624
011-39-02-290-35-477

U.S. Secret Service
Moscow
American Embassy, PSC 77 (USSS)
APO AE 09721
011-7-095-252-2451

U.S. Secret Service
Montreal
c/o U.S. Consulate—Montreal
P.O. Box 847
Champlain, NY 12919-0847
(514) 398-9488

U.S. Secret Service
Nicosia
American Embassy—Nicosia, PFC-815
FPO AE 09836
011-357-2-776-400-2549

U.S. Secret Service
Ottawa 613-569-4180
American Embassy (USSS)
P.O. Box 5000
Ogdensburg, NY 13669

U.S. Secret Service
Paris, France
American Embassy—Paris
USSS PSC 116/Box D306
APO AE 09777
011-331- 4312-7100

U.S. Secret Service
Rome
American Embassy—Rome
PSC 59 Box 62, USSS
APO AE 09624
011-39-06-4674-1

U.S. Secret Service
Vancouver
145 Tyee Drive
Pt. Roberts, WA 98371-9602
(604) 689-3011

U.S. DEPARTMENT OF STATE OPPORTUNITIES

This last section in the chapter describes positions available in the State Department.

Diplomatic Security Service (DSS) Careers

```
┌─────────────────────────────┐
│ Diplomatic Security Service │
└─────────────────────────────┘
       │
       ├─ Special Agent
       ├─ Security Engineering Officer
       ├─ Security Technical Specialist
       └─ Diplomatic Courier
```

Department of State
Diplomatic Security Service
2201 C Street, N.W.
Washington, DC 20520
(202) 647-7284
www.ds.state.gov/

POSITIONS

Special Agent *FS-6*		$43,094–$64-519
Security Engineering Officer	*FS-6*	$43,094–$64-519
Security Technical Specialist	*FP-6*	$34,776–$46,736
Diplomatic Courier *FP-6*		$34,776–$46,736

MAIN MISSION

Department of State special agents work both overseas and within the United States. They are responsible for personnel security investigations, special protection of dignitaries, and the handling of sensitive information. Diplomatic security service staff conduct special investigations and provide protection to embassy personnel and facilities. In addition, the State Department enforces the laws pertaining to the issuance, use, and manufacture of passports and visas.

HOMELAND SECURITY MISSION

Prevention
Deterrence
Crisis Management
Consequence Management
Attribution

REQUIREMENTS
Age:	21 to 35 years	
Education:	Bachelor's degree	and/or
Experience:	3 years general	FS-6
	1 year specialized	

OPPORTUNITIES   ✪Over 700 Agents (in the next four years)

TERRORISM'S DARK HISTORY

U.S. Embassy Bombings in East Africa, August 7, 1998: A bomb exploded at the rear entrance of the U.S. embassy in Nairobi, Kenya, killing 12 U.S. citizens, 32 foreign service nationals, and 247 Kenyan citizens. About 5,000 Kenyans, six U.S. citizens, and 13 foreign service nationals were injured. The U.S. embassy building sustained extensive structural damage. Almost simultaneously, a bomb detonated outside the U.S. embassy in Dar es Salaam, Tanzania, killing seven foreign service nationals and three Tanzanian citizens and injuring one U.S. citizen and 76 Tanzanians. The explosion caused major structural damage to the U.S. embassy facility. The U.S. government held Osama bin Laden responsible.

Source: U.S. Department of State

COMMENTS   Must qualify for a top secret security clearance. Special agents are most frequently assigned first to a domestic field office for 2 years.

EMPLOYMENT CONDITIONS   The foreign service requires international assignment. Candidates with language skills have an edge. Training occurs at the Federal Law Enforcement Training Center, Glynco, GA.

WHERE TO APPLY
Civil Service Personnel Office
24-hour job phone line (202) 647-7284
www.ds.state.gov/
DSRecruitment@state.gov

Department of State
Civil Service
2201 C Street, N.W.
Washington, DC 20520

Security Officer Recruitment Division
P.O. Box 9317
Rosslyn Station
Arlington, VA 22219

Foreign Service
P.O. Box 9317
Arlington, VA 22210
(703) 875-7490

Investigative Field Offices

Phoenix, AZ	(602) 640-4842
Los Angeles, CA	(213) 894-3290
San Diego, CA	(619) 557-6194
San Francisco, CA	(415) 705-1176
Denver, CO	(303) 236-2782
Stamford, CT	(203) 975-0820
Washington, DC	(703) 204-6101
Miami, FL	(305) 536-5781
Atlanta, GA	(404) 331-3521
Honolulu, HI	(808) 541-2854
Chicago, IL	(312) 353-6163
New Orleans, LA	(504) 589-2010
Boston, MA	(617) 565-8200
New York, NY	(212) 264-1292
Greensboro, NC	(336) 547-4292
Philadelphia, PA	(215) 861-3370
San Juan, PR	(809) 766-5704
Dallas, TX	(214) 767-0702
Houston, TX	(713) 209-3482
Seattle, WA	(206) 220-7721

"All that is necessary for evil to triumph is for good men to do nothing."

Edmund Burke

SECTION

2

EMERGENCY PREPAREDNESS AND RESPONSE CAREERS

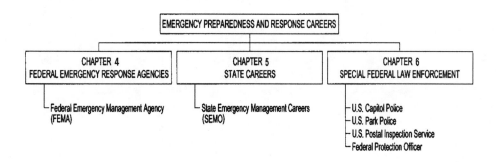

Chapter 4

FEDERAL EMERGENCY RESPONSE AGENCY OPPORTUNITIES

☐ **Federal Emergency Management Agency (FEMA) Careers**

☐ **U.S. Fire Administration (USFA) Careers**

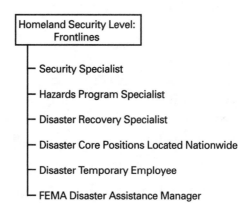

Career opportunities in the field of Federal Emergency Response are mostly limited to jobs within the Federal Emergency Management Agency (FEMA) and the U.S. Fire Administration.

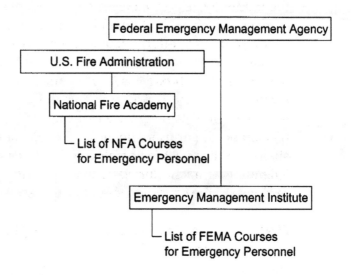

FEDERAL EMERGENCY MANAGEMENT AGENCY (FEMA) CAREERS

Federal Emergency Management Agency
Federal Center Plaza
500 C Street, S.W.
Washington, D.C. 20472
(202) 566-1600
www.fema.gov
Hire.Me@fema.gov

POSITIONS			
Security Specialist	*GS-5/7/9*		$25,822–$44,783
Hazards Program Specialist	*GS-5/7/9*		$25,822–$44,783
Disaster Recovery Specialist	*GS-5/7/9*		$25,822–$44,783
Disaster Assistance Manager	*GS 5/7/9*		$25,822–$44,783
Disaster Core Positions			Pay Varies
Disaster Temporary Employee			Pay Varies
Student Interns			Pay Varies

MAIN MISSION

The Federal Emergency Management Agency (FEMA) is the central agency within the federal government for emergency planning, preparedness, mitigation, response, and recovery. The Federal Emergency Management Agency, created in 1979, reports directly to the White House and manages the president's Disaster Relief Fund. By working closely with state and local governments, FEMA funds emergency programs, offers technical guidance and training, and makes available federal resources in events of disaster. Its coordinated activities ensure that broad-based programs protect life and property and provide recovery assistance after disasters. FEMA's special duties include off-site planning for emergencies at commercial nuclear power plants and the army's chemical stockpile sites, emergency food and shelter funding for the homeless, plans to ensure the continuity of the federal government during national security emergencies, and federal response to the consequences of major terrorist incidents.

FEMA also administrates the Emergency Management Institute (EMI) at Emmitsburg, Maryland, which offers professional courses for the nation's emergency managers. FEMA also runs the U.S. Fire Administration (USFA) and its National Fire Academy (NFA), providing national leadership in fire safety and prevention. The U.S. Fire Administration has responsibility for all fire prevention and public fire safety education.

NATURAL DISASTERS
- Earthquakes
- Extreme heat
- Floods and flash floods
- Hurricanes
- Landslides and mudflows
- Thunderstorms and lightning
- Tornadoes
- Tsunamis
- Volcanoes
- Wildland fires
- Winter driving
- Winter storms
- Winter preparedness safety tips

TECHNOLOGICAL DISASTERS
- Hazardous materials
- Finding hazards in the home
- Hazardous materials in the home
- House and building fires
- Radiological accidents—under revision
- Nuclear power plant emergency
- Terrorism

HOMELAND SECURITY MISSION	Crisis Management Consequence Management

PROFILE OF AGENCY	Personnel:	Approximately 2300 full-time & 4000 temporary and reserve employees

REQUIREMENTS	Age:	Open
	Education:	Open/Diverse
	Background Investigation	
	Top secret security clearance	

OPPORTUNITIES Over 200 nationwide (*during staffing-up period)

COMMENTS Whenever an event happens, Americans, maybe even your family, friends, and neighbors, need help. FEMA employees either coordinate the emergency response or have trained the folks on the scene. This is a critical need area. There exist full-time, part-time, and temporary disaster employee opportunities that can be a great entry level to a homeland security career. FEMA has its own Emergency Management Institute to train and instruct in a wide variety of related subjects— some for college credit. Also included in this section is a little-known opportunity for those in fire departments and in other emergency positions: the national Fire Academy. It provides state-of-the-art training and coursework, including higher-level college credits in emergency response and disaster planning.

FEMA DISASTER CORE POSITIONS LOCATED NATIONWIDE

This is on-call employment. Positions are term appointments for up to four years, with the possibility for a one-year extension. Depending on the level of disaster activity, the incumbent is subject to release to a nonpay status and recall to duty within 48 hours to meet the fluctuating work requirements. Travel to disaster areas may be required with very short notice at any time of the year. Relocation expenses will not be paid.

Source: FEMA

INTERNSHIP PROGRAM   Yes

STUDENT PROGRAMS   Yes

WHERE TO APPLY   Applicants must complete the online application at **www.appl.fema.gov/career/**

Contact information: Job Hotline at (800) 225-3304
E-mail: **Hire.Me@fema.gov**

Federal Emergency Management Agency
Human Resources Division/Regional Services Branch
16825 South Seton Avenue
Building E, Room 113
Emmitsburg, MD 21727

"It is not the critic who counts, not the man who points out how the strong man stumbled, or where the doer of deeds could have done better. The credit belongs to the man who is actually in the arena; whose face is marred by the dust and sweat and blood; who strives valiantly; who errs and comes short again and again; who knows the great enthusiasms, the great devotions, and spends himself in a worthy course; who, at the best, knows in the end the triumph of high achievement, and who, at worst, if he fails, at least fails while daring greatly; so that his place shall never be with those cold and timid souls who know neither victory or defeat."

President Theodore Roosevelt, 1910

FEMA Personnel Offices and Jurisdiction

Federal Emergency Management Agency
Federal Center Plaza
500 C Street, S.W.
Washington, DC 20472
(202) 566-1600

FEMA Region I

442 J. W. McCormack
Post Office and Courthouse Building
Boston, MA 02109
(617) 223-9540

Jurisdiction: Maine, New Hampshire, Vermont, Rhode Island, Connecticut, and Massachusetts.

FEMA Region II

26 Federal Plaza
New York, NY 10278
(212) 680-3600

Jurisdiction: New York, New Jersey, Puerto Rico, and U.S. Virgin Islands.

FEMA Region III

615 Chestnut Street
Philadelphia, PA 10106
(215) 931-5608

Jurisdiction: District of Columbia, Delaware, Maryland, Pennsylvania, Virginia, and West Virginia.

FEMA Region IV

3003 Chamblee-Tucker Road
Atlanta, GA 30341
(770) 220-5200

Jurisdiction: Alabama, Florida, Georgia, Kentucky, Mississippi, North Carolina, South Carolina, and Tennessee.

FEMA Region V

536 South Clark Street
Chicago, IL 60605
(312) 408-5500

Jurisdiction: Illinois, Indiana, Michigan, Minnesota, Ohio, and Wisconsin.

FEMA Region VI

Federal Regional Center
800 N. Loop 288
Denton, TX 76209
(940) 898-5399

Jurisdiction: Arkansas, Louisiana, New Mexico, Oklahoma, and Texas.

FEMA Region VII

2323 Grand Boulevard
Suite 900
Kansas City, MO 64108
(816) 283-7061

Jurisdiction: Iowa, Kansas, Missouri, and Nebraska.

FEMA Region VIII

Building 710, Box 25267
Denver, CO 80225-0267
(303) 235-4800

Jurisdiction: Colorado, Montana, North Dakota, South Dakota, Utah, and Wyoming.

FEMA Region IX

1111 Broadway, Suite 1200
Oakland, CA 94607
(415) 923-7100

Jurisdiction: Arizona, California, Hawaii, Nevada, the Territory of American Samoa, the Territory of Guam, the Commonwealth of the Northern Mariana Islands, the Republic of the Marshall Islands, the Federated States of Micronesia, and the Republic of Palau.

FEMA Region X

Federal Regional Center
130 228th St. SW
Bothell, WA 98021
(206) 487-4765

Jurisdiction: Alaska, Idaho, Oregon, and Washington.

SPECIAL FEMA TRAINING

TERRORISM TRAINING AND RESOURCES

FEMA provides special training and preparedness education to help communities and individuals prepare to deal with the consequences of terrorism.

FEMA Training Resources for Community Preparedness

Resident Courses at EMI

E417	Community Emergency Response Team (CERT) Train-the-Trainer Course
S301	Radiological Emergency Response Operations Course
S302	Advanced Radiation Incident Operations Course
S425	Radiological Series Train-the-Trainer
S915	Integrated Emergency Management Course (IEMC): Consequences of Terrorism

EMI Courses Taught by State Offices of Emergency Management

G190	Incident Command System (ICS) for Law Enforcement Personnel
G191	Incident Command System (ICS)/Emergency Operations Center (EOC) Interface
G192	Incident Command System (ICS) for Public Works Officials
G194	Incident Command System (ICS) for Public Officials Conference
G195	Intermediate Incident Command System (ICS)
G196	Advanced Incident Command System (ICS)
G120	Exercise Design Course
G130	Exercise Evaluation Course
G202	Debris Management
G250.11	Continuity of Operations (COOP) Workshop in Emergency Management (WEM)
G250.12	Senior Officials Workshop on Terrorism
G310	Weapons of Mass Destruction
G310.1	Weapons of Mass Destruction: Nuclear Scenario
G310.2	Weapons of Mass Destruction: Radiological Scenario
G310.3	Weapons of Mass Destruction: Chemical-Sarin Scenario
G310.4	Weapons of Mass Destruction: Chemical-Vx Scenario
G310.5	Weapons of Mass Destruction: Biological-Anthrax Scenario
G320	Fundamentals Course for Radiological Response Teams
G346	Hospital Emergency Department Management of Hazardous Materials Accidents
G357	Emergency Response to Criminal and Terrorist Incidents
G386	Mass Fatalities Incident Response

Independent Study Courses

IS3	Radiological Emergency Management
IS195	Basic Incident Command System (ICS)
IS301	Radiological Emergency Response
IS330	Refresher Course for Radiological Response
IS346	Orientation to Hazardous Materials for Medical Personnel

A HIGHER-EDUCATION COURSE

Terrorism and Emergency Management

A college-level course covering various terrorism issues.
Chemical Stockpile Emergency Preparedness Program (CSEPP) Courses
Joint Information Center (JIC) Joint Information System (JIS) Course
ACT FAST (Agent Characterization and Toxicity First Aid and Special
Treatment)

U.S. FIRE ADMINISTRATION (USFA) CAREERS

U.S. Fire Administration
National Fire Academy
16825 S. Seton Ave.
Emmitsburg, MD 21727
(301) 447-1000
www.usfa.fema.gov/nfa

POSITIONS   *Fire Program Specialist (Research)*   *GS-9* $34,451–$44,783

Program Specialist (Emergency Response)   *GS-9*
$34,451–$44,783

MAIN   The National Fire Academy (NFA) was created in 1974 and offers a
MISSION   comprehensive curriculum of courses to assist firefighters, emergency
medical personnel, and other first responders to be prepared to deal
with terrorist incidents. NFA touts that since 1975 over 1,400,000 students have been trained, so countless lives have been saved and
property losses prevented thanks to the instruction.

"To respond to terrorists, we have to anticipate their moves. We cannot be
everywhere at once. Our resources won't allow it. More importantly, our
freedoms won't allow it. Our National Strategy will be guided by an over-
arching philosophy: risk management—focusing our resources where they
will do the most good and achieve the maximum protection of lives and
property."

President George W. Bush, April 29, 2002

HOMELAND SECURITY MISSION	Crisis Management Consequence Management
PROFILE OF AGENCY	See FEMA

REQUIREMENTS

Age:	Open
Education:	Open/Diverse
Background Investigation	
Top secret security clearance	

OPPORTUNITIES   Very small—seeking extremely specialized staff

COMMENTS   Opportunity is extremely limited with the NFA. The main focus of this entry is to indentify the outstanding training and education being given.

America's fire death rate is one of the highest per capita in the industrialized world. Fire kills over 4,000 and injures more than 22,000 people each year. Also, approximately 100 firefighters die in the line of duty each year. Direct property losses due to fire exceed $11 billion a year. Most of these deaths and losses can be prevented!

Source: USFA

INTERNSHIP PROGRAM   No

STUDENT PROGRAMS   No

WHERE TO APPLY   **www.appl.fema.gov/career/**
Contact information: Job Hotline at (800) 225-3304
E-mail: **Hire.Me@fema.gov.**

NFA Course Methods

- **At the resident facility in Emmitsburg, Maryland:** The academy conducts specialized training courses and advanced management programs of national impact. Programs target middle- and top-level fire officers, fire service instructors, technical professionals, and representatives from allied professions including allied professionals, such as police, military, or personnel from other government agencies who need to understand the fire service perspectives on incident management. Any person with substantial involvement in fire prevention and control, emergency medical services, or fire-related emergency management activities is eligible to apply for Academy courses.

- **Throughout the nation with state and local fire training organizations:** Many volunteer and career fire service personnel do not have the time to attend on-campus programs. To reach these students, the academy offers courses through a distance delivery training system. NFA two-day courses are available for direct delivery in states and local communities. Students can attend select one- and two-week NFA courses within their geographical region.

- **Local colleges and universities:** NFA has a program involving a network of seven colleges and universities for those interested in pursuing the degrees at a distance program. Fire service personnel who cannot attend college due to work hours and locations are able to earn a degree in fire technology and management through independent study.

SPECIAL NFA TRAINING

Main Focus

Fundamentals of Fire Protection
Fire Protection Systems
Fire Behavior and Combustion
Fire Protection Hydraulics and Water Supply
Building Construction for Fire Protection
Fire Prevention

Arson Curriculum

R205	Fire/Arson Investigation
R207	Management for Arson Prevention and Control
R208	Interviewing-Interrogation Techniques and Courtroom Testimony
R811	Fire Cause Determination for Company Officers (VIP)

Emergency Medical Services Curriculum

R150   Management of Emergency Medical Services
R151   Advanced Leadership Issues in Emergency Medical Service
R247   Advanced Life Support Response to Hazardous Materials
        Incidents
R152   Emergency Medical Services: Special Operations
R822   Advanced Incident Safety Operations and Management (VIP)

Emergency Response to Terrorism Curriculum

R817   Emergency Response to Terrorism: Incident Management
        (VIP)

Fire Prevention: Management Curriculum

R101   Code Management: A Systems Approach
R225   Management of Fire Prevention Programs
R280   Leading Community Risk Reduction
R309   Strategic Analysis of Community Risk Reduction

Hazardous Materials Curriculum

R229   Hazardous Materials Operating Site Practices
R243   Hazardous Materials Incident Management
R814   Hazardous Materials Incident Management (VIP)

Management Science Curriculum

R107   Fire Service Communications
R331   Organizational Theory in Practice
R332   Interpersonal Dynamics in Fire Service Organizations

FACTS ABOUT FIRST RESPONDERS

There are over 1 million firefighters in the United States, of which approximately 750,000 are volunteers. Local police departments have an estimated 556,000 full-time employees, including about 436,000 sworn law enforcement personnel. Sheriffs' offices reported about 291,000 full-time employees, including about 186,000 sworn officers. There are over 155,000 nationally registered emergency medical technicians.

Source: Homeland Security Agency

Chapter 5

OPPORTUNITIES WITH INDIVIDUAL STATE EMERGENCY MANAGEMENT ORGANIZATIONS (SEMOs)

☐ **SEMO Listings by State**

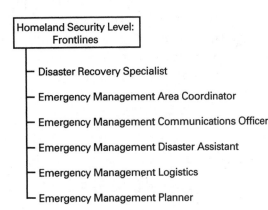

STATE EMERGENCY MANAGEMENT ORGANIZATIONS

Unlike previous chapters, this one does not discuss federal organizations. Instead, it focuses on state emergency management organizations (SEMOs). It includes a listing of SEMOs by state.

**POSITIONS
(TYPICAL)**

Emergency Management Area Coordinator
Emergency Management Communications Officer
Emergency Management Disaster Assistant
Emergency Management Logistics
Emergency Management Planner
Information Technology Systems Technician
Radio Operator
Student Intern/Aide

(*See Special Comments)

**MAIN
MISSION**

The main missions of state emergency management organizations (SEMOs) is to minimize the loss of life and property from disasters. SEMO coordinates its state emergency services and the efforts of governmental agencies to reduce the impact of disasters on persons and property. SEMOs are responsible for the administration of statewide planning, training, and coordination of effective emergency response to natural and technological emergencies. They prevent loss of life or property resulting from any natural or man-made cause. This is not limited to terrorism, fire, flood, earthquake, windstorm, wave action, oil spill, or other water contamination requiring emergency action to avert danger or damage, epidemic, air contamination, blight, drought, infestation, explosion, riot, or terrorism.

**HOMELAND
SECURITY
MISSION**

Prevention
Deterrence
Crisis Management
Consequence Management

**PROFILE OF
AGENCY**

Unknown

REQUIREMENTS   Vary per position by state

> "Terrorism is the premeditated, deliberate, systematic murder, mayhem, and threatening of the innocent to create fear and intimidation in order to gain a political or tactical advantage, usually to influence an audience."
>
> James M. Poland

COMMENTS The positions listed on page 98 do not reflect the actual positions for each state SEMO agency but a typical position as they vary slightly in name and description from state to state. Like police departments in the United States, each SEMO is slightly different. Some, like the one in Hawaii, are just an extension of the National Guard. Most SEMOs utilize existing state employees in various agencies for staffing. However, opportunities still exist, and approaching them to work as an intern or volunteer could lead to enhancing your résumé.

SPECIAL NOTE

Most states are in the process of establishing state homeland agencies. However, at the time of this publication, most are token efforts at best and are housed with the state's SEMO or governor's offices.

INTERNSHIP PROGRAM Yes

STUDENT PROGRAMS Yes

**FIRST RESPONDER'S GUIDE TO TERRORISM INCIDENTS
THE TEN "-ATES"**

- Evacuate the area as quickly and safely as possible.
- Isolate the site to restrict access by all personnel.
- Hesitate. Fools rush in. Don't be one.
- Evaluate the situation and your potential response actions before entering the scene.
- Communicate your conclusions and call for assistance as necessary (because of bomb danger, use NO radios or cellular phones closer than 300 yards). Notify hospitals as appropriate.
- Infiltrate. Go in carefully, only when it is time to do so.
- Procrastinate. Take no action until it is as safe as possible and only when necessary. ↓

- Investigate. Remember, this is a crime scene. Do not exceed your authority, but support and assist the investigation as appropriate.
- Cooperate with other responders (teamwork!) and with those in charge.
- Decontaminate and clean up carefully to avoid accidental removal of evidence and to avoid endangering others.

Source: Pennsylvania Emergency Management Agency

WHERE TO APPLY   Applicants should send a letter stating you are interested in applying for a position and a résumé to any of the organizations listed below. Samples of both are shown in Chapter 11.

SEMOs by State

Alabama Emergency Management Agency
5898 County Road 41
P.O. Box 2160
Clanton, AL 35046
(205) 280-2200
(205) 280-2495
www.personnel.state.al.us

Alaska Division of Emergency Services
Dept. of Miltary and Veteran Affairs
P.O. Box 5750
Fort Richardson-Camp Denali, AK
    99505-5750
(205) 428-6030
www.ak-prepared.com/

Arkansas Department of Emergency
    Management
P.O. Box 758
Conway, AR 72033-0758
(501) 730-9750
www.adem.state.ar.us/

Arizona Division of Emergency
    Management
5636 East McDowell Road
Phoenix, AZ 85008-3495
(602) 244-0504
(800) 411-2336
www.dem.state.az.us/

California Governor's Office of
    Emergency Services
P.O. Box 419047
Rancho Cordova, CA 95741-9047
(916) 845-8321
Exam/Job Information (916) 845-8324
Fax: (916) 845-8910
www.oes.ca.gov/

Colorado Office of Emergency
    Management (COEM)
15075 South Golden Road
Golden, CO 80401-3979
Office: (303) 273-1622
Fax: (303) 273-1795
www.dlg.oem2.state.co.us
www.dola.state.co.us/oem/
    oemindex.htm

Connecticut Office of Emergency
    Management
Military Department
360 Broad Street
Hartford, CT 06105
(860) 566-3180
Fax: (860) 247-0664
www.mil.state.ct.us/oem.htm

Delaware Emergency Management
  Agency
165 Brick Store Landing Road
Smyrna, DE 19977
(302) 659-3362
Fax: (302) 326-6045
www.state.de.us/dema/index.htm

District of Columbia Emergency
  Management Agency
2000 14th Street, N.W., 8th Floor
Washington, DC 20009
(202) 727-2775
Fax: (202) 673-2290
www.dc.gov/

Florida Division of Emergency
  Management
2555 Shumard Oak Boulevard
Tallahassee, FL 32399-2100
(850) 413-9900
www.floridadisaster.org

Georgia Emergency Management Agency
P.O. Box 18055
Atlanta, GA 30316-0055
(404) 635-7000
Fax: (404) 635-7205
www.2.state.ga.us/GEMA/

Hawaii State Civil Defense
920 Ululani Street
Hilo, HI 96720
(808) 935-6460
Fax: (808) 935-6460
www.sed.state.hi.us/index.html

Idaho Bureau of Disaster Services
Military Division
Building 600
Boise, ID 83705-5004
(208) 422-5268
www.state.id.us/bds/bds.html

Illinois Emergency
  Management Agency
110 East Adams Street
Springfield, IL 62701
(217) 782-2700
Fax: (217) 524-7967
www.state.il.us/iema

Indiana State Emergency Management
  Agency
302 West Washington Street
Room E208A
Indianapolis, IN 46204
(317) 232-3986
Fax: (317) 232-3895

State of Idaho—Bureau of Disaster
  Services
www.state.id.us/bds/bds.html
www.ai.org/sema/index.html

Iowa Emergency Management Division
Department of Public Defense
Hoover Office Building
Des Moines, IA 50319
(515) 281-3231
Fax: (515) 281-7539
www.state.ia.us/government/
  dpd/emd/index.htm

Kansas Division of Emergency
  Management
2800 S.W. Topeka Boulevard
Topeka, KS 66611-1287
(785) 274-1401
Fax: (785) 274-1426
www.ink.org/public/kdem/

Louisiana Office of Emergency
  Preparedness
P.O. Box 44217
Baton Rouge, LA 70804
(225) 342-5470
www.loep.state.la.us

Maine Emergency Management Agency
72 State House Station
Augusta, ME 04333-0072
(207) 626-4503
Fax: (207) 626-4499
**www.state.me.us/mema/
memahome.htm**

Maryland Emergency Management
Agency
Camp Fretterd Military Reservation
5401 Rue Saint Lo Drive
Reistertown, MD 21136
(410) 517-3600
Fax: (410) 517-3610
www.mema.state.md.us/

Massachusetts Emergency Management
Agency
400 Worcester Road
Framingham, MA 01702-5399
(508) 820-2000
Fax: (508) 820-2030
www.state.ma.us/mema

Michigan Department of State Police
Emergency Management Division
4000 Collins Road
P.O. Box 30636
Lansing, MI 48909
(517) 333-5042
Fax: (517) 333-4987
**www.msp.state.mi.us/division/
emd/emdweb1.htm**

Minnesota Department of Public Safety
Division of Emergency Management
444 Cedar Street
Suite 223
St. Paul, MN 55101
(651) 296-0450
Fax: (651) 296-0459
www.dps.state.mn.us/emermgt/

Missouri State Emergency Management
Agency
P.O. Box 116
Jefferson City, MO 65102
(573) 526-9101
Fax: (573) 634-7966
www.sema.state.mo.us/semapage.htm

Mississippi Emergency Management
Agency
1410 Riverside Drive
Jackson, MS 39202-1297
(601) 352-9100 (24 Hours)
Fax: (601) 352-8314
www.msema.org/index.htm

Nebraska Emergency Management
Agency
1300 Military Road
Lincoln, NE 68508-1090
(402) 471-7410
Fax: (402) 471-7433
www.nebema.org

New Hampshire Governor's Office of
Emergency Management
State Office Park South
107 Pleasant Street
Concord, NH 03301-3809
(603) 271-2231
Fax: (603) 225-7341
www.nhoem.state.nh.us/

New Jersey Office of Emergency
Management
P.O. Box 7068
West Trenton, NJ 08628-0068
(609) 538-6050
Fax: (609) 538-0345
www.state.nj.us/njoem/

New Mexico Division of Emergency
  Management
P.O. Box 1628
Santa Fe, NM 87504-1628
(505) 476-9606
www.dps.nm.org/emc.htm

New York State Emergency Management
  Office
1220 Washington Avenue
Building 22, Suite 101
Albany, NY 12226-2251
(518) 457-2222
Fax: (518) 457-9995
www.nysemo.state.ny.us/

North Carolina Division of Emergency
  Management
Administration Building
116 West Jones Street
Raleigh, NC 27699-4713
(919) 733-3867
www.dem.dcc.state.nc.us/

North Dakota, Department of
  Emergency Management
P.O. Box 5511
Bismark, ND 58506-5511
(701) 328-8100
(701) 328-8181
www.state.nd.us/dem

Nevada Division of Emergency
  Management
2525 South Carson Street
Carson City, NV 89701
(775) 687-4240
Fax: (775) 687-6788
www.dem.state.nv.us/index.htm

Ohio Emergency Management Agency
2855 West Dublin-Granville Road
Columbus, OH 43235
(614) 889-7150
Fax: (614) 889-7183
www.state.oh.us/odps/division/ema/

Oklahoma Department of Civil
  Emergency Management
P.O. Box 53365
Oklahoma City, OK 73152-3365
(405) 521-2481
www.onenet.net/~odcem/

Oregon Emergency Management
595 Cottage Street, N.E.
Salem, OR 97310
(503) 378-2911
www.osp.state.or.us/oem/oem.htm

Pennsylvania Emergency Management
  Agency
2605 Interstate Drive
Harrisburg, PA 17110-9364
(717) 651-2001
Fax: (717) 651-2021
www.pema.state.pa.us

Puerto Rico State Emergency
  Management Agency
Office of the Governor
P.O. Box 966597
San Juan, PR 00906-6597
(787) 724-0124
Fax: (787) 725-4244

Rhode Island Emergency Management
  Agency
645 New London Avenue
Cranston, RI 02920
(401) 946-9996
Fax: (401) 944-1891
www.state.ri.us/riema/riemaaa.html

South Carolina Emergency Management
  Division
1100 Fish Hatchery Road
West Columbia, SC 29172
(803) 737-8500
www.state.sc.us/emd/sitemap.htm

South Dakota Division of Emergency
Management
500 East Capitol
Pierre, SD 57501-5070
(605) 773-3231
Fax: (605) 773-3580
www.state.sd.us/military/sddem.htm

Tennessee Emergency Management
Agency (TEMA)
3041 Sidco Drive
Nashville, TN 37204
or
P.O. Box 45102
Nashville, TN 37204
(800) 258-3300 (24 hour) out-of-state
Fax: (615) 242-9635
www.tnema.org

Texas Division of Emergency
Management
P.O. Box 4087
Austin, TX 78773-0001
(512) 424-2138
www.txdps.state.tx.us/dem/

Utah, Division of Emergency Services
and Homeland Security
Room 1110, State Office Building
Salt Lake City, UT 84114
(801) 538-3400
Toll-free (800) SL-FAULT
Fax: (801) 538-3770
www.des.utah.gov/
www.cem.ps.state.ut.us

Vermont Division of Emergency
Management
103 S. Main Street
Waterbury, VT 05671-2101
(802) 244-8721
Fax: (802) 244-8655
E-mail: **evonturk@dps.state.vt.us**
www.dps.state.vt.us/

Virginia Department of Emergency
Management
10501 Trade Court
Richmond, VA 23236-3713
(804) 897-6500
Fax: (804) 897-6506
www.vdem.state.va.us

Virgin Islands Territorial Emergency
Management Agency
A & Q Building
#2C Estate Contant
St. Thomas, VI 00820
(340) 774-2244
Fax: (340) 774-1491
www.gov.vi/

Washington Emergency Management
Division
WA Military Department
Camp Murray, WA 98453-5122
(253) 512-7001
www.wa.gov/wsem/

West Virginia Office of Emergency
Services
Building 1, Room EB-80
1900 Kanawha Boulevard, East
Charleston, WV 25305-0360
(304) 558-5380
Fax: (304) 344-4538

Wisconsin Emergency Management
2400 Wright Street
P.O. Box 7865
Madison, WI 53707
(608) 242-3232
Fax: (608) 242-3247

Wyoming Emergency Management
Agency
5500 Bishop Boulevard
Cheyenne, WY 82009-3320
(307) 777-4900
Fax: (307) 635-6017
www.wema.state.wy.us

WHAT YOU CAN DO TO PREPARE

Develop a disaster plan together as a family.

1. Create an emergency communications plan.
   - Choose an out-of-town contact your family will call or e-mail to check on each other should a disaster occur.
   - Make sure every household member has that contact's, and each other's, e-mail addresses and telephone numbers (home, work, pager, and cell).

2. Establish a meeting place.
   - Have a predetermined meeting place away from your home.

3. Assemble a disaster supplies kit.
   - Prepare a disaster supplies kit in an easy-to-carry container such as a duffel bag or small plastic trash can. Include special needs items for any member of your household (diapers, medicines, and so on), first aid supplies, change of clothing, sleeping bags, a battery-powered radio or television and extra batteries, food, bottled water, and tools.
   - Include some cash and copies of important family documents.

4. Check on the school emergency plan of any school-age children you may have.
   - You need to know if the school will keep children at school until a parent or designated adult can pick them up or send them home on their own. Be sure that the school has updated information about how to reach parents and responsible caregivers to arrange for pickup.

Source: American Red Cross

Chapter 6

SPECIAL FEDERAL LAW ENFORCEMENT OPPORTUNITIES

☐ **U.S. Capitol Police Careers**

☐ **Federal Protective Service (FPO) Careers**

☐ **National Park Service (NPS) Careers**

☐ **U.S. Postal Inspection Service Careers**

Homeland Security Level:
Frontlines

— U.S. Capitol Police Officer

— Federal Protection Officer

— U.S. Park Police Officer

— U.S. Postal Inspector

There are four different agencies that are classified as special law enforcement: the Capitol Police, the Federal Protection Service, the Park Police, and the Postal Inspection Service. This chapter explains the positions available in these services.

U.S. CAPITOL POLICE CAREERS

United States Capitol Police
119 D Street, N.W.
U.S. Capitol Building
Washington, DC 20510-7218
(202) 224-9820
www.uscapitolpolice.gov

POSITION   *United States Capitol Police Officer* $39,427–$44,682

MAIN MISSION

Provide police services for the U.S. Capitol building and property. In addition, the U.S. Capitol police provide special protection to the members of Congress, officers of Congress, and their families. U.S. Capitol police have several specialty units such as drug enforcement, emergency response, K-9, and bicycle patrol, to name a few. In the wake of September 11, 2001, they earned more respect for their swift actions.

HOMELAND SECURITY MISSION

Prevention
Deterrence
Crisis Management
Consequence Management

"For terrorists fleeing Afghanistan—for any terrorist looking for a base of operations, there must be no refuge, no safe haven. By driving terrorists from place to place, we disrupt the planning and training for further attacks on America and the civilized world. Every terrorist must be made to live as an international fugitive, with no place to settle or organize, no place to hide, no governments to hide behind, and not even a safe place to sleep."

President George W. Bush, March 11, 2002

PROFILE OF AGENCY   Personnel: 1,000+   (Currently increasing staff)

REQUIREMENTS   Age: 21 to 37 years
                    Education: High school
                    Vision: 20/20 corrected
                                                            20/100 uncorrected

                    Background Investigation

OPPORTUNITIES   Over 100 (*during staffing-up period)

COMMENTS   All duty takes place in the U.S. Capitol building in Washington, DC.

INTERNSHIP PROGRAM   Unknown. Inquire with the department for details.

STUDENT PROGRAMS   Unknown. Inquire with the department for details.

WHERE TO APPLY   United States Capitol Police
                      119 D Street, N.W.
                      U.S. Capitol Building
                      Washington, DC 20510-7218
                      (202) 224-9820
                      Recruiting@Cap-Police.Senate.Gov

QUICK REFERENCE REMINDERS FOR ALL FIRST RESPONDERS TO THE SCENE OF A TERRORIST INCIDENT

Remember this is a crime scene. It is the scene of a deliberately violent and lethal act. There may be more.

- Do not touch anything at a crime scene or remove anything from a crime scene unless it is absolutely necessary for the performance of your official duties or it is done concurrently with the appropriate law enforcement personnel.

Words to live by:

- Do not create more casualties "rescuing" the dead.
- Life safety—of 1) responders and 2) victims—is the first priority.
- The second priority is preservation of evidence.
- Examine victims for injuries and weapons. A perpetrator may have been injured, too.   ↓

Chemical incident:
- Approach from upwind if possible.
- Use personal protective equipment.
- Stay clear of spills, vapors, fumes, and smoke.

Bomb incident:
- Assume there are more! Responders may be terrorist targets, too.
- Do not use radios or cellular phones within 300 yards of the site.
- Remove the injured as quickly and carefully as possible; leave the dead for coroners.

Biological/nerve agents incident:
- Count the number of people or animals exhibiting similar symptoms of illness.
- Look for human or animal remains with no apparent trauma.

Nuclear/radiological incident:
- This is not detectable without monitoring equipment.
- Distance is the best immediate protection; enforce a bomb exclusion zone.
- Remember: time, distance, shielding.

Source: Pennsylvania Emergency Management Agency

FEDERAL PROTECTIVE SERVICE (FPO) CAREERS

Important Update Information:
On March 1, 2003, functions of several border and security agencies (including the Federal Protective Service) were transitioned into the U.S. Department of Homeland Security.

Federal Protective Service
18th Street, N.W.
U.S. Capitol Building
Washington, DC 20510
(202) 708-5082
www.gsa.gov
www.dhs.gov

POSITION   *Federal Protective Officer*   **GS-5** $25,822–$41,585

MAIN MISSION   Federal protective officers (FPO) provide police services and security for federal buildings and property nationwide. FPOs protect federal employees, investigate crimes, and maintain special security devices to protect federal buildings.

TERRORISM'S DARK HISTORY

Bombing of the Federal Building in Oklahoma City, April 19, 1995: Right-wing extremists Timothy McVeigh and Terry Nichols destroyed the Federal Building in Oklahoma City with a massive truck bomb that killed 166 and injured hundreds more in what was up to then the largest terrorist attack on American soil.

Source: U.S. Department of State

HOMELAND SECURITY MISSION

Prevention
Deterrence
Crisis Management
Consequence Management

PROFILE OF AGENCY

Law Enforcement Personnel:	732
Major States of Assignment:	CA, DC, IL, MA, MO, NY, TX

REQUIREMENTS

Age:	21 to 37 years	
Education:	Bachelor's degree	and/or
Experience:	3 years general	GS-5
	1 year specialized	GS-7
Vision:	20/20 corrected	

Background Investigation
Top secret security clearance
Complete the training program conducted at the Federal Law Enforcement Training Center, Glynco, GA.

OPPORTUNITIES Over 50 (*during staffing-up period)

COMMENTS In the wake of the both the bombing of the Oklahoma Federal Building and September 11, it is expected that a reexamination of federal protection staffing may occur. A sharp increase in hiring could possibly occur in the near future.

INTERNSHIP PROGRAM Unknown. Inquire with the department for details.

STUDENT PROGRAMS Unknown. Inquire with the department for details.

WHERE TO APPLY

GSA Pacific Rim Region
450 Golden Gate Avenue
San Francisco, CA 94102
(415) 522-3001

GSA Rocky Mountain Region
Buidling 41, Denver Federal Center
Denver, CO 80225
(303) 236-7329

GSA National Capital Region
7th and D Streets S.W.
Washington, DC 20407
(202) 708-9100

GSA Southeast Sunbelt Region
77 Forsyth Street, Suite 600
Atlanta, GA 30303
(404) 331-3200

GSA Great Lakes Region
230 South Dearborn Street
Chicago, IL 60604
(312) 353-5395

GSA New England Region
10 Causeway Street
Boston, MA 02222
(617) 565-5860

GSA Heartland Region
1500 East Bannister Road
Kansas City, MO 64131
(816) 926-7201

GSA Northeast and Caribbean Region
26 Federal Plaza
New York, NY 10278
(212) 264-2600

GSA Mid-Atlantic Region
The Strawbridge Building
20 North Eighth Street
Philadelphia, PA 19107-3191
(215) 446-5100

GSA Greater Southwest Region
819 Taylor Street
Fort Worth, TX 76102
(817) 978-2321

GSA Northwest/Arctic Region
400 15th Street S.W.
Auburn, WA 98001
(253) 931-7000

NATIONAL PARK SERVICE (NPS) CAREERS

National Park Service
U.S. Park Police
1100 Ohio Drive, S.W.
Washington, DC 20024
(202) 619-7056
www.nps.gov

POSITIONS			
U.S. Park Police Officer	GS-5/7		$25,822–$41,585
U.S. Park Police Ranger	GS-5/7		$25,822–$41,585

MAIN MISSION

The U.S. park police and rangers contribute to resource protection through the use of law enforcement methods and techniques designed to fit the nature of the offenses committed or suspected on national park system properties. Offenses may range from homicides, rapes, assaults, burglaries, car theft, use of alcoholic beverages to excess, and use of and trafficking in illegal drugs. Rangers perform duties educating the public about the park's resources and requirements pertaining to their use. They also have specialized duties directed toward the protection of the park's natural and cultural resources and the safety and security of park visitors, park employees, contract and concessionaire employees, and other members of the public. They also protect public and private property.

HOMELAND SECURITY MISSION

Prevention
Deterrence
Crisis Management
Consequence Management

PROFILE OF AGENCY	Law Enforcement Personnel:	660 Police Officers/ 1,500 Rangers	

REQUIREMENTS	Age:	21 to 37 years	
	Education:	High school diploma	and/or
	Experience:	3 years general	GS-5
		1 year specialized	GS-7
	Vision:	20/20 corrected	
		20/100 uncorrected	

"Don't hit at all if it is possible to avoid hitting; but never hit soft."
—President Theodore Roosevelt

OPPORTUNITIES Inquire with the department for details.

COMMENTS Both park police and rangers may be required to work weekends, holidays, evenings, and during special events or snow emergencies. This is a required occupancy position. Rangers will be required to live in government quarters, if available. Prolonged walking, standing, and occasional running are required. Police and rangers may be required to work frequent overtime with little or no notice. Training occurs at the Federal Law Enforcement Training Center, Glynco, GA.

INTERNSHIP PROGRAM Yes

STUDENT PROGRAMS Inquire with the department for details.

WHERE TO APPLY The main address or at the following personnel offices.

U.S. Park Police
1100 Ohio Drive, S.W.
Washington, DC 20242
(202) 619-7056

U.S. Ranger Division
1849 C Street, N.W.
Washington, DC 20240
(202) 208-5093

National Park Service
Seasonal Employment Unit
P.O. Box 37127
Washington, DC 20013
(202) 619-7056

U.S. POSTAL INSPECTION SERVICE CAREERS

U.S. Postal Inspection Service
Office of Recruitment
9600 Newbridge Drive
Potomac, MD 20854-4436
(301) 983-7400
**www.usps.com/postalinspectors/
employmt.htm**

POSITION	*U.S. Postal Inspector*	*GS-5/12*	$28,164–$64,944
	U.S. Postal Police Officer	*GS-5*	$25,822–$41,585

**MAIN
MISSION**
The Postal Inspection Service is the law enforcement and audit arm of the Postal Service, which has jurisdiction in criminal matters affecting the integrity and security of the mail. Further, it acts as the inspector general for the Postal Service. The U.S. Postal Inspection Service investigates and seeks to prevent criminal assaults against the Postal Service or its employees and misuse of the nation's postal system. Its responsibilities include offenses such as armed robberies; the murder of, or assault upon, postal employees; burglaries or theft of mail; mailings of obscene matter, child pornography, bombs, and drugs; and use of the mail to swindle the public. In addition, the U.S. Postal Police Force provides police and security service at U.S. post office properties nationwide.

**HOMELAND
SECURITY
MISSION**
Prevention
Deterrence
Crisis Management
Consequence Management

**PROFILE OF
AGENCY**
Law Enforcement Personnel: 3,587

REQUIREMENTS
Age: 21 to 37 years
Education: Bachelor's degree   and/or
Experience: 3 years general   GS-5
                          1 year specialized   GS-7
Vision: 20/20   corrected

TERRORISM'S DARK HISTORY

In January 1997, a series of letter bombs with Alexandria, Egypt, postmarks were discovered at Al-Hayat newspaper bureaus in Washington, New York City, London, and Riyadh, Saudi Arabia. Three similar devices, also postmarked in Egypt, were found at a prison facility in Leavenworth, Kansas. Bomb disposal experts defused all the devices, but one detonated at the Al-Hayat office in London, injuring two security guards and causing minor damage.

Source: U.S. Department of State

OPPORTUNITIES   Over 50 (Postal Inspector)
Over 50 (Postal Police Officer)

COMMENTS   Preferred Degree Fields: Accounting, Criminal Justice, Law
Training Location: U.S. Postal Inspector Course, Potomac, MD

INTERNSHIP PROGRAM   Unknown

STUDENT PROGRAMS   N/A

WHERE TO APPLY   At the main address or at the closest regional office.

Regional Offices

United States Postal Inspection Service
P.O. Box 20666
Phoenix, AZ 85036
(602) 223-3660

United States Postal Inspection Service
P.O. Box 882000
San Francisco, CA 94188
(415) 550-5700

United States Postal Inspection Service
P.O. Box 2000
Pasadena, CA 91102
(818) 405-1200

United States Postal Inspection Service
P.O. Box 329
Denver, CO 80201
(303) 295-5320

United States Postal Inspection Service
P.O. Box 2110
San Diego, CA 92112
(619) 233-0610

United States Postal Inspection Service
P.O. Box 96096
Washington, DC 20066
(202) 636-2300

United States Postal Inspection Service
3400 Lakeside Drive, 6th Floor
Miramar, FL 33027
(305) 436-7200

United States Postal Inspection Service
P.O. Box 22526
Tampa, FL 33622
(813) 281-5200

United States Postal Inspection Service
P.O. Box 16489
Atlanta, GA 30321
(404) 765-7369

United States Postal Inspection Service
433 W. Van Buren Street MPO
Chicago, IL 60669
(312) 765-4500

United States Postal Inspection Service
P.O. Box 51690
New Orleans, LA 70151
(504) 589-1200

United States Postal Inspection Service
P.O. Box 2217
Boston, MA 02205
(617) 654-5825

United States Postal Inspection Service
P.O. Box 330119
Detroit, MI 48232
(313) 226-8184

United States Postal Inspection Service
P.O. Box 64558
St. Paul, MN 55164
(612) 293-3200

United States Postal Inspection Service
Suite 850
3101 Broadway
Kansas City, MO 64111
(816) 932-0400

United States Postal Inspection Service
1106 Walnut Street
St. Louis, MO 63199
(314) 539-9300

United States Postal Inspection Service
1200 Main Place Tower
Buffalo, NY 14202
(716) 853-5300

United States Postal Inspection Service
P.O. Box 555
James Farley Building
New York, NY 10116
(212) 330-3844

United States Postal Inspection Service
P.O. Box 509
Newark, NJ 07101
(210) 596-5400

United States Postal Inspection Service
2901 I-85 South GMF
Charlotte, NC 28228
(704) 329-9120

United States Postal Inspection Service
P.O. Box 14487
Cincinnati, OH 45250
(513) 684-5700

United States Postal Inspection Service
P.O. Box 5726
Cleveland, OH 44101
(216) 443-4000

United States Postal Inspection Service
P.O. Box 7500
Philadelphia, PA 19101
(215) 895-8450

United States Postal Inspection Service
1001 California Avenue
Pittsburgh, PA 15290
(412) 359-7900

United States Postal Inspection Service
P.O. Box 363667
San Juan, PR 00936
(809) 749-7600

United States Postal Inspection Service
P.O. Box 1276
Houston, TX 77251
(713) 238-4400

United States Postal Inspection Service
P.O. Box 3180
Memphis, TN 38173
(901) 576-2077

United States Postal Inspection Service
P.O. Box 25009
Richmond, VA 23260
(804) 775-6267

United States Postal Inspection Service
P.O. Box 162929
Fort Worth, TX 76161
(817) 625-3400

United States Postal Inspection Service
P.O. Box 400
Seattle, WA 98111
(206) 442-6300

"If you see a snake, just kill it. Don't appoint a committee on snakes."

H. Ross Perot

A Note on Recommended Reading:

For a more detailed selection of specific law enforcement opportunities:

Barron's Guide to Law Enforcement Careers, 2nd Edition
by Donald B. Hutton and Anna Mydlarz

Barron's Educational Series, Inc.
250 Wireless Boulevard
Hauppauge, New York 11788
(631) 434-3311
www.barronseduc.com

SECTION

3

CHEMICAL, BIOLOGICAL, RADIOLOGICAL, AND NUCLEAR COUNTERMEASURES CAREERS

CHEMICAL, BIOLOGICAL, RADIOLOGICAL, AND NUCLEAR COUNTERMEASURES CAREERS

CHAPTER 7

DEPARTMENT OF HEALTH & HUMAN SERVICES (HHS)

└ Food and Drug Administration
└ Centers for Disease Control

ENVIRONMENTAL PROTECTION AGENCY

DEPARTMENT OF ENERGY

National Labs

└ National Nuclear Security Administration
└ Office of Security

CHEMICAL, BIOLOGICAL, RADIOLOGICAL, AND NUCLEAR COUNTERMEASURES OPPORTUNITIES

☐ **Food and Drug Administration (FDA) Careers**

☐ **Environmental Protection Agency (EPA) Careers**

☐ **U.S. Department of Energy Careers**

☐ **Centers for Disease Control and Prevention Careers**

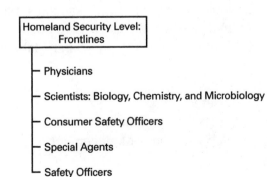

Several different agencies offer homeland security careers involving chemical, biological, radiological, and nuclear countermeasures. This chapter discusses four federal organizations.

FOOD AND DRUG ADMINISTRATION (FDA) CAREERS

Food and Drug Administration
Office of Human Resources and
    Management Services
Room 7B-44, Parklawn Building
5600 Fishers Lane
Rockville, MD 20857
(301) 443-1969
www.fda.gov

POSITIONS

Physicians GS-14		$79,060–$99,391
Scientists GS-9/11/12/13		$35,656–$82,180
Consumer Safety Officers GS-9/11/12/13		$35,656–$82,180

MAIN MISSION

The Food and Drug Administration (FDA) protects the health and welfare of American consumers by both science and law enforcement methods. The areas of jurisdiction include:

Food	Food-borne illness, nutrition, dietary supplements
Drugs	Prescription, over-the-counter, generic
Medical devices	Pacemakers, contact lenses, hearing aids
Biological	Vaccines, blood products
Animal feed and drugs	Livestock, pets
Cosmetics	Safety, labeling

HOMELAND SECURITY MISSION

Prevention
Deterrence
Crisis Management
Consequence Management

PROFILE OF AGENCY	Personnel:	Nearly 11,000 people in a variety of technical, scientific, professional, and administrative occupations

REQUIREMENTS Age: Open
Education: Open/diverse
Undergraduate and/or graduate degrees in biology, chemistry, and microbiology
Background Investigation

OPPORTUNITIES Over 500 nationwide (during staffing-up period)

COMMENTS None

INTERNSHIP PROGRAM No

STUDENT PROGRAMS Yes

WHERE TO APPLY
Food and Drug Administration
Office of Human Resources and Management Services
Room 7B-44, Parklawn Building
5600 Fishers Lane
Rockville, MD 20857
(301) 443-1969
www.fda.gov

"Forgive your enemies, but never forget their names."

President John F. Kennedy

ENVIRONMENTAL PROTECTION AGENCY (EPA) CAREERS

Environmental Protection Agency
401 M Street, S.W.
Washington, DC 20009
(202) 382-3055
(800) 338-1350
www.epa.gov

POSITIONS

Criminal Investigators	*GS-5/7*	$25,822–$41,585
Consumer Safety Officers	*GS-9/11/12/13*	$35,656–$82,180

MAIN MISSION

The overall mission of the Environmental Protection Agency (EPA) is to protect and enhance our national environment today and for future generations to the fullest extent possible under the laws enacted by Congress. EPA controls and abates pollution in the areas of air, water, solid waste, pesticides, radiation, and toxic substances. Its mandate is to mount an integrated, coordinated attack on environmental pollution in cooperation with state and local governments. Specifically, EPA will

- provide planning and response expertise and resources prior to and during a terrorist incident,

- help state and local responders plan for emergencies and responses to deliberate chemical releases that might occur in a terrorist incident, and

- train first responders to respond effectively and safely to potential terrorist attacks in which chemical or biological agents have been used against a civilian population.

Tokyo Subway Station Attack, March 20, 1995: Twelve persons were killed, and 5,700 were injured in a sarin nerve gas attack on a crowded subway station in the center of Tokyo, Japan. A similar attack occurred nearly simultaneously in the Yokohama subway system. The Aum Shinri-kyu cult was blamed for the attacks.

Source: U.S. Department of State

HOMELAND SECURITY MISSION	Prevention
	Deterrence
	Crisis Management
	Consequence Management

| **PROFILE OF AGENCY** | Personnel: | 8,000 personnel nationwide |

| **REQUIREMENTS** | Age: | Open |
| | Education: | Open/diverse |

Undergraduate and/or graduate degrees in biology, chemistry, and microbiology

Background Investigation

Top secret security clearance

OPPORTUNITIES Undetermined

COMMENTS None

INTERNSHIP PROGRAM Yes

STUDENT PROGRAMS Unknown

WHERE TO APPLY
EPA Headquarters
(Washington, DC Metropolitan Area)
1200 Pennsylvania Avenue, N.W.
Washington, DC 20460
For employment: ezhire@epa.gov

Regional Offices

Region 1 (CT, MA, ME, NH, RI, VT)
Environmental Protection Agency
1 Congress Street, Suite 1100
Boston, MA 02114-2023
(617) 918-1111
www.epa.gov/region01

Region 2 (NJ, NY, PR, VI)
290 Broadway
New York, NY 10007-1866
(212) 637-3000
www.epa.gov/region2

Region 3 (DC, DE, MD, PA, VA, WV)
1650 Arch Street
Philadelphia, PA 19103-2029
(215) 814-5000
www.epa.gov/region03

Region 4 (AL, FL, GA, KY, MS, NC, SC, TN)
Atlanta Federal Center
61 Forsyth Street, S.W.
Atlanta, GA 30303-3104
(404) 562-9900
www.epa.gov/region04

Region 5 (IL, IN, MI, MN, OH, WI)
77 West Jackson Boulevard
Chicago, IL 60604-3507
(312) 353-2000
www.epa.gov/region5

Region 6 (AR, LA, NM, OK, TX)
Fountain Place, 12th Floor, Suite 1200
1445 Ross Avenue
Dallas, TX 75202-2733
(214) 665-2200
www.epa.gov/region06

Region 7 (IA, KS, MO, NE)
901 North 5th Street
Kansas City, KS 66101
(913) 551-7003
www.epa.gov/region07

Region 8 (CO, MT, ND, SD, UT, WY)
999 18th Street, Suite 500
Denver, CO 80202-2466
(303) 312-6312
www.epa.gov/region08

Region 9 (AZ, CA, HI, NV)
75 Hawthorne Street
San Francisco, CA 94105
(415) 744-1305
www.epa.gov/region09

Region 10 (AK, ID, OR, WA)
1200 Sixth Avenue
Seattle, WA 98101
(206) 553-1200
www.epa.gov/region10

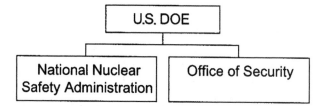

U.S. DEPARTMENT OF ENERGY (DOE) CAREERS

U.S. Department of Energy
1000 Independence Avenue, S.W.
Washington, DC 20585
(202) 586-5000
www.energy.gov

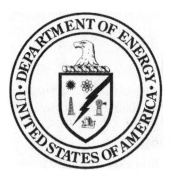

POSITIONS		
Physicians GS-14		$79,060–$99,391
Scientists GS-9/11/12/13		$35,656–$82,180
Consumer Safety Officers GS-9/11/12/13		$35,656–$82,180
Security Agents GS-9/11/12/13		$35,656–$82,180

MAIN MISSION

The U.S. Department of Energy (DOE) is a large organization with many subdivisions. However, only two subagencies along with a host of national labs will be discussed here. The DOE provides training to emergency responders for nuclear and radiological incidents and provides personal protective equipment and detection and diagnostic instruments, on a selective basis, to state and local law enforcement officials. The DOE works with public health partners on strategies to improve bioterrorism-related expertise, facilities, and procedures at local, state, and national levels.

The National Nuclear Safety Administration maintains and enhances the safety, reliability, and performance of the United States nuclear weapons stockpile. It also works to reduce global danger from weapons of mass destruction.

The Office of Security manages security operations for DOE facilities. It also establishes and implements a comprehensive security program to protect Department of Energy headquarters facilities, personnel, and classified and sensitive matter from dissident, terrorist, foreign intelligence, criminal, and insider threats.

HOMELAND SECURITY MISSION

Prevention
Deterrence
Crisis Management
Consequence Management

A *dirty bomb* is a conventional explosive or bomb containing radioactive material. The conventional bomb is used as a means to spread radioactive contamination. It is not a nuclear bomb and does not involve a nuclear explosion. Because a dirty bomb explosion could expose people to loose radioactive material in the air, which could be inhaled, people are advised to move away from the immediate area quickly.

Source: U.S. Department of Energy

PROFILE OF AGENCY

Personnel: Unknown

REQUIREMENTS

Age: Open
Education: Open/diverse
Undergraduate and/or graduate degrees in biology, chemistry, and microbiology
Background Investigation
Top secret security clearance

OPPORTUNITIES   Over 500 nationwide (during staffing-up period)

INTERNSHIP   Yes
PROGRAM

STUDENT   Yes
PROGRAMS

WHERE TO   U.S. Department of Energy
APPLY   1000 Independence Avenue, S.W.
Washington, DC 20585
(202) 586-5000
www.energy.gov

National Labs

California
Berkeley: Lawrence Berkeley National Laboratory Employment
Livermore: Lawrence Livermore National Laboratory Employment
Menlo Park: Stanford Linear Accelerator Center Employment
Oakland: Oakland Operations Office Employment

Colorado
Golden: Denver Regional Office Employment
                   Golden Field Office Employment
                   National Renewable Energy Laboratory Employment
                   Rocky Flats Closure Project Employment
Grand Junction: Grand Junction Project Office Employment
Lakewood: Western Area Power Administration Employment

Georgia
Atlanta: Atlanta Regional Office Employment
Elberton: Southeastern Power Administration Employment

Iowa
Ames: Ames National Laboratory Employment

Illinois
Argonne: Argonne National Laboratory Employment
                   New Brunswick Laboratory Employment
Batavia: Fermi National Accelerator Laboratory Employment
Chicago: Chicago Operations Office Employment
                   Chicago Regional Office Employment

Idaho
　Idaho Falls:　Idaho National Engineering Laboratory Employment
　　　　　　　　Idaho Operations Office Employment
　Scoville:　　Argonne National Laboratory (West) Employment

Louisiana
　New Orleans:　Strategic Petroleum Reserve Employment

Maryland
　Germantown:　Department of Energy Headquarters Employment

Massachusetts
　Boston:　　Boston Regional Office Employment

Missouri
　Kansas City:　Kansas City Plant Employment

Nevada
　Las Vegas:　Nevada Operations Office Employment
　　　　　　　Yucca Mountain Project Employment

New Jersey
　Princeton:　Princeton Plasma Physics Laboratory Employment

New Mexico
　Albuquerque:　Albuquerque Operations Office Employment
　　　　　　　　Sandia National Laboratory Employment
　Los Alamos:　Los Alamos National Laboratory Employment

New York
　Upton:　　Brookhaven National Laboratory Employment
　West Valley:　West Valley Demonstration Project Employment

Ohio
　Cincinnati:　Fernald Environmental Management Project Employment
　Miamisburg:　Mound Environmental Management Project Employment
　　　　　　　Ohio Field Office Employment

Oklahoma
　Tulsa:　　Southwestern Power Administration Employment

Oregon
　Albany:　Albany Research Center Employment
　Portland:　Bonneville Power Administration Employment

Pennsylvania

Philadelphia:	Philadelphia Regional Office Employment
Pittsburgh:	National Energy Technology Laboratory Employment
West Mifflin:	Bettis Atomic Power Laboratory Employment

South Carolina

Aiken:
Savannah River Operations Office Employment
Savannah River Site Employment
Savannah River Ecology Laboratory Employment

Tennessee

Oak Ridge:
Oak Ridge Operations Office Employment
Oak Ridge National Laboratory Employment
Y-12 Plant Employment

Texas

Amarillo: Pantax Plant Employment

Virginia

Newport News: Thomas Jefferson Laboratory Employment

Washington

Richland:
Pacific Northwest National Laboratory Employment
Richland Operations Office Employment
River Protection Office Employment
Seattle: Seattle Regional Office Employment

West Virginia

Morgantown: National Energy Technology Laboratory Employment

POTASSIUM IODIDE

Potassium iodide is a salt, similar to table salt. Its chemical symbol is KI. It is routinely added to table salt to make it iodized. Potassium iodide, if taken in time and at the appropriate dosage, blocks the thyroid gland's uptake of radioactive iodine and thus could reduce the risk of thyroid cancers and other diseases that might otherwise be caused by exposure to radioactive iodine that could be dispersed in a severe nuclear accident.

Source: U.S. Department of Energy

CENTERS FOR DISEASE CONTROL AND PREVENTION (CDC) CAREERS

**Centers for Disease Control
and Prevention**
Human Resources Management Office
Mail Stop K-16
4770 Buford Highway
Atlanta, GA 30341-3724
(888) CDC-HIRE
www.cdc.gov

POSITIONS

Physicians	*GS-14*	$79,060–$99,391
Scientists	*GS-9/11/12/13*	$35,656–$82,180
Consumer Safety Officers	*GS-9/11/12/13*	$35,656–$82,180

**MAIN
MISSION**

The Centers for Disease Control and Prevention (CDC) is recognized as the leading federal agency for protecting the health and safety of people by developing and applying disease prevention and control, environmental health, and health promotion and education activities designed to improve the health of the people of the United States. The CDC monitors health, detects and investigates health problems, conducts research to enhance prevention, develops and advocates sound public health policies, implements prevention strategies, promotes healthy behaviors, fosters safe and healthful environments, and provides leadership and training throughout the nation and world.

**HOMELAND
SECURITY
MISSION**

Prevention
Deterrence
Crisis Management
Consequence Management

**PROFILE OF
AGENCY**

Personnel: 8,500

ANTHRAX

Anthrax is an acute infectious disease caused by the spore-forming bacterium *Bacillus anthracis*. Anthrax most commonly occurs in wild and domestic lower vertebrates (cattle, sheep, goats, camels, antelopes, and other herbivores), but it can also occur in humans when they are exposed to infected animals or tissue from infected animals. Anthrax can also be spread by eating undercooked meat from infected animals. It is rare to find infected animals in the United States. Inhalation anthrax is usually fatal.

Source: Centers for Disease Control

REQUIREMENTS   Age: Open
Education: Open/diverse
Undergraduate and/or graduate degrees, health and medical related
Background Investigation
Top secret security clearance

OPPORTUNITIES   Over 400 nationwide (during staffing-up period)

INTERNSHIP PROGRAM   Yes

STUDENT PROGRAMS   Yes

WHERE TO APPLY
Centers for Disease Control and Prevention
Human Resources Management Office
Mail Stop K-16
4770 Buford Highway
Atlanta, GA 30341-3724
(888) CDC-HIRE
www.cdc.gov

CDC Key Facilites Locations
Anchorage, Alaska
Fort Collins, Colorado
Atlanta, Georgia
Research Triangle Park, North Carolina
Cincinnati, Ohio
Pittsburgh, Pennsylvania
San Juan, Puerto Rico
Spokane, Washington
Morgantown, West Virginia

IF DISASTER STRIKES

- Remain calm and be patient.
- Follow the advice of local emergency officials.
- Listen to your radio or television for news and instructions.
- If the disaster occurs near you, check for injuries. Give first aid, and get help for seriously injured people.
- If the disaster occurs near your home while you are there, check for damage using a flashlight. Do not light matches or candles or turn on electrical switches. Check for fires, fire hazards, and other household hazards. Sniff for gas leaks, starting at the water heater. If you smell gas or suspect a leak, turn off the main gas valve, open windows, and get everyone outside quickly.
- Shut off any other damaged utilities.
- Confine or secure your pets.
- Call your family contact—do not use the telephone again unless it is a life-threatening emergency.
- Check on your neighbors, especially those who are elderly or disabled.

Source: American Red Cross

TERRORISM'S DARK HISTORY

"We... have the ability to make and use chemicals and poisonous gas. And those gases and poisons are made from the simplest ingredients, which are available in the pharmacies, and we could, as well, smuggle them from one country to another if needed. And this is for use against vital institutions and residential populations and drinking water sources and others."

U.S. v. *Ramzi Ahmed Yousef*, Government Exhibit 528-T, August 26, 1998

SECTION

4

INFORMATION ANALYSIS AND INFRASTRUCTURE PROTECTION CAREERS

DEFENSE / INTELLIGENCE CAREERS CHAPTER 8		
Central Intelligence Agency	National Security Agency	U.S. Naval Criminal Investigative Service

Chapter 8

DEFENSE AND INTELLIGENCE OPPORTUNITIES

☐ **Central Intelligence Agency (CIA) Careers**

☐ **National Security Agency (NSA) Careers**

☐ **U.S. Naval Criminal Investigative Service (NCIS) Careers**

Homeland Security Level:
Frontlines

— Intelligence Agent

— Security Specialist

— Open Source Officer

— Foreign Language Instructors

— Middle Eastern Language Specialist

— Research Analyst

This chapter discusses careers in defense and intelligence. The three agencies presented here are in the front lines of homeland security.

CENTRAL INTELLIGENCE AGENCY (CIA) CAREERS

Central Intelligence Agency
Recruitment Center
Attn: (fill in position applying for)
P.O. Box 4090, Dept: Internet
Reston, VA 20195
www.cia.gov

POSITIONS

Professional Positions	$43,500–$60,400
Technical Positions	$43,500–$60,400
Language Positions	$43,500–$60,400
Analytical Positions	$43,500–$60,400
Clandestine Positions	$43,500–$60,400

(*Salary depends on position)

Professional Positions

Architect
Attorney
Auditor
Auditor—Info Systems
Bookbinder
Cartographer Entry Level
College Students
Contracting Officer—Experienced COs
Cost Analyst—Senior Level
Cost Estimator
Cross-Cultural Psychologists
Early Childhood Education Teacher
Environmental Safety Engineer
Facilities Maintenance Specialist
Finance Assistant
Finance Officer—Expert, Midlevel, and Entry Level
Geographer
Graphic Artist/Multimedia Specialist
Graphic Designer
Human Resource Administrator

Human Resource Generalist
Information Manager
Leadership/Training Instructor
Librarian
Logistics Co-op
Logistics Officer
Management Analyst

Technical Positions

College Students
Desktop Technology Consultant
Electronic Specialist
Engineering Specialist
Facilities Engineers—EE, ME
Information Systems Security
Network Design and Management
Project Management Engineer
Satellite Reconnaissance
Software and Applications Development
Systems Engineers
Technical Operations Officer
Telecom Info Systems Officer
Web Developer
Web Developer Co-op

Language Positions

Open Source Officer
Foreign Language Instructors
Middle Eastern Language Specialist

Analytical Positions

College Students
Counterterrorism Analyst
Economist
Engineer—Analyst
Leadership—Analyst
Military Analyst
Political Analyst
Statistician

Clandestine Positions

Operations Officer
Staff Operations Officer
Collection Management Officer
Professional Trainee Program

MAIN MISSION The Central Intelligence Agency (CIA) provides accurate, evidence-based, comprehensive, and timely foreign intelligence related to national security. It conducts counterintelligence activities, special activities, and other functions related to foreign intelligence and national security. The CIA is responsible for bringing the latest foreign political, military, economic, and technical information from the foreign media to the intelligence analysis, warning, and operations processes.

TERRORISM'S DARK HISTORY

March 16, 1984: CIA Beirut station chief William Buckley is kidnapped by militant Islamic extremists in Lebanon. He is said to have died after prolonged torture. His body was found on December 27, 1991 in southern Beirut, nearly eight years after his abduction.

Source: U.S. Department of State

HOMELAND SECURITY MISSION Prevention
Deterrence
Crisis Management
Consequence Management

PROFILE OF AGENCY Personnel: Classified (36,000+)

REQUIREMENTS Age: Open
Education: Open/diverse
Undergraduate and/or graduate degrees in area studies and international relations. Advanced level foreign language reading and listening comprehension skills. Excellent English language writing skills. Strong critical thinking skills. Foreign travel, foreign language proficiency, previous residency abroad, and military experience are pluses.

OPPORTUNITIES Up to 2,000

COMMENTS The CIA is particularly interested in candidates with backgrounds in Central Eurasian, East Asian, and Middle Eastern languages.

"What are the threats that keep me awake at night?

"International terrorism, both on its own and in conjunction with narcotics traffickers, international criminals, and those seeking weapons of mass destruction. You need go no further than Osama bin Laden . . . ."

George J. Tenet, Director, CIA, October 18, 1999

INTERNSHIP PROGRAM   Yes

STUDENT PROGRAMS   Undergraduate Student Trainee (Co-op) Program
Graduate Studies Program

WHERE TO APPLY   Mail your résumé and cover letter to:
Recruitment Center
Attn: (fill in position applying for)
P.O. Box 4090, Dept: Internet
Reston, VA 20195
www.cia.gov

"And in order to make sure that we're able to conduct a winning victory, we've got to have the best intelligence we can possibly have. And my report to the nation is, we've got the best intelligence we can possibly have thanks to the men and women of the CIA."

President George W. Bush to the CIA Employees, September 27, 2001

NATIONAL SECURITY AGENCY (NSA) CAREERS

National Security Agency
NSA Headquarters
Fort Meade, MD
(301) 688-6524
www.nsa.gov

POSITIONS

Language Analyst and Intelligence Analyst	$31,397–$55,694
Electronic and Computer Engineer, Signals Analyst	$46,728–$80,075
Computer Scientist, Mathematician, Cryptanalyst	$45,831–$69,694

(*Salary depends on position)

Information Assurance Directorate

- Network Security
- Firewalls/Router Security
- Vulnerability Analysis
- Security Hardware Design/Development
- Public Key Infrastructure (PKI)
- Customer Support
- Security Testing/Red Teaming
- Defense Information Operations (DIO)
- Firewalls/Router Security
- Special Processing Laboratory (SPL)
- Security Software Design/Development (Object-Oriented Programming—C++/Java)
- Microelectronics Research Laboratory (MRL)
- Networking
- Packet Based Optical Network Management
- Internet/Intranets Advanced Research
- Protocol Development

Signals Intelligence Directorate

- Traditional Communications
- RF Voice
- Non-RF Data
- Telephony Fiber Optics
- Wireless

- Processing Technology
- Speech Multimedia
- Image Processing
- Digital Signals Processing
- Security Encryption
- Information Protection Tools
- Exploitation Network
- Multilevel Secure Operating Systems Enterprise
- Digital Design ("Build What We Can't Buy")
- Systems Chip Level Board ASICs
- Hardware Exploitation
- Software Exploitation
- Network Exploitation
- Software Design/Development (Object-Oriented Programming—C++/Java)
- Hardware Design/Development
- Information Operations

Research Associate Directorate

- Mathematics Research
- Information Assurance Research
- Cryptology Research
- Secure Network Technology
- Secure Systems Research Biometrics
- Intrusion Detection
- Wireless Security
- High-Speed Networking Security
- Laboratory for Physical Sciences
- Scientific Linguists
- Algorithm Research and Development

Information Technology Infrastructure Services (IT IS)

- Data Mining
- Database Management Systems
- Supercomputing
- NSA Internal Infrastructure
- NSA Operational Computer Security
- Enterprise Software
- Data Visualization
- Visualization High-Volume Data Storage and Processing

MAIN MISSION

The National Security Agency (NSA) is the nation's cryptological organization. It coordinates, directs, and performs highly specialized activities to protect U.S. information systems and produce foreign intelligence information. A high-technology organization, NSA is on the frontier of communications and data processing. It is also one of the most important centers of foreign language analysis and research within the government.

The NSA employs the country's premier code makers and code breakers. It is said to be the largest employer of mathematicians in the United States and perhaps the world. Its mathematicians contribute directly to the two missions of the agency: designing cipher systems that will protect the integrity of U.S. information systems and searching for weaknesses in adversaries' systems and codes.

Source: The National Security Agency

HOMELAND SECURITY MISSION

Prevention
Deterrence
Crisis Management
Consequence Management

PROFILE OF AGENCY

Personnel: Classified

REQUIREMENTS

Age: Open
Education: Open/diverse

Undergraduate and/or graduate degrees in area studies, international relations, and especially mathematics. Advanced-level foreign language reading and listening comprehension skills are needed, as are excellent English language writing skills and strong critical thinking skills. Foreign travel, foreign language proficiency, previous residency abroad, and military experience are pluses.

"Let us never forget that good intelligence saves American lives and protects our freedom."

President Ronald Reagan, 1981

OPPORTUNITIES   Up to 1,000

COMMENTS   Particularly interested in candidates with backgrounds in Central Eurasian, East Asian, and Middle Eastern languages:

Amharic	Pashto	Tigrinya
Arabic	Persian/Farsi	Turkmen
Chinese	Somali	Urdu/Punjabi
Dari	Swahili	Uzbek
Greek	Tagalog	

INTERNSHIP PROGRAM	Yes

STUDENT PROGRAMS	Undergraduate Student Trainee (Co-op) Program Graduate Studies Program

WHERE TO APPLY	NSA Headquarters Fort Meade, MD (301) 688-6524 **www.nsa.gov**

Note: The NSA prefers electronic submission of résumés.

U.S. Naval Criminal Investigative Service (NCIS) Careers —

Naval Criminal Investigative Service
(Code 0025AP)
716 Sicard Street, S.E.
Washington Navy Yard, DC 20388-5388
(800) 616-8891
www.ncis.navy.mil
jobs@ncis.navy.mil

POSITIONS	*NCIS Special Agent GS/7–GS/9*	$34,451–$44,783

MAIN MISSION

The Naval Criminal Investigative Service (NCIS) is a centrally directed, largely civilian organization responsible for criminal investigations and counterintelligence operations for the U.S. Navy. NCIS special agents are frequently detailed for protective service to U.S. military officials and are trained in antiterrorism tactics. In addition, the NCIS Special Agent Afloat Program stations an agent aboard military vessels to be responsible for all major criminal investigations and counterintelligence matters.

TERRORISM'S DARK HISTORY

Berlin Discoteque Bombing, April 5, 1986: Two U.S. soldiers were killed, and 79 American servicepeople were injured in a Libyan bomb attack on a nightclub in West Berlin, West Germany. In retaliation, U.S. military jets bombed targets in and around Tripoli and Benghazi.

Source: U.S. State Department

HOMELAND SECURITY MISSION	Prevention Deterrence		
PROFILE OF AGENCY	Personnel:	1,200 NIS Special Agents	
REQUIREMENTS	Age: Education: Experience: Vision:	21 to 37 years Bachelor's degree 3 years general 1 year specialized 20/20 corrected 20/70 uncorrected	and/ or GS-5 GS-7
	Background Investigation Top secret security clearance		
OPPORTUNITIES	Over 100 nationwide		
COMMENTS	During a 20-year career, an NCIS special agent can expect to do at least two years of duty overseas. Some NCIS special agents may be assigned to a military vessel for up to a year's tour of duty. Training occurs at the Federal Law Enforcement Training Center, Glynco, GA.		
INTERNSHIP PROGRAM	No		
STUDENT PROGRAMS	Unknown		

"We sit by and watch the barbarian. We tolerate him in the long stretches of peace, we are not afraid. We are tickled by his irreverence; his comic inversion of our old certitudes and our fixed creed refreshes us; we laugh. But as we laugh we are watched by large and awful faces from beyond, and on these faces there are no smiles."

Hilaire Belloc

**WHERE TO
APPLY**

Naval Criminal Investigative Service Headquarters
(Code 0025AP)
716 Sicard Street, S.E.
Washington Navy Yard, DC 20388-5388
(800) 616-8891
jobs@ncis.navy.mil

Regional Offices

Middle East Field Office
Manama, Bahrain
PSC 451, Box 32
FPO AE 09834-2800
973-724-437

San Diego Field Office
Box 368130
3405 Welles Street, Suite 1
San Diego, CA 92136-5050
(619) 556-1364

Los Angeles Field Office
1317 W. Foothill Boulevard
Suite 120
Upland, CA 91786
(909) 985-2264

Washington Field Office
Washington Navy Yard
Building 200
Washington, DC 20374
(202) 433-3858

Mayport Field Office
P.O. Box 280076
Naval Station
Mayport, FL 32228-0076
(904) 270-5361

Gulf Coast Field Office
341 Saufley Street
Pensacola, FL 32508-5133
(904) 452-3835

Hawaii Field Office
449 South Avenue
Pearl Harbor, HI 96860-4988
(808) 474-1218

European Field Office
Naples, Italy
PSC 817, Box 36
FPO AE 09622
011-39-081-568-6002

Far East Field Office
Yokosuka, Japan
PSC 473, Box 76
FPO AP 96349-2500
011-81-311-743-7745

Carolinas Field Office
H-32 Julian C. Smith Boulevard
Camp Lejeune, NC 28547-1600
(910) 451-8071

Northeast Field Office
344 Meyerkord Avenue
Naval Education and Training Center
Newport, RI 02841-1607
(401) 841-2241

Norfolk Field Office
1329 Bellinger Boulevard
Norfolk, VA 23511-2395
(757) 444-7327

Northwest Field Office
Land Title Professional Building
9657 Levin Road N.W., Suite L20
Silverdale, WA 98383
(360) 396-4660

Resident Locations

Yuma, AZ
Manama, Bahrain
Camp Pendleton, CA
China Lake, CA
Lemoore, CA
Los Angeles, CA
Point Mugu, CA
Port Hueneme, CA
San Diego, CA
Twentynine Palms, CA
New London, CT
Souda Bay, Crete
Guantanmo Bay, Cuba
Washington, DC
Jacksonville, FL
Key West, FL
Mayport, FL
Miami, FL
Orlando, FL
Panama City, FL
Tampa, FL
Marseille, France
Kings Bay, GA
Frankfurt, Germany
Munich, Germany
Guam
Honolulu, HI
Kaneohe, HI
Keflavik, Iceland
Great Lakes, IL
Gaeta, Italy
La Maddelena, Italy
Rome, Italy
Sigonella, Italy
Atsugi, Japan
Camp Hansen, Japan
Iwakuni, Japan
Misawa, Japan
Okinawa, Japan
Sasebo, Japan
Yokosuka, Japan
Chinhae, Korea
Pusan, Korea

Seoul, Korea
New Orleans, LA
Annapolis, MD
Baltimore, MD
Bethesda, MD
Patuxent River, MD
Brunswick, ME
Gulfport, MS
Meridian, MS
Pascagoula, MS
Camp Lejeune, NC
Cherry Point, NC
New River, NC
Portsmouth, NH
Earle, NJ
Lakehurst, NJ
Fallon, NV
New York, NY
Mechanicsburg, PA
Philadelphia, PA
Manila, Philippines
Roosevelt Roads, PR
San Juan, PR
Singapore
Charleston, SC
Parris Island, SC
Rota, Spain
Memphis, TN
Corpus Christi, TX
Dallas, TX
London, UK
Dahlgren, VA
Little Creek, VA
Norfolk, VA
Oceana, VA
Portsmouth, VA
Quantico, VA
Bremerton, WA
Everett, WA
Puget Sound, WA
Seattle, WA
Whidbey Island, WA

Afloat Assignments

USS *Constellation* (CV-64)
USS *Dwight D. Eisenhower* (CVN-69)
USS *Enterprise* (CVN-65)
USS *John F. Kennedy* (CV-67)
USS *Kitty Hawk* (CV-63)
USS *Abraham Lincoln* (CVN-72)
USS *Nimitz* (CVN-68)
USS *Theodore Roosevelt* (CVN-71)
USS *Harry S. Truman* (CVN-75)
USS *John C. Stennis* (CVN-74)
USS *Carl Vinson* (CVN-70)
USS *George Washington* (CVN-73)

SECTION

MILITARY
CAREERS

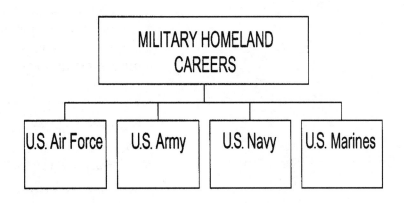

Chapter 9

MILITARY OPPORTUNITIES

- [ ] **Overview of the Military**
- [ ] **Military Careers**
- [ ] **Branch Profiles**
  - — U.S. Air Force (USAF) Careers
  - — U.S. Army Careers
  - — U.S. Navy Careers
  - — U.S. Marine Corps (USMC) Careers
- [ ] **Military Careers Related to Homeland Security**

OVERVIEW OF THE MILITARY

There is no greater service one can provide to this country than serving in the U.S. military. All military members serve to protect this country no matter what their assignment or rank. They are all at the frontlines of the homeland security efforts. Although there are hundreds of career choices to make, specific focus will be given in each branch for specialties relating to counterterrorism, intelligence, and the homeland protection critical need areas. Even now, new units are being created in each branch relating to stealth and overt antiterrorism.

> "A young man who does not have what it takes to perform military service is not likely to have what it takes to make a living."
>
> President John F. Kennedy

The military provides some outstanding opportunities. There are hundreds of career occupational specialities for a candidate to choose from, law enforcement being one of them. Most civilian agencies give credit or consideration to veterans. Many people make the military a career and retire early enough after 20 years to begin another career. Opportunities for education, travel, and to gain personnel and management experience exist in the U.S. military.

MILITARY OPPORTUNITIES

Enlisted

Enlisted personnel begin at the lowest rank in the military. The military prefers candidates with a high school education. Although beginning at a low point, with time, good service, and education, enlisted personnel can steadily advance.

Officers

Officers begin at a supervisory rank. They must have a four-year college degree from an accredited institution. Pathways to becoming a commissioned officer include:

- Service academies
- Officer Candidate School (OCS)
- Reserve Officer Training Corps (ROTC)
- Direct appointments

Promotions in the Military

The military offers a wide area of advancement, provided you are motivated. A military person can start as a lowly private (E-1 pay grade) and retire as a full colonel (O-7). Promotions in the military are based on several factors that include:

- Length of time in the military (plus time in rank)
- Time in present pay grade
- Job performance
- Leadership ability
- Awards or commendations
- Job speciality
- Educational achievement through technical, on-the-job, or civilian instruction

	UNITED STATES ARMED FORCES RANKS AND PAY GRADES				
Pay Grade	**Army**	**Air Force**	**Navy**	**Marine**	**Coast Guard**
O-10	General	General	Admiral	General	Admiral
O-9	Lieutenant General	Lieutenant General	Vice Admiral	Lieutenant General	Vice Admiral
O-8	Major General	Major General	Rear Admiral	Major General	Rear Admiral
O-7	Brigadier General	Brigadier General	Rear Admiral Lower Half	Brigadier General	Rear Admiral Lower Half
O-6	Colonel	Colonel	Captain	Colonel	Captain
O-5	Lieutenant Colonel	Lieutenant Colonel	Commander	Lieutenant Colonel	Commander
O-4	Major	Major	Lieutenant Commander	Major	Lieutenant Commander
O-3	Captain	Captain	Lieutenant	Captain	Lieutenant
O-2	First Lieutenant	First Lieutenant	Lieutenant Junior Grade	First Lieutenant	Lieutenant Junior Grade
O-1	Second Lieutenant	Second Lieutenant	Ensign	Second Lieutenant	Ensign
W-4	Chief Warrant	Chief Warrant	Chief Warrant	Chief Warrant	Chief Warrant
W-3	Chief Warrant	Chief Warrant	Chief Warrant	Chief Warrant	Chief Warrant
W-2	Chief Warrant	Chief Warrant	Chief Warrant	Chief Warrant	Chief Warrant
W-1	Warrant Officer	Warrant Officer	Warrant Officer	Warrant Officer	Warrant Officer
E-9	Sergeant Major	Chief Major Sergeant	Master Chief Petty Officer	Sergeant Major	Master Chief Petty Officer
E-8	Master Sergeant	Senior Master Sergeant	Senior Chief Petty Officer	Master Sergeant	Senior Chief Petty Officer
E-7	Sergeant First Class	Master Sergeant	Chief Petty Officer	Gunnery Sergeant	Chief Petty Officer
E-6	Staff Sergeant	Technical Sergeant	Petty Officer First Class	Staff Sergeant	Petty Officer First Class
E-5	Sergeant	Sergeant	Petty Officer Second Class	Sergeant	Petty Officer Second Class
E-4	Corporal	Senior Airman	Petty Officer Third Class	Corporal	Petty Officer Third Class
E-3	Private First Class	Airman First Class	Seaman	Lance Corporal	Seaman
E-2	Private	Airman	Seaman Apprentice	Private First Class	Seaman Apprentice
E-1	Private	Airman Basic	Seaman Recruit	Private	Seaman Recruit

O = Officer Ranks / W = Warrant Officer Ranks / E = Enlisted Ranks

2002 MILITARY PAY CHART*

(Monthly pay rates in dollars for military personnel)

Years of Service

Rank	0	2	4	6	8	10	12	14	16	18	20
COMMISSIONED OFFICERS											
O-10	0.00	0.00	0.00	0.00	0.00	0.00	0.00	0.00	0.00	0.00	11516.70
O-9	0.00	0.00	0.00	0.00	0.00	0.00	0.00	0.00	0.00	0.00	10147.50
O-8	7180.20	7415.40	7571.10	7614.90	7809.30	8135.10	8210.70	8519.70	8608.50	8874.30	9259.50
O-7	5966.40	6371.70	6371.70	6418.20	6657.90	6840.30	7051.20	7261.80	7472.70	8135.10	8694.90
O-6	4422.00	4857.90	5176.80	5176.80	5196.60	5418.90	5448.60	5448.60	5628.60	6305.70	6627.00
O-5	3537.00	4152.60	4440.30	4494.30	4673.10	4673.10	4813.50	5073.30	5413.50	5755.80	5919.00
O-4	3023.70	3681.90	3927.60	3982.50	4210.50	4395.90	4696.20	4930.20	5092.50	5255.70	5310.60
O-3	2796.60	3170.40	3421.80	3698.70	3875.70	4070.10	4232.40	4441.20	4549.50	4549.50	4549.50
O-2	2416.20	2751.90	3169.50	3276.30	3344.10	3344.10	3344.10	3344.10	3344.10	3344.10	3344.10
O-1	2097.60	2183.10	2638.50	2638.50	2638.50	2638.50	2638.50	2638.50	2638.50	2638.50	2638.50
WARRANT OFFICERS											
W-5	0.00	0.00	0.00	0.00	0.00	0.00	0.00	0.00	0.00	0.00	4965.60
W-4	2889.60	3108.60	3198.00	3285.90	3437.10	3586.50	3737.70	3885.30	4038.00	4184.40	4334.40
W-3	2638.80	2862.00	2862.00	2898.90	3017.40	3152.40	3330.90	3439.50	3558.30	3693.90	3828.60
W-2	2321.40	2454.00	2569.80	2654.10	2726.40	2875.20	2984.40	3093.90	3200.40	3318.00	3438.90
W-1	2049.90	2217.60	2330.10	2402.70	2511.90	2624.70	2737.80	2850.00	2963.70	3077.10	3189.90
ENLISTED MEMBERS											
E-9	0.00	0.00	0.00	0.00	0.00	0.00	3423.90	3501.30	3599.40	3714.60	3830.40
E-8	0.00	0.00	0.00	0.00	0.00	2858.10	2940.60	3017.70	3110.10	3210.30	3314.70
E-7	1986.90	2169.00	2251.50	2332.50	2417.40	2562.90	2645.10	2726.40	2808.00	2892.60	2975.10
E-6	1701.00	1870.80	1953.60	2033.70	2117.40	2254.50	2337.30	2417.40	2499.30	2558.10	2602.80
E-5	1561.50	1665.30	1745.70	1828.50	1912.80	2030.10	2110.20	2193.30	2193.30	2193.30	2193.30
E-4	1443.60	1517.70	1599.60	1680.30	1752.30	1752.30	1752.30	1752.30	1752.30	1752.30	1752.30
E-3	1303.50	1385.40	1468.50	1468.50	1468.50	1468.50	1468.50	1468.50	1468.50	1468.50	1468.50
E-2	1239.30	1239.30	1239.30	1239.30	1239.30	1239.30	1239.30	1239.30	1239.30	1239.30	1239.30
E-1(>4)	1105.50	1105.50	1105.50	1105.50	1105.50	1105.50	1105.50	1105.50	1105.50	1105.50	1105.50
E-1(<4)	1022.70										

*subject to change without notice

More than 400,000 new military personnel in over 100 career occupations need to be recruited each year to replace those who complete their enlistment or retire.

Source: U.S. Department of Defense

What Do You Want to Do?

Basically, your interest in seeking a military career or opportunity has assigned you to a complex investigation that you may find both thrilling and time-consuming. First, however, you have to make a choice—what do you want to do? Although you may presently think you want to work in one particular branch or service, you should keep an open mind and consider all other options.

"Saddle up!"

John Wayne in *The Sands of Iwo Jima*

Plan Your Course of Action

You should not just walk into a military career. Most successful candidates planned a course of action that enabled them to obtain their desired position. Make a list of several positions you are interested in. Check the qualifications for those positions. Do you qualify? If not, obtain more education and experience. As you plan your career, ask yourself some important questions:

1. *Are you ready for a military life?*
   Military life is not for everyone. The pay is predominantly low to start, a majority of personnel are stationed on overseas bases, personnel are subject to transfer at a moment's notice, and, most important, they have signed a commitment, meaning they cannot simply quit if they do not like the service.

2. *Are you willing to travel and be reassigned?*
   Military personnel may be transferred throughout the world several times during their careers, which means they may have to live on military bases until retirement. They may also have to conduct extensive travel for their duties. Not everyone can handle the military life. If you are single, it is your decision alone. However, if you have a family, it must be a family decision.

3. *How do you feel about submarines, ships, and planes?*
   Before you sign up for a career that takes you into the air or under the sea, make sure that you are prepared for it. Do not make a career decision based on a movie or CD-ROM attraction.

4. *Are you ready for military responsibility?*
   Being a member of the military entails more than a job; the duties and responsibilities for the most part are a significant burden that an individual must accept both on and off duty, 24 hours a day.

Therefore, the decision to pursue a particular position must be well thought out and planned in advance. Unlike civilian jobs, you cannot simply tell the boss you quit and then leave. When you sign on, you are obligated to serve for a certain time.

Do You Want a Full-Time or Part-Time Military Career?

The next question you should ask should be the degree of commitment you are willing to make. The military is flexible and has several full-time and part-time options.

Regular Service

In the regular service, personnel serve on a full-time basis. After enlisting in the service, members are sent to basic training. After graduation, they are sent to specialty job-training schools. Upon completion, they are assigned to a station or unit for duty. After 20 years of regular service, members qualify for a military retirement.

Reserve Service

The reserves are part-time military soldiers. Personnel serve an initial period on active duty after attending basic training and job training. After the training period, which usually lasts several months, reservists are free to return to civilian life. For the remainder of the service obligation, though, they attend training sessions and perform work in the job specialty one or two days a month with their local unit. Once a year, reservists participate in an active-duty training session for 14 days. It is important to know that reservists can be called to active duty at any time, as many were during Operation Desert Storm. When reservists have completed 20 years of service and have reached age 60, they are entitled to retirement, based on reserve pay.

National Guard

In addition to reserve forces, the army and air force have national guard units in every state. Duty is similar to that of a reservist. Over the years, the function and mission of the national guard units have increased to include domestic emergencies as well as drug and illegal alien interdiction efforts. National guard members can earn a retirement after 20 years of service and after reaching age 60.

"In defending the peace, we face a threat with no precedent . . . . The only path to safety is the path of action. And this nation will act. We will not leave the safety of America, and the peace of the planet, at the mercy of a few mad terrorists and tyrants."

President George W. Bush (Address to West Point Graduates), 2002

Military Academies

The military services maintain educational institutions that offer specialized academic educational opportunities like that of major colleges and universities. The differences are that graduates not only receive a baccalaureate degree after four years but also a regular commission as an officer. It should be noted that military academies are strict educational institutions. The selection process is rigid. For further information regarding particular requirements and admission procedures, contact the following academies:

United States Military Academy
Admissions Office
Taylor Hall, Building 600
West Point, NY 10996-1788
(845) 938-2006
www.usma.edu

United States Air Force Academy
Admissions Office
2304 Cadet Drive, Suite 320
U.S. Air Force Academy, CO 80840-5016
(719) 472-2990
www.usafa.af.mil/flash

United States Naval Academy
Admissions Office
121 Blake Road
Annapolis, MD 21402-5000
(410) 267-2291
www.nadn.navy.mil/homepage.html

United States Coast Guard Academy
Admissions Office
15 Mohegan Avenue
New London, CT 06320-4195
(203) 444-8270
www.sga.edu

Reserve Officer Training Corps (ROTC)

Numerous universities and colleges maintain active ROTC programs that include military police or military law enforcement units. Like the academy programs, after four years, the candidate not only receives a baccalaureate degree but also a reserve commission. Typically candidates perform weekend drills and summer military service activity toward their enlistment commitment.

Check with the colleges, universities, or military units in the areas you are interested in to learn if a military ROTC and law enforcement unit is available.

THE MILITARY BRANCHES: YOUR CHOICE

Branches	Main Mission
U.S. Air Force Air Force Reserve Air National Guard	Defends the United States through control of air and space; flies and maintains aircraft, missiles, and spacecraft; air force personnel are stationed worldwide.
U.S. Army Army Reserve Army National Guard	Protects and defends the United States and its interests by way of ground troops, tanks, helicopters, and missile systems; conducts land-based operations around the world.
U.S. Coast Guard Coast Guard Reserve	A branch of the armed services and a service within the U.S. Department of Transportation; the primary maritime law enforcement agency for the United States.
U.S. Marine Corps Marine Corps Reserve	An elite fighting force that is part of the Department of the Navy; marines serve on ships, protect naval bases, guard U.S. embassies, and provide a quick, ever-ready strike force to protect U.S. interests worldwide.
U.S. Navy Navy Reserve	Maintains freedom on the seas; defends the United States and its allies, and enables them to travel and trade freely on the world's oceans; navy personnel serve on ships, on submarines, in aviation positions, and at shore bases around the world.

GENERAL ENLISTMENT REQUIREMENTS

Age	Must be between the ages of 17 and 35 years. If age 17, parents' signed consent is required.
Citizenship	Must be a U.S. citizen or have been legally admitted to the United States for permanent residence and possess immigration and naturalization documents.
Males: physical condition (Some military occupations have additional requirements)	Height: 5'0" to 6'8" Weight: 100 lb. to 255 lb.
Females: physical condition (Some military occupations have additional requirements)	Height: 4'10" to 6'8" Weight: 90 lb. to 227 lb.
Vision (in general) (Some military occupations have additional requirements)	At least 20/400 or 20/200 vision corrected to 20/20 with eyeglasses or contact lenses; Depth perception and and color blindness is also tested.
General health	Must be able to pass a medical exam.
Education	High school is now a requirement in most enlisted occupations.
Aptitude	Must qualify for enlistment on the Armed Services Vocational Aptitude Battery (ASVAB) test.
Background investigation	Background investigation must reveal that person is of strong moral character.
Marital status and dependents	May be either single or married, with or without dependents.

Enlisting in the Military

Step 1: → Meet with a recruiter

Step 2: → Qualify for enlistment

Step 3: → Select a military occupation speciality (MSO). Make sure that you receive a guaranteed agreement for the speciality training program after basic enlisted or officer training.

Step 4: → Agree on the service obligation in years. Enlist in the service.

SPECIAL HINT

On recruiters: Be careful, and sign nothing on your first meeting. Recruiters are geared for high-pressure dealings and will try to have you sign up on the first meeting. Meet with recruiters or representatives from all of the services in which you are interested. Obtain all the publications that will clearly explain the programs in which you are interested.

BRANCH PROFILES

U.S. Air Force (USAF) Careers

United States Air Force
☆ United States Air Force Reserve
☆ Air National Guard
United States Air Force
Recruiting Command
Arlington, VA 22203
(800) 423-USAF
www.USAF.MIL

OVERVIEW   The air force (USAF) is the youngest of all of the U.S. military services. It was created two years after World War II (ending a 40-year association with the U.S. Army to become a separate service). The Department of the Air Force was created when President Truman signed the National Security Act of 1947. The air force offers a wide variety of career and educational opportunities. Both the air force reserve and the air national guard offer career fields the same as the active air force.

MAIN MISSION

The main mission of the air force is to defend the United States through the control and exploitation of air and space. The air force flies and maintains aircraft and the bases that house them. Air force personnel are stationed worldwide. The air force:

- Establishes air superiority, interdicts the enemy, and provides air support of combat ground forces; defends the nation against air and missile attack;

- provides major space research and development support for the Department of Defense; and

- provides assistance to the National Aeronautics and Space Administration in conducting our nation's space program.

Special Operation Forces

Special Operations Command (AFSOC)
The AFSOC provides specialized air power for worldwide deployment and assignment to conduct unconventional warfare, special reconnaissance, counterterrorism, and foreign internal defense. It also provides humanitarian assistance, psychological operations, personnel retrieval, and counternarcotics. AFSOC has approximately 9,700 personnel assigned.

OPPORTUNITY   ✪ Recruits over 30,000 new personnel each year

PROFILE OF AIR FORCE PERSONNEL

U.S. Army Careers

United States Army
☆ United States Army Reserve
☆ Army National Guard
U.S. Army Recruiting Command
Building 1307, Third Avenue
Fort Knox, KY 40121-2726
(800) USA-ARMY
www.goarmy.com

OVERVIEW

The army is the oldest of the military services, technically established on June 4, 1775, by the Continental Congress. The U.S. Army protects the security of the United States and its vital resources. The army stands ready to defend American interests and the interests of our allies through land-based operations anywhere in the world.

The army is the largest of the military services and offers a wide variety of careers and opportunities. Both the army reserve and the army national guard offer the same career fields as the active-duty army.

MAIN MISSION

The main missions of the army include the following:

- Projection of land forces and contingency operations

- Peacetime and wartime reinforcement

- Evacuation and protection of U.S. citizens

- Support of the nation's war on drugs

- Assistance to friendly nations

- Support of national assistance and civil affairs

Special Operations Forces

Green Berets
The Green Berets are special forces soldiers that conduct guerrilla warfare techniques, collect strategic intelligence, conduct raids, perform infiltration missions, and conduct unconventional warfare.

Airborne Rangers

The Airborne Rangers are special Army soldiers who have been qualified through rigorous training to parachute from airplanes.

THE RANGER CREED

R ecognizing that I volunteered as a Ranger, fully knowing the hazards of my chosen profession, I will always endeavor to uphold the prestige, honor, and high esprit de corps of the Rangers.

A cknowledging the fact that a Ranger is a more elite soldier who arrives at the cutting edge of battle by land, sea, or air, I accept the fact that as a Ranger my country expects me to move further, faster, and fight harder than any other soldier.

N ever shall I fail my comrades. I will always keep myself mentally alert, physically strong, and morally straight, and I will shoulder more than my share of the task whatever it may be, one hundred percent and then some.

G allantly will I show the world that I am a specially selected and well-trained soldier. My courtesy to superior officers, neatness of dress, and care of equipment shall set the example for others to follow.

E nergetically will I meet the enemies of my country. I shall defeat them on the field of battle for I am better trained and will fight with all my might. Surrender is not a Ranger word. I will never leave fallen comrades to fall into the hands of the enemy and under no circumstances will I ever embarrass my country.

R eadily will I display the intestinal fortitude required to fight on to the Ranger objective and complete the mission, though I be the lone survivor.

Source: U.S. Army Rangers

Delta Force

Combat Applications Group (CAG): Delta Force is one of the U.S. government's principal units tasked with counterterrorist operations. U.S. Army Colonel Charles Beckwith created Delta Force in 1977 in direct response to numerous, well-publicized terrorist incidents that occurred in the 1970s. In 1993, as part of Task Force Ranger, Delta Force took part in numerous operations to apprehend warlord Mohamad Farah Aidid in Mogadishu, Somalia, which was depicted in the movie *Black Hawk Down*.

OPPORTUNITIES ✪ Recruits over 80,000 new personnel each year

PROFILE OF ARMY PERSONNEL

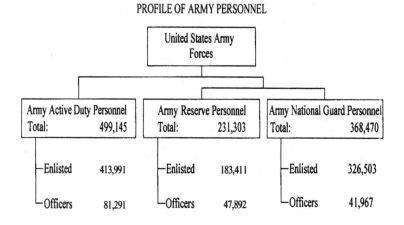

Army Active Duty Personnel	Army Reserve Personnel	Army National Guard Personnel
Total: 499,145	Total: 231,303	Total: 368,470
Enlisted 413,991	Enlisted 183,411	Enlisted 326,503
Officers 81,291	Officers 47,892	Officers 41,967

U.S. Navy Careers

United States Navy
☆ United States Navy Reserve
Navy Recruiting Command
801 North Randolph Street
Arlington, VA 22203
(800) 327-Navy
www.navy.job

OVERVIEW   The navy is one of the oldest military services, having been established in 1775 by the Continental Congress. Throughout American history, wars were decided by the navy's sea power. The Department of the Navy is responsible for the Marine Corps and, in a time of war or if the president directs, the U.S. Coast Guard as well. The navy offers a wide variety of career and educational opportunities, especially in the nuclear and engineering fields. The navy reserve offers the same career fields as does the active navy.

MAIN MISSION   The navy maintains freedom in the seas. It defends the rights of our country and its allies to travel and trade freely on the world's oceans and helps protect our country during times of international conflict. Navy sea and air power make it possible for our country to use the oceans when and where our national interests require it. Navy personnel serve on ships, on submarines under the sea, in aviation positions on land, and at shore bases around the world.

Special Operations Forces

Sea-Air-Land (SEAL)

Formally known as the Underwater Demolition Teams, the navy SEALs are lightly armed units who operate with stealth, concealment, and surprise to accomplish their operations. Navy SEALs conduct search and destroy missions, clear underwater mine fields, and go behind enemy lines.

"Verily, thou art not paid for thy methods, but for thy results, by which meaneth thou shalt kill thine enemy by any means available before he killeth you."

Richard Marcinko, Former Seal Team Six Unit Founder and Leader

---

OPPORTUNITY   ✪ Recruits 60,000 new people each year

Profile of U.S. Navy Personnel

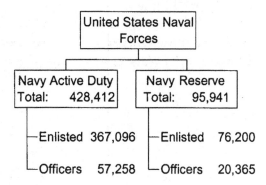

Major Commands

U.S. Atlantic Fleet Headquarters—Norfolk, VA
Atlantic, Mediterranean, Indian Ocean Areas

U.S. Pacific Fleet Headquarters—Pearl Harbor, HI
Pacific Ocean Regions

TERRORISM'S DARK HISTORY

On October 12, 2000, a small dinghy carrying explosives rammed the destroyer U.S.S. *Cole* in Aden, Yemen, killing 17 sailors and injuring 39 others. Supporters of Osama bin Laden were suspected.

Source: U.S. Department of State

Where They Serve

Total of personnel assigned ashore (bases):   272,410
Total of personnel assigned afloat (ships and submarines):   162,207

U.S. Marine Corps (USMC) Careers

United States Marine Corps
☆ U.S. Marine Corps Reserve
U.S. Marine Corps Recruiting
   Command
2 Navy Annex
Washington, DC 20380
(800) Marines
www.usmc.mil/marines

OVERVIEW

The Marine Corps is one of the oldest military services. It was established on November 10, 1775, by the Continental Congress as a service to act as landing forces with the fleet. On July 11, 1798, the United States Marine Corps was established as a separate service. In 1834, it was made part of the Department of the Navy. The Marine Corps offers a wide variety of career and educational opportunities. The Marine Corps Reserve offers career fields the same as the active Marine Corps.

> "Some people live an entire lifetime and wonder if they have ever made a difference in the world, but the Marines don't have that problem."
>
> President Ronald Reagan

MAIN MISSION

The marines are an elite fighting force, which are part of the Department of the Navy and operate in close cooperation with U.S naval forces at sea. Marines serve on U.S. navy ships, protect naval bases, guard U.S. embassies, and provide a quick, ever-ready strike force to protect U.S. interests anywhere in the world. The Marine Corps is also responsible for developing programs including tactics, techniques, and equipment used by landing forces.

Special Operation Forces

Marine Expeditionary Unit (MEW)
The MEW is a small tactical unit of the Marine Corps Air Ground Task Force. The elite MEW has approximately 2,200 members. The MEW

mission is an "expeditionary intervention force with the ability to rapidly organize for combat operations in virtually any environment. Naval Special Warfare encompasses operations generally accepted as being unconventional in nature and clandestine in character, including use of specially trained and equipped forces."

OPPORTUNITY   ✪ Recruits 41,000 new people each year

PROFILE OF USMC PERSONNEL

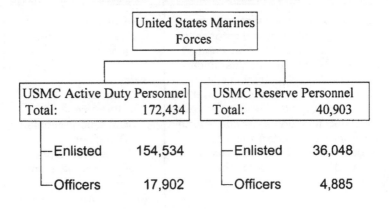

United States Marines Forces	
USMC Active Duty Personnel Total: 172,434	**USMC Reserve Personnel** Total: 40,903
─Enlisted 154,534	─Enlisted 36,048
└Officers 17,902	└Officers 4,885

TERRORISM'S DARK HISTORY

Bombing of Marine Barracks, Beirut, October 23, 1983: Simultaneous suicide truck-bomb attacks were made on American and French compounds in Beirut, Lebanon. A 12,000-pound bomb destroyed the U.S. compound, killing 242 Americans, while 58 French troops were killed when a 400-pound device destroyed a French base. Islamic Jihad claimed responsibility.

Source: U.S. Department of State

Where They Serve

Total of personnel assigned ashore (bases):   169,431
Total of personnel assigned afloat (ships):   5,208

MILITARY CAREERS RELATED TO HOMELAND SECURITY

SPECIAL OPERATIONS FORCES (SOF)		
Enlisted Occupations	**Available Positions by Branch**	**Opportunities in Civilian Life**
SOF are elite combat units that operate with stealth, concealment, and surprise to accomplish their operations. SOF conduct search and destroy missions, clear underwater mine fields, and go behind enemy lines. SOF provide specialized air power for worldwide deployment and are assigned to conduct unconventional warfare, special reconnaissance, counterterrorism, foreign internal defense, humanitarian assistance, psychological operations, personnel retrieval, and counternarcotics. *Special Comment:* For the most part, special operations are not entry-level positions. The military is looking for service members who have already proven themselves prior to special operations duty. *Restricted:* At the present time, special forces occupations are restricted to male military members only. However, things may change.	**Air Force** 　Special operations 　Pararescue **Army** 　Green Berets 　Delta Force 　SO weapons sergeant 　SO engineer 　SO medical sergeant 　SO communications **Marine Corps** 　MEW team member 　SO weapons sergeant 　SO engineer 　SO medical sergeant 　SO communications **Navy** 　SEAL team member	**Federal Jobs** 　CIA agent 　FBI agent 　ATF agent **Civilian Jobs** 　Corporate security

SPECIAL OPERATIONS FORCES (SOF)		
Officer Careers	**Available Positions by Branch**	**Opportunities in Civilian Life**
SOF are elite combat units that operate with stealth, concealment, and surprise to accomplish their operations. SOF conduct search and destroy missions, clear underwater mine fields, and go behind enemy lines. SOF provide specialized air power for worldwide deployment and are assigned to conduct unconventional warfare, special reconnaissance, counterterrorism, foreign internal defense, humanitarian assistance, psychological operations, personnel retrieval, and counternarcotics. *Special Comment:* For the most part, special operations are not entry-level positions. The military is looking for service members who have already proven themselves prior to special operations duty. *Restricted:* At the present time, special forces occupations are restricted to male military members only. However, things may change. *Education Requirement:* Four-year college degree	**Air Force** Special operations **Army** Green Berets officer **Marine Corps** MEW team officer **Navy** SEAL team officer	**Federal Jobs** CIA agent FBI agent ATF agent **Civilian Jobs** Corporate security

INTELLIGENCE, LAW ENFORCEMENT, AND SECURITY		
Enlisted Careers	**Available Positions by Branch**	**Opportunities in Civilian Life**
Intelligence Specialists: Gather information from a variety of sources, including aerial photographs, electronic monitoring, and human observation. Analyze and prepare detailed intelligence reports. Position requires clearance. *Intelligence Specialist Specialities:* Language interrogation Image interpretation Operation intelligence Psychological operations Counterintelligence Signal intelligence Human intelligence	**Air Force** OSI Intelligence specialist **Army** CID Intelligence analyst Imagery analyst Imagery ground station Ground surveillance Unmanned aerial vehicle operator Counterintelligence assistant Interrogator Signal security specialist Translator/interpreter **Coast Guard** CGI Intelligence specialist **Marine Corps** Intelligence specialist **Navy** ONI Intelligence specialist	**Federal Jobs** Federal police U.S. Marshal U.S. Customs Border Patrol **Civilian Jobs** State police Sheriff's deputy City police
Investigation (Law Enforcement) Investigates criminal conduct involving personnel and property within military jurisdictions. **Military Police** Conduct patrols, maintain law and order on military installation. In addition, support battlefield activity by conducting prisoner of war activities.	**Air Force** OSI investigator Security police **Army** CID investigator Military police **Coast Guard** CGI investigator Port security **Marine Corps** Criminal investigator Military police **Navy** NIS investigator Master-at-arms	**Federal Jobs** Federal police U.S. Marshal U.S. Customs Border Patrol **Civilian Jobs** State police Sheriff's deputy City police

INTELLIGENCE, LAW ENFORCEMENT, AND SECURITY (continued)		
Enlisted Careers	**Available Positions by Branch**	**Opportunities in Civilian Life**
Corrections Specialists Control and counsel military prisoners and manage correctional treatment programs.	**Air Force** Corrections specialist Corrections officer **Army** Corrections specialist Corrections officer **Marine Corps** Corrections officer **Navy** Corrections specialist	**Federal Jobs** Corrections specialist Corrections officer **Civilian Jobs** Corrections specialist Corrections officer
Security (Military Guards) Maintain security patrol or posts at installments or specific sensitive locations.	**Air Force** Security specialist **Army** Guard **Marine Corps** Guard **Navy** Security guard	**Federal Jobs** Federal guard **Civilian Jobs** Security specialist Security guard

Emergency Management Specialists
Plan and maintain disaster operations. Train military personnel and civilians on disaster preparedness.
	Air Force
	Disaster preparedness
	  specialist
	
	Army
	Disaster preparedness
	  specialist
	Safety inspector
	
	Navy
	Damage control
		Federal Jobs
		Emergency
		  management
		  specialists
		
		Civilian Jobs
		Emergency
		  management
		  specialists

INTELLIGENCE, LAW ENFORCEMENT, AND SECURITY (continued)		
Enlisted Careers	**Available Positions by Branch**	**Opportunities in Civilian Life**
Nuclear, Biological, and Chemical Warfare, and Ordnance Specialists Transport, store, inspect, prepare, and destroy weapons and ammunition, including large shells, missiles, chemicals, and nuclear devices. Nuclear, biological, and chemical (NBC) warfare.	**Air Force** Nuclear weapons specialist NBC specialist Munitions specialist Explosive ordnance disposal specialist **Army** Ammunition specialist Explosive ordnance Nuclear ordnance NBC specialist Disposal specialist **Coast Guard** Gunner's mate **Marine Corps** Ammunition technician Explosive ordnance Disposal technician **Navy** Gunner's mate Mineman	**Federal Jobs** Munitions Nuclear regulatory **Civilian Jobs** Civil disaster coordinator Disposal expert
Firefighters Responsible for protecting lives and property from fire on military bases and ships.	**Air Force** Firefighter **Army** Firefighter **Coast Guard** Damage control **Marine Corps** Firefighter **Navy** Damage control	**Federal Jobs** Firefighter (DOVA) **Civilian Jobs** Firefighter

INTELLIGENCE AND LAW ENFORCEMENT		
Officer Careers	**Available Positions by Branch**	**Opportunities in Civilian Life**
Intelligence Gather information critical to national defense. The means by which the information is gathered leads to numerous specialities within the intelligence field. "Intell" officers help plan military missions and direct sea, ground, and human surveillance. *Specialities:* Language interrogation Image interpretation Operation intelligence Psychological operations Counterintelligence Signal intelligence Human intelligence *Education Requirement:* Four-year college degree (numerous fields)	**Air Force** Intelligence officer Signals intelligence Imagery intelligence **Army** Military intelligence Strategic intelligence Tactical intelligence Human intelligence Signals intelligence Imagery intelligence Counterintelligence **Coast Guard** CGI Intelligence officer **Marine Corps** Intelligence officer **Navy** ONI Intelligence officer Psychology ops Operational intelligence Tactical intelligence	**Federal Jobs** CIA agent NSA agent FBI agent DIS agent **Civilian Jobs** Corporate intelligence
Law Enforcement and Military Police Law Enforcement and Military Police "Officers" direct and supervise military police officers much like a chief of police, oversee physical security, criminal investigations, and correction activities. *Education Requirement:* Four-year college degree (numerous fields)	**Air Force** OSI Security police **Army** CID Military police Corrections **Coast Guard** CGI Investigations **Marine Corps** NIS Military police Corrections **Navy** NIS Security officer Shore patrol officer	**Federal Jobs** FBI agent U.S. customs agent ATF agent Corrections **Civilian Jobs** Chief of police Director of security Warden State trooper Police officer

Recommended Reading:

For a more detailed selection of military opportunities, refer to:

Barron's Guide to Military Careers
by Donald B. Hutton

Barron's Educational Series, Inc.
250 Wireless Boulevard
Hauppauge, New York 11788
(631) 434-3311
www.barronseduc.com

Military Careers: A Guide to Military Occupations and Selected Military Career Paths
U.S. Department of Defense
Washington, DC

SECTION

YOUR APPLICATION AND BACKGROUND CHECK

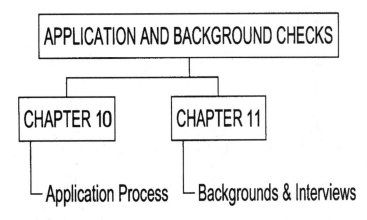

APPLICATION AND BACKGROUND CHECKS

CHAPTER 10

CHAPTER 11

Application Process

Backgrounds & Interviews

Chapter 10

PLAN YOUR COURSE OF ACTION

☐ **The General Process**

☐ **The Federal Process**

☐ **Major Federal Employment Benefits**

☐ **U.S. Office of Personnel Management**

THE GENERAL PROCESS

1. Call or write and ask for position announcements and required applications.

2. Read the announcements carefully, and then fill out the applications.

3. Submit the applications (and your résumé, if applicable).

4. Take the required tests. Wait for the results and information about the next steps.

5. If at first you do not succeed, reexamine what when wrong and . . . TRY . . . TRY . . . AGAIN!!!

Plan Your Course of Action

You will not accidently walk into a homeland security position. Most successful candidates have planned a course of action that guided them to their desired position. Make a list of several positions in which you are interested. The more positions you apply for, the better your chances of obtaining a position. Check the qualifications for the positions. Do you qualify? If not, continue to enhance your background by obtaining more qualifying education and experience.

What are you willing to do for a law enforcement position? Are you willing to

- move?

- attend college?

- gain experience as an intern?

- join the military?

- obtain employment experience?

You need to set the parameters of what you are willing to do to obtain a homeland security position. If you answered "yes" to the above questions, you are on the right path toward your goal. Remember, you must not be just a qualified candidate; you must be a desirable candidate! A candidate who has a well-rounded package of experience, education, and the ability to relocate has the tactical edge.

SAMPLE LETTER TO HOMELAND SECURITY AGENCY

Name
Address
City, State Zip Code
Phone number

Agency Title
Address
City, State Zip Code

Date

Dear Personnel Administrator:

I am interested in applying for a position as a _____ with the _____ Agency. Please send me the position's announcement, required application forms, and information on the selection process and qualifications. Thank you for your time and consideration.

Sincerely,

Your name

Résumé Hints

For the most part, applicants to homeland security positions are required to fill out an official form, which is essentially a narrative résumé. You should also have a narrative history-style résumé on hand that lists your education or experience in reverse chronological order, meaning your most recent employment first.

- Type your résumé on standard 8 1/2" × 11" paper. If possible, have your résumé printed with a laser printer so as to provide the best-quality lettering.

- Make clear and presentable copies. Nothing is worse than a hazy photocopy of a résumé. It sends a message that the person that submitted it has sent out a mass of copies and may not really care about the position. Remember, your résumé is the first impression a perspective employer will have of you.

- Avoid long-winded descriptions of your experience. Write short and concise sentences, using the key buzz words indicating your experience. Proofread your résumé, or have someone else do it for you. Misspelled words or grammer errors can be a fatal mistake.

SAMPLE LETTER TO CIVIL SERVICE OR PERSONNEL DEPARTMENTS

Name
Address
City, State Zip Code
Phone Number

Civil Service Department
Address
City, State Zip Code

Date

Dear Personnel Administrator:

I am interested in applying for the position of _____. Please send me any announcements for current homeland security positions, the required application forms, and information on the selection process and qualifications. Thank you for your time and consideration.

Sincerely,

Your name

SAMPLE RÉSUMÉ

Chris Candidate
123 Address, Street
Buffalo, New York 12345
(716) 123-4567

EDUCATION

1995–1997   SUNY Empire State College at Buffalo, NY
Bachelor's Degree: Criminal Justice

1993–1995   Sam Houston State University, Huntsville, TX
Bachelor's Degree: Criminal Justice

INTERNSHIP

1993   Sam Houston State University, Public Safety Department,
Huntsville, TX
PUBLIC SAFETY INTERN
Conducted safety patrol as assigned by campus police supervisor. Instructed and completed uniform crime report for
department. Assigned a special statistical project and received
a letter of recommendation from the chief of the department
for my assistance.

EXPERIENCE

1995, 1996   United States Customs Service, Niagara Falls, NY
U.S. CUSTOMS INSPECTOR (Summer)
Protected the United States border. Controlled carriers, persons,
and cargo entering and departing U.S. Prevented fraud and
smuggling. Assessed and collected customs duties, excise tax on
imported goods. Worked during summer break from college.

1994–1995   State Protection Services, Huntsville, TX
SECURITY OFFICER
Worked as a uniformed security guard. Assigned to high-crime
areas. Conducted both foot and vehicle patrols. Entrusted
with several special protection projects.

State Agencies

The procedures to apply to state agencies varies slightly from state to state. However, for the most part, you are advised to contact the hiring agency directly for information and to request an application. In some states, you may be redirected to the state civil service or personnel department for the application and examination requirements. However, the best advice is to send a letter to the state agencies and the corresponding civil service and personnel departments. Not only will you receive the information you are looking for, but you may also receive information you need but did not know to ask for.

"A great people has been moved to defend a great nation. Terrorist attacks can shake the foundations of our biggest buildings, but they cannot touch the foundation of America. These acts shattered steel, but they cannot dent the steel of American resolve. America was targeted for attack because we're the brightest beacon for freedom and opportunity in the world. And no one will keep that light from shining."

President George W. Bush, Address to the Nation, September 11, 2001

SAMPLE ANNOUNCEMENT

POLICE DEPARTMENT
CIVIL SERVICE ANNOUNCEMENT

POLICE OFFICER—EXAMINATION

An application fee of $10.00 must accompany your application

Benefits
Salary $31,489 a year
Full pay during academy training
Family and domestic partner health and dental coverage
Paid Vacation, Sick Leave, and Holidays

TEST DATES: To Be Announced
LOCATION: To Be Announced

SELECTION PROCESS

- Written examination
- Physical agility test
- Psychological evaluation
- Extensive background investigation
- Polygraph test
- Medical screening and examination
- Urinalysis

GENERAL REQUIREMENTS

In addition to completing the competitive examinations given by the State's Civil Service Division successfully, candidates must meet several standards established by the State Law Enforcement Division:

Area of recruitment:
Candidates must be citizens of the United States. Residents of the city will be given preference in appointment to the position of police officer.

Minimum Age:
Candidates must be at least 20 years old on the date of the competitive examination and at least 21 years old on the date of appointment.

Maximum Age:
Candidates must not have reached their 35th birthday on the date of appointment. Candidates with military service in their background, as defined in section 243 of the military law, may use service time to extend the age limit with up to a 5-year limit. Applicable provisions of federal law may also have an impact on the maximum age requirement.

Education:
Candidates must have graduated from a registered high school or possess a state high school equivalency diploma prior to appointment. Military GED and high school

(continued)

equivalency diplomas from other states must be converted to this state's standards. *(Possible)* In addition, all candidates must have completed a minimum of 45 credit hours at an accredited college at the time of appointment. The State Law Enforcement Administration may waive 30 credit hours for candidates who have an honorable discharge from the United States military or candidates who have prior law enforcement experience and have successfully graduated from a certified police academy.

Residence:

Candidates must be U.S. citizens and must be a resident of this state on the date of employment and maintain that residency as long as employed by the State Law Enforcement Agency.

Criminal Record:

Candidates with felony convictions are automatically disqualified. Conviction for other crimes and offenses are subject to evaluation by the administrative staff.

Driver's License:

Candidate must possess a valid state license at the time of appointment.

Veteran's Preference:

Candidates who have active duty service in their background and possess an honorable discharge may apply for a veteran's credit on the examination.

Medical Fitness:

Since the physical activities of the position as a state law enforcement officer often demand extreme exertion in emergency situations, sound health and physical condition are required of all candidates. A complete medical examination will be given prior to appointment during which hearing, vision, weight, dental, and general fitness will be determined. Vision must be no worse than 20/40 in each eye uncorrected; corrected to 20/20. Color blindness is a disqualifying factor. Weight must be in proportion to height and build. (Minimum/maximum height standards have been removed from many states). Candidates will be required to provide blood and urine samples for analysis of drug abuse.

An Equal-Opportunity Employer

GENERAL INFORMATION

Eligible List:

The term of the eligible list resulting from this examination will be one year and may be extended for four years. Candidates will be ranked on the resulting eligible list in the order of their final ratings, with the name of the candidates with the highest final rating first.

Salary:

The salary for this position is subject to change from time to time.

Veterans:

If you are entitled to veteran's credits, you should claim these credits when you file your application.

Residence:

Residence is required for all positions at appointment date.

The General Application Form

Most agencies utilize personnel or civil service application forms for the initial application process. These forms request certain information for the position the candidate is seeking. Blocks are designated for background, experience, education, and veteran's preference. In addition, questions regarding employment background, criminal records, and financial history may also be asked.

On the following pages you will find a sample New York State civil service application form (for reference only).

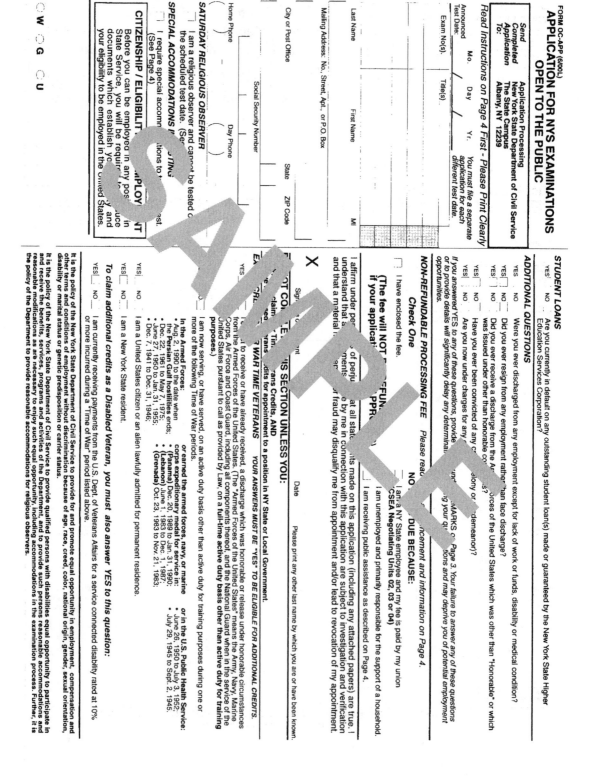

O W G U

FORM OC-APP (6/00L)

APPLICATION FOR NYS EXAMINATIONS
OPEN TO THE PUBLIC

Send Completed Application To:
Application Processing
New York State Department of Civil Service
The State Campus
Albany, NY 12239

Read Instructions on Page 4 First - Please Print Clearly

You must file a separate application for each different test date.

Exam No(s).

Announced Test Date: Mo. / Day / Yr.   Title(s).

Last Name   First Name   MI

Mailing Address: No., Street, Apt., or P.O. Box   Social Security Number

City or Post Office   State   ZIP Code

Home Phone   Day Phone

SATURDAY RELIGIOUS OBSERVER
I am a religious observer and cannot be tested on the scheduled test date.

SPECIAL ACCOMMODATIONS
I require special accommodations to...

CITIZENSHIP / ELIGIBILITY FOR EMPLOYMENT
Before you can be employed in any position in State Service, you will be required to produce documents which establish your identity and your eligibility to be employed in the United States.

STUDENT LOANS
YES NO   Are you currently in default on any outstanding student loan(s) made or guaranteed by the New York State Higher Education Services Corporation?

ADDITIONAL QUESTIONS
YES NO   Were you ever discharged from any employment except for lack of work or funds, disability or medical condition?
YES NO   Did you ever resign from any employment rather than face discharge?
YES NO   Did you ever receive a discharge from the Armed Forces of the United States which was other than "Honorable" or which was issued under other than honorable conditions?
YES NO   Have you ever been convicted of any felony or misdemeanor?
YES NO   Are you now under charges for any felony or misdemeanor?

If you answered YES to any of these questions, provide details... READ REMARKS on Page 3. Your failure to answer any of these questions or to provide details will significantly delay any determination regarding your qualifications and may deprive you of potential employment opportunities.

NON-REFUNDABLE PROCESSING FEE   Please read announcement and information on Page 4.
Check One
☐ I have enclosed the fee.
☐ NO FEE DUE BECAUSE:
   I am a NY State employee and my fee is paid by my union CSEA Negotiating Units 02, 03 or 04)
(The fee will NOT BE REFUNDED if your application...)
   I am unemployed and primarily responsible for the support of a household.
   I am receiving public assistance as described on Page 4.

I affirm under penalty of perjury that all statements made on this application (including any attached papers) are true. I understand that any statement made by me in connection with this application are subject to investigation and verification and that a material false statement or fraud may disqualify me from appointment and/or lead to revocation of my appointment.

X _____   _____
   Signature   Date

Please print any other last name by which you are or have been known.

DO NOT COMPLETE THIS SECTION UNLESS YOU:

EXTRA CREDITS — WAR TIME VETERANS   YOUR ANSWERS MUST BE "YES" TO BE ELIGIBLE FOR ADDITIONAL CREDITS.

I am now serving, or have served, on an active duty basis other than active duty for training purposes during one or more of the following Time of War periods.

...to receive or have already received, a discharge which was honorable or release under honorable circumstances from the Armed Forces of the United States. ("The 'Armed Forces' means the Army, Navy, Marine Corps, Air Force and Coast Guard, including all components thereof, and the National Guard when in the service of the United States pursuant to call as provided by Law, on a **full-time active duty basis other than active duty for training purposes.**)

In the Armed Forces:
• Aug. 2, 1990 to the date when the Persian Gulf hostilities ends;
• Dec. 22, 1961 to May 7, 1975;
• June 27, 1950 to Jan. 31, 1955;
• Dec. 7, 1941 to Dec. 31, 1946;

or earned the armed forces, navy, or marine corps expeditionary medal for service in:
• (Panama) Dec. 20, 1989 to Jan. 31, 1990;
• (Lebanon) June 1, 1983 to Dec. 1, 1987;
• (Grenada) Oct. 23, 1983 to Nov. 21, 1983;

or in the U.S. Public Health Service:
• June 26, 1950 to July 3, 1952;
• July 29, 1945 to Sept. 2, 1945.

YES NO   I am a United States citizen or an alien lawfully admitted for permanent residence.

YES NO   I am a New York State resident.

To claim additional credits as a Disabled Veteran, you must also answer YES to this question:
YES NO   I am currently receiving payments from the U.S. Dept. of Veterans Affairs for a service connected disability rated at 10% or more incurred during a Time of War period listed above.

It is the policy of the New York State Department of Civil Service to provide and promote equal opportunity in employment, compensation and other terms and conditions of employment without discrimination because of age, race, creed, color, national origin, gender, sexual orientation, disability or marital status or genetic predisposition or carrier status.

It is the policy of the New York State Department of Civil Service to provide qualified persons with disabilities equal opportunity to participate in and receive the benefits, services, programs and activities of the Department, and to provide such persons reasonable accommodations in the examination process. Further, it is reasonable modifications as are necessary to enjoy such equal opportunity, including accommodations in the examination process. Further, it is the policy of the Department to provide reasonable accommodations for religious observers.

OC–APP (6/00L)   **Application for NYS Examinations Open to the Public**   **Page 2**

YOUR EDUCATION:

Read the exam announcement for educational requirements, if any. If specialized coursework is required, attach a copy of the transcript or a list of the required courses and the number of credit hours you completed.

Do you have a High School or Equivalency Diploma?	☐ Yes ☐ No	If YES, Name and location of High School or Issuing Governmental Authority:						

College, University, Professional or Technical School(s)	Semester Credits Received	Quarter Hours Received	Type of Degree Received	Major Subject or Type of Course	Did You Graduate	Degree Expected
Name					☐ Yes ☐ No	MO. YR. /
Address (City, State)						
Name					☐ Yes ☐ No	MO. YR. /
Address (City, State)						

LICENSE OR CERTIFICATION:

Complete the following if a license, certificate or other authorization to practice a trade or profession is required ... ouncement(s).

Trade or Profession	License Number	Date License First Issued	Re tration FROM MO. YR. / TO MO.		If you are not currently licensed, check this box: ☐
Specialty	Granted by (licensing agency)			State	

DESCRIBE YOUR EXPERIENCE:

Beginning with your most recent, list all employment, military service, o... teer exp... ce that show. you meet the minimum qualifications for the examination(s). We cannot interpret omissions or vagueness in y... r. Y... responsible for an accurate and clear description of your experience. Do not send your resume. Under DUTIES de... ibe the ... e work which you personally performed including the estimated percentage of time spent on each type of activity. If ... ervised, ... now many people and the nature of such supervision.

LENGTH OF EMPLOYMENT MO. YR. MO. YR. FROM / TO /	FIRM NAME	S	CITY AND STATE
EARNINGS (Circle One) $ / WK. / MO / YR.	DUTIES:		
TYPE OF BUSINESS			
YOUR EXACT TITLE			
NAME OF YOUR SUPERVISOR			
SUPERVISOR'S			
No. of hours worked per we (exclusive of overtime):			

LENGTH OF EMPLOYMENT MO. YR. MO. FROM / TO /	F ME	ADDRESS	CITY AND STATE
EARNINGS (Circle One) $ / WK. / MO / YR.	DUTIES:		
TYPE OF BUSINESS			
YOUR EXACT TITLE			
NAME OF YOUR SUPERVISOR			
SUPERVISOR'S TITLE			
No. of hours worked per week (exclusive of overtime):			

BE SURE TO READ THE REQUIRED QUALIFICATIONS ON THE EXAMINATION ANNOUNCEMENT(S)
ALL STATEMENTS ARE SUBJECT TO VERIFICATION

OC–APP (6/00L)   **Application for NYS Examinations Open to the Public**   **Page 3**

LENGTH OF EMPLOYMENT	FIRM NAME	ADDRESS	CITY AND STATE
MO. YR. MO. YR. FROM / TO /			
EARNINGS (Circle One) $ / WK. / MO / YR.	DUTIES:		
TYPE OF BUSINESS			
YOUR EXACT TITLE			
NAME OF YOUR SUPERVISOR			
SUPERVISOR'S TITLE			
No. of hours worked per week (exclusive of overtime):			

LENGTH OF EMPLOYMENT	FIRM NAME	ADDRESS	STATE
MO. YR. MO. YR. FROM / TO /			
EARNINGS (Circle One) $ / WK. / MO / YR.	DUTIES:		
TYPE OF BUSINESS			
YOUR EXACT TITLE			
NAME OF YOUR SUPERVISOR			
SUPERVISOR'S TITLE			
No. of hours worked per week (exclusive of overtime):			

LENGTH OF EMPLOYMENT	FIRM NAME	ADDRESS	CITY AND STATE
MO. YR. MO. YR. FROM / TO /			
EARNINGS (Circle One) $ / WK. / MO / YR.	DUTIES:		
TYPE OF BUSINESS			
YOUR EXACT TITLE			
NAME OF YOUR SUPERVISOR			
SUPERVISOR'S TITLE			
No. of hours worked per week (exclusive of overtime):			

REMARKS:

Attach additional 8 1/2" x 11" sheets if necessary.

OC–APP (6/00L)   **Application for NYS Examinations Open to the Public**   **Page 4**

EXAMINATION APPLICATION

Use this form to apply for New York State Civil Service exams which are open to the public (The five-digit Examination Numbers beginning with 2 or 8). Read each exam announcement carefully to be sure that you meet the Minimum Qualifications.

You must file a separate application for each different test date. You may list up to eight exam numbers on one application, as long as they are all being held on the same date.

Unless the exam announcement has different instructions, mail your application (and the required processing fee, if any) to Application Processing: NYS Department of Civil Service, The State Campus, Albany, NY 12239.

ADMISSION TO EXAMINATION

We usually review your application before the test to be sure that you qualify. Generally we will advise you if we need more information. You may be admitted to the test pending a full review of your application. If you take the test but your application is disapproved later, you will not receive a test score. If your application disapproved, we will notify you of the reason.

If you are applying for a written test and you do not receive a notice from us by ___ days ___ re the test date, immediately call (518) 457-5483 if taking the test in Albany; (518) 457-6556 ___ ew Y___ City Test Centers; and (518) 457-7022 for all other Test Centers. We cannot accept collect calls.

PLACE OF EXAMINATION

Unless the exam announcement states otherwise, written tests are held in the following locations, although some may not be open for every examination. You will be assigned to the nearest open location based on the postal ZIP code for your mailing address.

Oral tests are usually held in Albany only.

Albany	Kingston	Rochester
Amste	Middletown	Saranac Lake
Bingham	New York City (Bronx)	Saratoga
Buffalo	ew York Cit nhattan)	Selden
ia	ck	Syracuse
	hu	Troy
Horn	Pe le	Utica
		Watertown

SATURDAY REL US OF RVER

Most written tests are held on Saturdays. If you are a religious ob___ ___ou cannot take the test on the announced test date, check the box, "I am a religious observer and cannot b___ ed on ___uled test date." We will make arrangements for you to take the test on a different date (usually the following ___

SPECIAL ACC M TION TESTING

We provide reasonable accommodations for ___s with a ___ab ___ take a est. If you need a reasonable accommodation, check the box, "I require special accommodations ___ test." ___ or b ___ the last date for filing applications, write to the Department of Civil Service or call (518) 457-3416 or T___ ___ D ___ e fo ___ Deaf) (518) 457-8480 and describe the accommodation you need.

NON-RE ABE PROCESSING FEE

Refer to the front of the exam ___ ent for the r___ d processing fee. Enclose a check or money order for the total amount required, **made payable to NY___ ___ f Civil S___ e. DO NOT SEND CASH. If your application is disapproved, the fee will not be refunded.** Check the ___ "I ___ sed the fee."

If you are a NYS employee in a ___ion r___ by CSEA, you are not required to submit a processing fee under current negotiated agreements. Check the ___ "I ___ NY___ mployee and my fee is paid by my union **(CSEA Negotiati___ 02, 03 &___** ___ runds will not be issued to employees covered by the agreements if they submit a fee.

No fee is due ___ ou are une___ ed ar ___ marily responsible for the support of a household. Do not enclose any payment with your application. ___ ck the b ___ hemp ed and primarily responsible for the support of a household."

No fee is due ___ ___ termi ___ ligible for Medicaid, or receiving Supplemental Social Security payments, or Public Assistance (Temporary As___ ___ e for Nee ___ amilies/Family Assistance or Safety Net Assistance) or are certified Job Training Partnership Act/Workforce Investment Ac ___ gible through a state or local social service agency. Do not enclose any payment with your application. Check the ___ receiving public assistance."

All claims are subject ___ ___ cation. Those not supported by appropriate documentation are grounds for barring or rescinding an appointment.

EXTRA CREDITS FOR WAR TIME VETERANS

Answering these questions means that you are requesting the extra credits. Do not answer the questions if you are not a wartime active duty member of the armed forces or a war time veteran or if you do not want to request the extra credits. If you are currently in the Armed Forces on full-time active duty (other than for training) or if you are a War Time Veteran or Disabled Veteran, you are eligible for extra credits added to your exam score if you pass. These extra credits can be used only once for any permanent government employment in New York State. If you want to have these extra credits added to your exam score, you must answer the questions now. You can waive the extra credits later if you wish. At the time of interview and appointment you will be required to produce the documentation, such as discharge papers, to prove that you are eligible for the extra credits.

PERSONAL PRIVACY PROTECTION LAW NOTIFICATION

The information which you are providing on this application is being requested pursuant to Section 50.3 of the New York State Civil Service Law for the principal purpose of determining the eligibility of applicants to participate in the examination(s) for which they have applied. This information will be used in accordance with Section 96(1) of the Personal Privacy Protection Law, particularly subdivisions (b), (e), and (f). Failure to provide this information may result in disapproval of the application. This information will be maintained by the Director, Division of Staffing Services, Department of Civil Service, The State Campus, Albany, New York 12239. For further information, relating *only* to the Personal Privacy Protection Law, call (518) 457-9375. **(For examination information, call (518) 457-6216.)**

THE FEDERAL PROCESS

You may apply for most federal jobs with a résumé or a special application form called OF612. However, if your résumé or application does not provide all the information requested on the form and in the job vacancy announcement, you may lose consideration for a job. Type or print clearly in dark ink. Help speed the selection process by keeping your application brief and sending only the requested information. If you must attach additional pages, include your name and social security number on each page.

Job Information

- Announcement number

- Title and grade(s) of the job you are applying for

Personal Information

- Full name, mailing address (with zip code), day and evening phone numbers (with area code)

- Social security number

- Country of citizenship (most federal jobs require U.S. citizenship)

- Veteran's preference

- Reinstatement eligibility

- Highest federal civilian grade held

Education

- High school

- Colleges or universities

- Send a copy of your college transcript only if the job vacancy announcement requests it

Work Experience

Provide the following information for your paid and nonpaid work experience related to the job you are applying for.

- Job title

- Duties and accomplishments

- Employers' names and addresses

- Supervisors' names and phone numbers

- Starting and ending dates

- Hours per week

- Salary

- Indicate if the agency may contact your current supervisor

Other Qualifications

- Job-related training courses

- Job-related skills, for example, speaking foreign languages or computer software/hardware expertise

- Job-related certificates and licenses

- Job-related honors, awards, and special accomplishments, for example, publications, memberships in professional or honor societies, leadership activities, public speaking, and performance awards

---

SPECIAL HINT

Make master copies of your OF612/federal résumé before you sign them. This way, you will have a clear legal signature on each copy you send to various agencies. You need to leave several questions blank on your master copy. This will allow you to apply for positions with different titles and announcement numbers. Always sign the copy that is being submitted, never send a photocopy of your signature.

Questions to leave blank on the master copy:
1. Job title
2. Grade
3. Announcement number

REMEMBER

- The more applications you submit, the greater your chances.

- Use a computer or have the OF612 or federal résumé typed.

- Do not sign the original. Use the original as a master and sign each copy.

- Make clear copies.

VETERAN'S PREFERENCE

The federal government gives preference in hiring qualified veterans. Veterans must fill out the Standard Form 15 (SF15), a blue form, and attach a copy of their DD214 as proof.

QUALIFYING FOR FEDERAL EMPLOYMENT

The keys to obtaining a position in federal employment are the ability to start out at a low rate of pay and the willingness to relocate for opportunities and advancement. Remember, in the federal system, once your foot is in the door, you can then apply to transfer to a desired position or area in which you wish to work.

Federal Requirements

All federal positions specifically require each of the following:

- U.S. citizenship
- Age range
- Education level
- Experience level
- Vision standard
- Physical
- Driver's license
- Polygraph
- Psychological assessment
- Intense background investigation
- Urinalysis testing

Basic Qualification Requirements for Federal Positions

The federal process allows for a possible mixture of education and experience to qualify for positions. Candidates can combine education with experience in order to qualify.

Grade	Education or Experience (or Equivalent Combination)
GS-5	4-year course of study above high school leading to a bachelor's degree *or* 3 years of general experience, 1 year of which at least equivalent to GS-4
GS-7	1 full academic year of graduate level education or law school or superior academic achievement *or* 1 year of specialized experience at least equivalent to GS-5
GS-9	2 full academic years of graduate level education *or* a master's degree *or* a graduate degree equivalent to a J.D. *or* 1 year of specialized experience at least equivalent to GS-7
GS-11	3 full academic years of graduate level education *or* a Ph.D. or an equivalent doctoral degree *or* 1 year of specialized experience at least equivalent to GS-9

General Experience

Candidates should have participated in administrative, law enforcement, or other work that shows ability to

- Deal with interpersonal relationships

- Learn and interpret facts

- Seek the cooperation of others in following procedures and regulations

Specialized experience

Work experience that demonstrates specific knowledge, skills, and abilities (KSA) in relationship to the law enforcement position is a plus. The ability to collect, develop, and evaluate facts, evidence, and other investigative data in compliance with laws, rules, or regulations is a positive.

SAMPLE FEDERAL ANNOUNCEMENT

POSITION: EMERGENCY MANAGEMENT PROGRAM SPECIALIST
GS-301-12/13 (PROMOTION POTENTIAL GS-13)

SALARY RANGE: $54,825–$84,751

ORGANIZATION: FEMA, REGION IV, NATIONAL PREPAREDNESS DIVISION

DUTIES: The incumbent in this position provides expert guidance and technical assistance to first responder and emergency management organizations in state and local government, and serves as the focal point in the integration with other divisions for response, training, planning, and preparedness related to domestic terrorism and weapons of mass destruction (WMD) events. Will also provide lead guidance, coordination, oversight, management, and leadership for the regional Continuity of Operations Plan (COOP) program. Conducts in-depth research and analysis of guidance and policies for assisting in state and local planning and preparation, and participates in studies to identify deficiencies in terrorism response. Provides expertise in coordinating and synthesizing terrorism-related issues across organization and program lines to meet the intent of program policies. Coordinates the development of all FEMA regional COOP and terrorism operations plans, including plans for test, training, and exercise (TT&E), multi-year management and strategy, implementation, and evacuation. Develops baseline budget estimates for funding of COOP-related equipment, plans, procedures, and other resources, and participates in the management of Terrorism Consequences Management Preparedness Assistance (TCMPA) grants to states and local communities for terrorism-related planning, training, and exercise activities. Participates with state and local partners in disseminating information on FEMA's terrorism preparedness strategy, mission, vision, and other activities directly related to the federal response plan and to all hazards policy. Interfaces with federal, state, and local counterparts to develop plans for maintaining lines of communication and support in an emergency situation.

QUALIFICATION REQUIREMENTS: Applicants must meet the basic qualification requirements as contained in OPM's (U.S. Office of Personnel Management) Qualifications Standards Operating Manual. These are available on-line at **www.opm.gov**. The manual states that one year of specialized experience equivalent to the next lower grade in the federal service is required. Specialized experience is experience that is indirectly or directly related to the line of work of the position to be filled and that has equipped the applicant with the particular knowledge, skills, and abilities to perform the duties of that position successfully.

Demonstrated experience working with COOP/terrorism programs at the local, state, or federal levels in the private sector.

KNOWLEDGE, SKILLS, AND ABILITIES:
1. Knowledge of current initiatives, policies, programs, structures, and legislation concerning response to and preparation for terrorism-related activities.
2. Ability to organize and coordinate with various stakeholders to implement program strategies and activities.

(continued)

3. Ability to research and analyze complex programs and issues and to synthesize findings and conclusions in a cogent manner.
4. Ability to negotiate effectively while maintaining focus on goals and objectives.

SECURITY CLEARANCE REQUIREMENT: This is a national security position that requires a background investigation. Appointment to the position is subject to the applicant or appointee successfully completing essential security investigation forms, the applicant or appointee cooperating with the investigator, the completion of the investigation, and the favorable adjudication of the investigation. Additionally, appointment could require that the employee satisfy additional security requirements established by FEMA or other federal departments or agencies. Failure to complete any aspect of the process satisfactorily is grounds for immediate termination. Applicants for the position may be required to submit to a urinalysis for illegal drug use prior to appointment.

DRUG TESTING: Applicants for this position may be required to submit to urinalysis for illegal drug use prior to appointment.

REGISTRATION FOR SELECTIVE SERVICE: The Defense Authorization Act of 1986 requires that all male applicants born after 12-31-59, who are required to register under the Military Selective Service Act, be registered or they are not eligible for appointment within this agency.

HOW AND WHERE TO APPLY: Applicants can apply for this position by submitting a résumé, the Optional Application for Federal Employment (OF-612), or any other written format including the SF-171 (Application for Federal Employment). The résumé or application must contain: (1) the employment opportunity number, title, and grade of the job being applied for (indicate the lowest grade level that you will accept if applying for a position advertised at multiple grade levels); (2) full name, mailing address, day and evening phone numbers, social security number, country of citizenship, and branch and date of military service, if applicable; (3) high school name and location, date of diploma or highest grade completed, college name and location, majors, and type and year of any degrees received; (4) work experience that includes job titles, duties and accomplishments, employers' names and addresses, supervisors' names and phone numbers, starting and ending dates, hours per week, and salary; and (5) list of other qualifications such as job-related training courses, job-related skills, job-related certificates, and job-related honors, awards, and special accomplishments.

You may apply for the position in several ways:

a. Mail—Use of a postage-paid federal government agency envelope to mail your application or résumé is not allowed. Applications received this way will not be considered. Complete application packages must be postmarked by the closing date of the announcement in order to receive consideration. All forms should be sent to:

> Federal Emergency Management Agency
> Human Resources Division/Regional Services Branch
> Building E, Room 113
> 16825 S. Seton Avenue
> Emmitsburg, MD 21727

(continued)

b. E-mail—**Hire.Me@fema.gov** Complete e-mail packages must be received by the closing date of the announcement. Please list the job opportunity announcement number in the subject line.

The following must be included:

- At a minimum, the application or résumé and the narrative responses to the knowledge, skills, and abilities (KSAs) and selective placement factor(s), if required.
- If claiming 5-point veteran preference, member copy 4 of the DD-214, Certificate of Release or Discharge from Active Duty, or other proof of entitlement.
- If claiming 10-point veteran preference, submit SF-15, Application for 10-point Veteran Preference, plus the proof required by that form.
- If applying as an ICTAP eligible, submit a copy of the Reduction in Force (RIF) or separation notice and a copy of the last performance appraisal.
- Status applicants with career or career-conditional status or reinstatement eligibility must submit a copy of their most recent Notification of Personnel Action (Standard Form 50) showing tenure group and highest grade held.

To obtain additional information about this vacancy, visit our Web site at **www.fema.gov** or call our employment opportunities hotline at (800) 225-3304.

The Federal Emergency Management Agency is committed to employing a highly qualified workforce that reflects the diversity of our nation. All applicants will receive consideration without regard to race, color, national origin, sex, age, political affiliation, nondisqualifying physical handicap, sexual orientation, and any other nonmerit factor. FEMA provides reasonable accommodations to applicants with disabilities. Anyone needing reasonable accommodation for any part of the application and/or hiring process shall notify FEMA at the number identified above. Reasonable accommodation will be granted on a case-by-case basis.

Source: U.S. FEMA

Form Approved
OMB No. 3206-0219

OPTIONAL APPLICATION FOR FEDERAL EMPLOYMENT - OF 612

You may apply for most jobs with a resume, this form, or other written format. If your resume or application does not provide all the information requested on this form and in the job vacancy announcement, you may lose consideration for a job.

1 Job title in announcement

2 Grade(s) applying for

3 Announcement number

4 Last name   First and middle names

5 Social Security Number

6 Mailing address

City   State   ZIP Code

7 Phone numbers (include area code)
Day   (   )

ing   (   )

WORK EXPERIENCE

8 Describe your paid and nonpaid work experience related to the job for which you are applying. Do **not** attach descriptions.

1)   Job title (if Federal, include series and grade)

From (MM/YY)	To (MM/YY)	Salary $	per	s per week

Employer's name and address   Supervisor's name and phone number
(   )

Describe your duties and accomplishments

2)   Job title (if Federal, include series and grade)

From (MM/YY)	To (MM/YY)	Salary $	per	Hours per week

Employer's name and address   Supervisor's name and phone number
(   )

Describe your duties and accomplishments

SAMPLE

50612-101   NSN 7540-01-351-9178   Optional Form 612 (September 1994)
U.S. Office of Personnel Management

9 May we contact your current supervisor?

YES ☐ NO ☐ ➡ If we need to contact your current supervisor before making an offer, we will contact you first.

EDUCATION

10 Mark highest level completed. Some HS ☐ HS/GED ☐ Associate ☐ Bachelor ☐ Master ☐ Doctoral ☐

11 Last high school (HS) or GED school. Give the school's name, city, State, ZIP Code (if known), and year diploma or GED received.

12 Colleges and universities attended. Do **not** attach a copy of your transcript unless requested.

	Name		Total Credits Earned		Major(s)	Degree - Year
1)			Semester	Quarter		(if any) Received
	City	State ZIP Code				
2)						
3)						

OTHER QUALIFICATIONS

13 **Job-related** training courses (give title and year). **Job-related** skills (othe   ages, com   software/har   are, tools, machinery, typing **speed**, etc. **Job-related** certificates and licenses (current only). **Job-related** honors, awards,   ecial   plishments(publications, memberships in professional/honor societies, leadership activities, public speaking, and performance a   rds.) Gi   onot send documents unless requested.

GENERAL

14 Are you a U.S. c   ☐ NO ☐ ➡ Give the country of your citizenship.

15 Do you claim   ans' prefere   ☐ YES ☐ ➡ Mark your claim of 5 or 10 points below.

  5 points ☐   14 o other proof. **10 points** ☐ ➡ Attach an *Application for 10-Point Veterans' Preference* (SF 15) and proof required.

16 Were you ever a   civilian empl   Series   Grade   From (MM/YY)   To (MM/YY)

  NO ☐ YES ☐ ➡ For highest civilian grade give:

17 Are you eligible for reins   ased on career or career-conditional Federal status?

  NO ☐ YES ☐ ➡ If requested, attach SF 50 proof.

APPLICANT CERTIFICATION

18 **I certify** that, to the best of my knowledge and belief, all of the information on and attached to this application is true, correct, complete and made in good faith. **I understand** that false or fraudulent information on or attached to this application may be grounds for not hiring me or firing me after I begin work, and may be punishable by fine or imprisonment. **I understand** that any information I give may be investigated.

SIGNATURE   DATE SIGNED

PRIVACY ACT AND PUBLIC BURDEN STATEMENT

The Office of Personnel Management is authorized to request this information under sections 1302, 3301, 3304, and 8716 of title 5 of the U.S. Code. Section 1104 of title 5 allows the Office of Personnel Management to delegate personnel management functions to other Federal agencies. If neces- sary, and usually in conjunction with another form or forms, this form may be used in conducting an investigation to determine your suitability or your ability to hold a security clearance, and it may be disclosed to authorized officials making similar, subsequent determinations.

Public burden reporting for this collection of information is estimated to vary from 5 to 30 minutes with an average of 15 minutes per response, including time for reviewing instructions, searching existing data sources, gathering the data needed, and completing and reviewing the collection of information. Send comments regarding the burden estimate or any other aspect of the collection of information, including suggestions for reducing this burden, to Reports and Forms Management Officer, U.S. Office of Personnel Management, 1900 E Street, N.W., Washington, D.C. 20415.

ROUTINE USES: Any disclosure of this record or information in this record is in accordance with routine uses found in System Notice OPM/GOVT-1, General Personnel Records. This system allows disclosure of information to training facilities; organizations deciding claims for retirement, insurance, unemployment, or health benefits; officials in litigation or administrative proceeding where the Government is a party; law enforcement agencies concerning a violation of law or regulation; Federal agencies for statistical reports and studies; officials of labor organizations recognized by law in connection with representing employees; Federal agencies or other sources requesting information for Federal agencies in connection with hiring or retaining, security clearance, security or suitability investigations, classifying jobs, contracting, or issuing licenses, grants, or other benefits; public and private organizations, including news media, which grant or publicize employee recognition and awards; the Merit Systems Protection Board, the Office of Special Counsel, the Equal Employment Opportunity Commission, the Federal

Labor Relations Authority, the National Archives, the Federal Acquisitions Institute, and Congressional offices in connection with their official functions; prospective non-Federal employers concerning tenure of employ- ment, civil service status, length of service, and the date and nature of action for separation as shown on the SF 50 (or authorized exception) of a specifically identified individual; requesting organizations or individuals concerning the home address and other relevant information on those who might have contracted an illness or been exposed to a health hazard; authorized Federal and non-Federal agencies for use in computer matching; spouses or dependent children asking whether the employee has changed from a self-and-family to a self-only health benefits enrollment; individuals working on a contract, service, grant, cooperative agreement, or job for the Federal government; non-agency members of an agency's performance or other panel; and agency- appointed representatives of employees con- cerning information issued to the employee about fitness-for-duty or agency-filed disability retirement procedures.

Optional Form 306 (EG)
September 1994
U.S. Office of Personnel
Management

Declaration for Federal Employme~~nt~~

Form Approved:
O.M.B. No. 3206-0182

GENERAL INFORMATION

1 FULL NAME

▶

2 SOCIAL ~~...~~ NUMBE~~R~~

▶

3 PLACE OF BIRTH (Include City and State or Country)

▶

4 DATE OF BIRT~~H~~ ~~/YY)~~

5 OTHER NAMES EVER USED (For example, maiden name, nic~~k~~)

▶

▶

6 ~~~E N~~~ ~~ER~~S (Include Area Codes)

DAY

NIGHT ▶

MILITARY SERVICE

7 Have you served in the United States Militar~~y Service~~ ~~if y...~~ ~~active~~ ~~as training in the~~ Reserves or National Guard, answer "NO~~".~~ . . .

	Yes	No

If you answered "YES", list the branch, dates (MM/DD/YY), and type of discharge for all active duty military service.

b~~ranch~~	FRO~~M~~	TO	TYPE OF DISCHARGE

BACKGROUND INF~~ORMATION~~

For all questions, provide a~~dditiona~~l ~~information under item 15 or on attached sheets. The circumstances of each event you list will be considere~~d~~ ~~however~~ ~~...es you can still be considered for Federal jobs.

For question~~s~~ ~~...and 10, you~~r~~ ~~...should include convictions resulting from a plea of nolo contendere *(no contest),* but omit (1) traffic ~~fines of~~ ~~...or less, (2)~~ ~~violation~~ of law committed before your 16th birthday, (3) any violation of law committed before your 18~~th bi~~rthday if finally decide~~d in ju~~venile court or under a Youth Offender law, (4) any conviction set aside under the Federal Youth ~~Corr~~ections Act ~~or Star~~ ~~...~~, and (5) any conviction whose record was expunged under Federal or State law.

		Yes	No
8	Du~~ring the last 10~~ years, ~~hav~~e you been convicted, been imprisoned, been on probation, or been on parole? (Inclu~~de felon~~ies, firear~~m or~~ explosives violations, misdemeanors, and all other offenses.) If "Yes", use item 15 t~~o provi~~de the date, explanation of the violation, place of occurrence, and the name and address of the ~~poli~~ce ~~dep~~artment or court involved.		
9	Have you be~~en convi~~cted by a military court-martial in the past 10 years? (If no military service, answer "NO".) If "Yes", use item 15 to provide the date, explanation of the violation, place of occurrence, and the name and address of the military authority or court involved.		
10	Are you now under charges for any violation of law? If "Yes", use item 15 to provide the date, explanation of the violation, place of occurrence, and the name and address of the police department or court involved. . .		
11	During the last 5 years, were you fired from any job for any reason, did you quit after being told that you would be fired, did you leave any job by mutual agreement because of specific problems, or were you debarred from Federal employment by the Office of Personnel Management? If "Yes", use item 15 to provide the date, an explanation of the problem and reason for leaving, and the employer's name and address.		
12	Are you delinquent on any Federal debt? (Includes delinquencies arising from Federal taxes, loans, overpayment of benefits, and other debts to the U.S. Government, plus defaults of Federally guaranteed or insured loans such as student and home mortgage loans.) If "Yes", use item 15 to provide the type, length, and amount of the delinquency or default, and steps that you are taking to correct the error or repay the debt. .		

ADDITIONAL QUESTIONS

		Yes	No
13	Do any of your relatives work for the agency or organization to which you are submitting this form? (Includes father, mother, husband, wife, son, daughter, brother, sister, uncle, aunt, first cousin, nephew, niece, father-in-law, mother-in-law, son-in-law, daughter-in-law, brother-in-law, sister-in-law, stepfather, stepmother, step-son, stepdaughter, stepbrother, stepsister, half brother, and half sister.) If "Yes", use item 15 to provide the name, relationship, and the Department, Agency, or Branch of the Armed Forces for which your relative works.		
14	Do you receive, or have you ever applied for, retirement pay, pension, or other pay based on military, Federal civilian, or District of Columbia Government service?		

Designed using Perform Pro, WHS/DIOR, Jan 95

CONTINUATION SPACE/AGENCY OPTIONAL QUESTIONS ───────

15 Provide details requested in items 8 through 13 and 17c in the continuation space below or on attached sheets. Be sure to identify attached sheets with your name, Social Security Number, and item number, and to include ZIP Codes in all addresses. If any questions are printed below, please answer as instructed (these questions are specific to your position, and your agency is authorized to ask them).

CERTIFICATIONS/ADDITIONAL QUESTION ───────

APPLICANT: If you are applying for a position and have not yet been selected. Carefully review your answers on this form and any attached sheets. When this form and all attached materials are accurate, complete item 16/16a.

APPOINTEE: If you are being appointed. Carefully review your answers on this form and all attached sheets including any other application materials that your agency has attached to this form. If any information requires correction to be accurate as of the date you are signing, make changes on this form or the attachments and/or provide additional information on additional sheets, initialing and dating all changes and additions. When this form and all attached materials are accurate, complete item 16b and answer item 17.

16 I certify that, to the best of my knowledge and belief, all of the information and attached to this Declaration for Federal Employment, including any attached application materials, is true, correct, complete, and made in good faith. **I understand** that a false or fraudulent answer to any question on any part of this declaration or its attachments may be grounds for not hiring me, or for firing me after I begin work, and may be punishable by fine or imprisonment. **I understand** that any information I give may be investigated for purposes of determining eligibility for Federal employment as allowed by law or Presidential order. I consent to the release of information about my ability and fitness for Federal employment by *employers, schools, law enforcement agencies, and other individuals and organizations to investigators, personnel specialists, and other authorized employees of the Federal Government.* I understand for financial or lending institutions, medical institutions, hospitals, health care professionals, and some other sources of information, a separate specific release may be needed, and I may be contacted for such a release at a later date.

16a Applicant's Signature *(Sign in ink)*	Date ▶

16b Appointee's Signature *(Sign in ink)*	Date ▶	APPOINTING OFFICER: Enter Date of Appointment or Conversion ▶

17 Appointee (*respond only if you have been employed by the Federal Government before*): Your elections of life insurance during previous Federal employment may affect your eligibility for life insurance during your new appointment. These questions are asked to help your personnel office make a correct determination.

	Date (MM/DD/YY)			
		Yes	No	Don't Know
17a When did you leave your last Federal job?				
17b When you left the Federal Government last time, did you waive Basic Life Insurance or any type of optional life insurance?				
17c If you answered "Yes" to item 17b, did you later cancel the waiver(s)? *If your answer to item17c is "No," use item 15 to identify the type(s) of insurance for which waivers were not cancelled.*				

Optional Form 306 (Back)   September 1994

Optional Form 306
U.S. Office of Personnel
Management

Declaration for Federal Employment

Form Approved:
O.M.B. No. 3206-0182

INSTRUCTIONS ───────

The information collected on this form is used to determine your acceptability for Federal employment and your enrollment status in the Government's Life Insurance program. You may be asked to complete this form at any time during the hiring process. Follow instructions that the agency provides. If you are selected, you will be asked to update your responses on this form and on other materials submitted during the application process and then to recertify that your answers are true before you are appointed.

Your Social Security Number is needed to keep our records accurate, because people may have the same name and birthdate. Executive Order 9397 also asks Federal agencies to use this number to help identify individuals in agency records. Giving us your SSN or other information is voluntary. However, if you do not give us your SSN or

any other information requested, we cannot process your application. Incomplete addresses and ZIP Codes may also slow processing.

You must answer all questions truthfully and completely. A false statement on any part of this declaration or attached forms or sheets may be grounds for not hiring you, or for firing you after you begin work. Also, you may be punished by fine or imprisonment (U.S. Code, title 18, section 1001.)

Either type your responses to this form or print clearly in dark ink. If you need additional space, attach letter-size sheets (8.5" X 11"), including your name, Social Security Number, and item number on each sheet. It is recommended that you keep a photocopy of your completed form for your records.

Standard Form 15 (Rev. 2/90) (EG)
U.S. Office of Personnel Management
FPM Supplement 296-33
FPM Chapter 211

**APPLICATION FOR 10-POINT
VETERAN PREFERENCE
(TO BE USED BY VETERANS & RELATIVES OF VETERANS)**

Form Approved:
O.M.B. Nn 3206-0001

PERSON APPLYING FOR PREFERENCE

1. Name (Last, First, Middle)

2. Name and Announcement Number of Civil Service or Postal Service Exam You Have Applied For or Position Which You Currently Occupy

3. Home Address (Street Number, City, State and ZIP Code)

4. Social Security Number

5. Date Exam Was Held or Application Submitted

VETERAN INFORMATION *(to be provided by person applying for preference)*

6. Veteran's Name (Last, First, Middle) Exactly As It Appears on Service Records

7. Veteran's Periods of Service

Branch of Service	From	To	Service Number

Veteran's Social Security Number

9. ...er, If Any

INSTRUCTIONS: Check the block which indicates the type of preference you are claiming. Answer all questions associated with that block. The "DOCUME... ...RE... ...D" column refers you to the back of this form for the documents you must submit to support your application. (PLEASE NOTE: Eligibility for veterans' preference is governed by 5 U.S.C. s 2108, ..., and FPM chapter 211. All conditions are not fully described in this form because of space restrictions. The office to which you apply can provide additional inform... Instructions on how to apply fo... ...reference are on SF 171, Application for Federal Employment, or PS Form 2591, Application for Employment (U.S. Postal Service Application).

DOCUMENTATION REQUIRED
(See reverse of this form.)

☐ 10. VETERAN'S CLAIM FOR PREFERENCE based on non-compensable service-connected disability; award of the Purple Heart; or receipt of disability pension under public laws administered by the VA.

→ A and B

☐ 11. VETERAN'S CLAIM FOR PREFERENCE based on eligibility for or receipt of compensation from the VA or disability retirement from a Service Department for a service-connected disability.

Per... ...isability ____%

→ A and C

☐ 12. PREFERENCE FOR A SPOUSE of a living veteran based on the fact that ... because of a service-connected disability, has been unable to qualify for a F... Government job, or any other position along the lines of his/her usual occupa... y... answer to item "a" is "NO," you are ineligible for preference and need not subm... ...om.

a. ...esently married to the ve... ☐ Yes ☐ No

C and H

☐ 13. PREFERENCE FOR WIDOW OR WIDOWER of a veteran... ..."NO" to ...e"... or "YES" to item "b," you are ineligible for preference and nee... ...om...)

a. ...ou married to the veteran ...n he or she died? ☐ Yes ☐ No

b. Have you remarried? (Do not count marriages that were annulled.) ☐ Yes ☐ No

A, D, E, and G
(Submit G when applicable.)

☐ 14. PREFERENCE FOR (NATURAL) MOT... ...onnected perma... ...t totally disabled, or deceased veteran provided... ...ed to the fathe... ...eteran, and your husband (either the veteran's ... r th... ...marriage) ...tally and permanently disabled, or you are now w... ...divorce... ...from the veteran's father and have not remarried, or you are... ...d or div... ...ran's father and have remarried, but are now widowed, divo... ...sepa... ...m ...band of your remarriage. (If your answer is "NO" to item "c"... ...eligible for preference and need not submit th...

a. Are you married? ☐ Yes ☐ No

b. Are you separated? If "YES", do not complete "c". Go to "d". ☐ Yes ☐ No

c. If married now, is your husband totally and permanently disabled? ☐ Yes ☐ No

d. If the veteran is dead, did he/she die in active service? ☐ Yes ☐ No

DISABLED VETERAN:
C, F, and H
(Submit F when applicable.)

DECEASED VETERAN:
A, D, E, and F
(Submit F when applicable.)

This Form Must Be Signed By All Persons Claiming 10-Point Preference

Signature of Person Claiming Preference

Date Signed *(Month, Day, Year)*

FOR USE BY APPOINTING OFFICER ONLY
Signature and Title of Appointing Officer

☐ Preference Entitlement Was Verified
Name of Agency

Date Signed *(Month, Day, Year)*

PREVIOUS 7-83 EDITION USABLE

15-1 10

NSN: 7540-00-634-3972
Designed using Perform Pro, WHS/DIOR, Apr 96

DOCUMENTATION REQUIRED - READ CAREFULLY
(PLEASE SUBMIT PHOTOCOPIES OF DOCUMENTS BECAUSE THEY WILL NOT BE RETURNED)

A. DOCUMENTATION OF SERVICE AND SEPARATION UNDER HONORABLE CONDITIONS

Submit any of the documents listed below as documentation, provided they are dated on or after the day of separation from active duty military service:

1. Honorable or general discharge certificate.

2. Certificate of transfer to Navy Fleet Reserve, Marine Corps Fleet Reserve, or enlisted Reserve Corps.

3. Orders of Transfer to Retired List.

4. Report of Separation from a branch of the Armed Forces.

5. Certificate of Service or release from active duty, provided honorable separation is shown.

6. Official Statement from a branch of the Armed Forces showing that honorable separation took place.

7. Notation by the Department of Veterans Affairs or a branch of the Armed Forces on an official statement, described in B or C below, that the veteran was honorably separated from military service,

8. Official statement from the Military Personnel Records Center that official service records show that honorable separation took place.

B. DOCUMENTATION OF SERVICE-CONNECTED DISABILITY (NON COMPENSABLE, I.E., LESS THAN 10%); PURPLE HEART; AND NONSERVICE-CONNECTED DISABILITY PENSION

Submit one of the following documents:

1. An official statement, dated within the last 12 months, from the Department of Veterans Affairs or from a branch of the Armed Forces, certifying to the present existence of the veteran's service-connected disability of less 10%.

2. An official citation, document, or discharge certificate, issued by a branch of the Armed Forces, showing the award to the veteran of the Purple Heart wound or injuries received in action.

3. An official statement, dated within the last 12 months, from the Department of Veterans Affairs, certifying that the veteran is receiving a non-service connected disability pension.

C. DOCUMENTATION OF SERVICE-CONNECTED DISABILITY (COMPENSABLE, I.E., 10% OR MORE)

Submit one of the following documents, indicated in item 11 on the front of this form:

1. An official statement, dated within the last 12 months, from the Department of Veterans Affairs or from a branch of the Armed Forces, certifying to the veteran's present receipt of compensation for a service-connected disability or disability retired pay.

2. An official statement, dated within the last 12 months, from the Department of Veterans Affairs or from a branch of the Armed Forces, certifying that the veteran has a service-connected disability of 10% or more.

3. An official statement or retirement orders from a branch of the Armed Forces, showing that the retired serviceman was retired because of permanent service-connected disability or was transferred to the permanent disability retirement list. The statement or retirement orders must indicate that the disability is 10% or more.

For spouses and mothers of disabled veterans checking Items 12 or 14, submit the following:

An official statement, dated within the last 12 months, from the Department of Veterans Affairs or from a branch of the Armed Forces, certifying: 1) the present existence of the veteran's service-connected disability, 2) the percentage and nature of the service-connected disability or disabilities (including the combined percentage), a notation as to whether or not the veteran is currently rated as "unemployable" due to the service-connected disability, and 4) a notation as to whether or not the service-connected disability is rated as permanent and total.

D. DOCUMENTATION OF VETERAN'S DEATH

1. If on active military duty at time of death, submit an official notice, from a branch of the Armed Forces, of death occurring under honorable conditions.

2. If death occurred while not on active military duty, submit death certificate.

E. DOCUMENTATION OF SERVICE OR DEATH DURING A WAR, IN A CAMPAIGN OR EXPEDITION FOR WHICH A CAMPAIGN BADGE IS AUTHORIZED, OR DURING THE PERIOD OF APRIL 28,1952 THROUGH JULY

Submit documentation of service or death during a war or during the period April 28, 1952, through July 1, 1955, or during a campaign or expedition for which a campaign badge is authorized.

F. DOCUMENTATION OF DECEASED OR DISABLED VETERAN'S MOTHER'S CLAIM FOR PREFERENCE BECAUSE OF HER HUSBAND'S TOTAL AND PERMANENT DISABILITY.

Submit a statement from husband's physician showing the prognosis of his disease and percentage of his disability.

G. DOCUMENTATION OF ANNULMENT OF REMARRIAGE BY WIDOW OR WIDOWER OF VETERAN

Submit either:

1. Certification from the Department of Veterans Affairs that entitlement to pension or compensation was restored due to annulment.

2. A certified copy of the court decree of annulment.

H. DOCUMENTATION OF VETERAN'S INABILITY TO WORK BECAUSE OF A SERVICE-CONNECTED DISABILITY

Answer questions 1 - 7 below:

1. Is the veteran currently working? ☐ YES ☐ NO If "NO", go to Item 3.	2. If currently working, what is the veteran's present occupation?
3. What was the veteran's occupation, if any, before military service?	4. What was the veteran's military occupation at the time of separation?

5. Has the veteran been employed, or is he/she now employed, by the Federal civil service or D.C. Government?			☐ YES ☐ NO	
A. Title and Grade of Position Most Recently, or Currently, Held	B. Name and Address of Agency		C. Dates of Employment From	To

6. Has the veteran resigned from, been disqualified for, or separated from a position in the Federal civil service or D.C. Government along the lines of his/her usual occupation because of service-connected disability?	☐ YES ☐ NO
If "YES", submit documentation of the resignation, disqualification, or separation.	

7. Is the veteran receiving a civil service retirement pension? ☐ YES ☐ NO	
If "YES", give the Civil Service or Federal Employee retirement annuity number ➤	**CSA**

STANDARD FORM 15 (REV. 2/90) BACK

MAJOR FEDERAL EMPLOYMENT BENEFITS

Federal Pay Scale

For the most part, federal employees are paid on the general schedule of pay known as the GS system. Most agencies start entry-level personnel at the GS-5 level.

Leave

Federal employees receive sick and vacation leave credits that increase with time.

Health

Federal employees have a variety of health insurance plans available.

Retirements

Federal law enforcement employees are eligible to retire at age 50 or with 20 years of service. Employees with 25 years' service are eligible to retire at any age.

Transfer

It is possible for federal employees to transfer from one position to another agency or position. Usually employees must have at least six months of service before transferring.

Federal Promotions

Federal agencies maintain a steady advancement track for employees who demonstrate their suitability for their position.

U.S. Office of Personnel Management									
Salary Table 2002-GS 2002 General Schedule Effective January 2002 **Annual Rates by Grade and Step**									
Steps	**1**	**2**	**3**	**4**	**5**	**6**	**7**	**8**	**9**	**10**
GS 1	14757	15249	15740	16228	16720	17009	17492	17981	18001	18456
GS 2	16592	16985	17535	18001	18201	18736	19271	19806	20341	20876
GS 3	18103	18706	19309	19912	20515	21118	21721	22324	22927	23530
GS 4	20322	20999	21676	22353	23030	23707	24384	25061	25738	26415
GS 5	22737	23495	24253	25011	25769	26527	27285	28043	28801	29559
GS 6	25344	26189	27034	27879	28724	29569	30414	31259	32104	32949
GS 7	28164	29103	30042	30981	31920	32859	33798	34737	35676	36615
GS 8	31191	32231	33271	34311	35351	36391	37431	38471	39511	40551
GS 9	34451	35599	36747	37895	39043	40191	41339	42487	43635	44783
GS 10	37939	39204	40469	41734	42999	44264	45529	46794	48059	49324
GS 11	41684	43073	44462	45851	47240	48629	50018	51407	52796	54185
GS 12	49959	51624	53289	54954	56619	58284	59949	61614	63279	64944
GS 13	59409	61389	63369	65349	67329	69309	71289	73269	75249	77229
GS 14	70205	72545	74885	77225	79565	81905	84245	86585	88925	91265
GS 15	82580	85333	88086	90839	93592	96345	99098	101851	104604	107357

U.S. OFFICE OF PERSONNEL MANAGEMENT

The federal government's employment information system provides worldwide job vacancy information, employment information fact sheets, job applications, and forms on-line. It has on-line résumé development and electronic transmission capabilities. Job seekers can apply for some positions on-line. The USAJOBS Web site is updated every business day from a database of more than 12,000 worldwide job opportunities and is available to job seekers in a variety of formats to ensure access for customers with differing physical and technological capabilities. It is convenient, user-friendly, accessible through the computer or telephone, and available 24 hours a day, seven days a week.

www.USAJOBS.opm.gov.
Automated Telephone System
(478) 757-3000 or TDD (478) 744-2299

Where to write or contact:

U.S. Office of Personnel Management
Huntsville Customer Service Office
150 West Park Loop
Huntsville, AL 35806-1762
(256) 837-1271
Fax: (256) 837-6071
E-mail: **Huntsville@opm.gov**

U.S. Office of Personnel Management
San Francisco Service Center
120 Howard Street, Room 735
San Francisco, CA 94105
(415) 281-7094
Fax: (415) 281-7095
E-mail: **SanFrancisco@opm.gov**

U.S. Office of Personnel Management
Denver Service Center
12345 Alameda Parkway
P.O. Box 25167
Denver, CO 80225
(303) 236-8550
Fax: (303) 236-8580
E-mail: **Denver@opm.gov**

U.S. Office of Personnel Management
Washington, DC Service Center
1900 E Street, N.W., Room 2469
Washington, DC 20415
(202) 606-2575
Fax: (202) 606-1768
E-mail: **Washington@opm.gov**

U.S. Office of Personnel Management
Atlanta Service Center
75 Spring Street, S.W., Suite 1000
Altanta, GA 30303
(404) 331-3455
Fax: (404) 730-9738
E-mail: **Atlanta@opm.gov**

U.S. Office of Personnel Management
Honolulu Customer Service Office
300 Ala Moana Boulevard
Box 50028
Honolulu, Hl 96850
(808) 541-2795
Fax: (808) 541-2788
E-mail: **Honolulu@opm.gov**

U.S. Office of Personnel Management
Chicago Service Center
230 South Dearborn Street, DPN 30-3
Chicago, IL 60604
(312) 353-6234
Fax: (312) 353-6211
E-mail: **Chicago@opm.gov**

U.S. Office of Personnel Management
Twin Cities Customer Service Office
One Federal Drive, Room 266
Fort Snelling, MN 55111-4007
(612) 725-3437
Fax: (612) 725-3725
E-mail: **TwinCities@opm.gov**

U.S. Office of Personnel Management
Kansas City Service Center
601 East 12th Street, Room 131
Kansas City, MO 64106
(816) 426-5705
Fax: (816) 426-5104
E-mail: **KansasCity@opm.gov**

U.S. Office of Personnel Management
Raleigh Service Center
4407 Bland Road, Suite 200
Raleigh, NC 27609-6296
(919) 790-2817
Fax: (919) 790-2824
E-mail: **Raleigh@opm.gov**

U.S. Office of Personnel Management
Philadelphia Service Center
600 Arch Street, Room 3400
Philadelphia, PA 19106
(215) 861-3031
Fax: (215) 861-3030
E-mail: **Philadelphia@opm.gov**

U.S. Office of Personnel Management
San Juan Customer Service Office
Torre de Plaza las Americas, Suite 1114
525 F. D. Roosevelt Avenue
San Juan, PR 00918
(787) 766-5259
Fax: (787) 766-5598
E-mail: **SanJuan@opm.gov**

U.S. Office of Personnel Management
San Antonio Service Center
8610 Broadway, Room 305
San Antonio, TX 78217
(210) 805-2423
Fax: (210) 805-2429
E-mail: **SanAntonio@opm.gov**

U.S. Office of Personnel Management
Norfolk Service Center
200 Granby Street, Room 500
Norfolk, VA 23510-1886
(757) 441-3373
Fax: (757) 441-6280
E-mail: **Norfolk@opm.gov**

Chapter 11

THE PROCESS

☐ Interviews

☐ Background Investigations

INTERVIEWS

The very nature of homeland security has made the need for in-depth interviews and background checks of candidates a priority. The interview process usually involves a panel that can ask the candidate several questions designed to test problem-solving abilities, respect for diversity, role adaptability, and personal accomplishments.

SPECIAL HINTS

- Practice with others. Have a family member or friend conduct a mock interview.
- If possible, videotape your practice interview. Note any behavior that reflects nervousness, such as foot tapping, arm crossing, and so on.
- Men should wear a business suit, white shirt, tie, and polished shoes.
- Women should wear a business suit, polished flat shoes, and a small, sensible purse. Leave the large purse home. Avoid wearing flashy jewelry.
- Arrive a few minutes early.
- Do not fidget during the interview.
- Interview questions are designed to put you to the test, so use common sense. Some questions are loaded and designed to get a reaction out of the candidate. Avoid displaying emotion or being baited into an argument. State your answers in a clear, concise manner.

MEDICAL EXAMINATION

As a candidate, you are expected to be in excellent health with no conditions that would restrict your ability to perform all the functions of the position. A designated physician usually conducts the medical examination to determine whether you meet the medical standards of the agency.

PSYCHOLOGY INTERVIEW

You may be interviewed and evaluated by a psychologist. The psychological parameters used are related to successful performance to determine if you are currently suited for such a difficult and stressful job.

POLYGRAPH

In certain positions, a polygraph examination may be used. The polygraph is a process that involves being physically connected to a polygraph machine while answering a series of questions about such things as:

- information you provided on the application

- prior employment

- possible alcohol and drug abuse

- economic situation

- possible criminal activities

The polygraph is not without controversy; many in law enforcement doubt its effectiveness in determining a candidate's background. However, it is currently in use at many agencies for employment and investigative applications.

BACKGROUND INVESTIGATIONS

Felony convictions or any misdemeanor conviction that would preclude you from carrying a gun can bar you from employment. Furthermore, a history of criminal or improper conduct, a poor employment or poor military record, or a poor driving record may affect your suitability for employment. You must also have a responsible financial history and a pattern of respect and honesty in your dealings with individuals and organizations.

For many of the positions noted in this book, candidates are fingerprinted and photographed. The investigative phase of the background process requires a thorough check of police records; personal, military, and employment histories; as well as field reference checks. Candidates are evaluated by the following standards: respect for the law; honesty; mature judgment; respect for others; positive employment, military, financial, and driving records; no use of illegal drugs; and responsible use of intoxicants. All candidates are required to submit comprehensive biographical information prior to their background investigation interview. Failure to provide complete and accurate information could result in disqualification. Depending on how sensitive in nature is the career that has been selected, the investigation may include a candidate's former schools, neighborhoods, and places of employment.

PUBLIC TRUST

This is a public trust position that requires a background investigation. Appointment to the position is subject to the applicant or appointee successfully completing essential security investigation forms, the applicant or appointee cooperating with the investigator, completion of the investigation, and favorable adjudication of the investigation. Failure to complete any aspect of this process satisfactorily is grounds for immediate termination. Applicants for this position may be required to submit to a urinalysis for illegal drug use prior to appointment.

Source: U.S. Office of Personnel Management

Security Clearance Terms

Security *clearances* are administrative determinations that an individual is eligible, from a security standpoint, for access to classified military information. Security *classifications* are levels of national security information and material and also the degree of damage that unauthorized disclosure would cause to national defense or foreign relations. Security classifications indicate the degree of protection required. There are three such categories:

Top Secret is the highest level of national security information or material, which requires the highest degree of protection. Unauthorized disclosure of top secret material could reasonably be expected to cause *exceptionally grave damage* to the national security.

Secret is a level that requires a substantial degree of protection. The unauthorized disclosure of secret national security information or material could reasonably be expected to cause serious damage to national security.

Confidential is a level that requires protection. The unauthorized disclosure of confidential material could reasonably be expected to cause damage to national security.

The sample forms provided on the following pages are similar to those the federal government and the military will use to complete a background check on you.

Standard Form 86
Revised September 1995
U.S. Office of Personnel Management
5 CFR Parts 731, 732, and 736

Form approved:
OMB No. 3206-0007
NSN 7540-00-634-4036
86-111

Questionnaire for National Security Positions

Follow instructions fully or we cannot process your form. Be sure to sign and date the certification statement on Page 9 and the release on Page 10. *If you have any questions,* call the office that gave you the form.

Purpose of this Form
The U.S. Government conducts background investigations and reinvestigations to establish that military personnel, applicants for or incumbents in national security positions, either employed by the Government or working for Government contractors, licensees, certificate holders, and grantees, are eligible for a required security clearance. Information from this form is used primarily as the basis for investigation for access to classified information or special nuclear information or material. Complete this form only after a conditional offer of employment has been made for a position requiring a security clearance.

Giving us the information we ask for is voluntary. However, we may not be able to complete your investigation, or complete it in a timely manner, if you don't give us each item of information we request. This may affect your placement or security clearance prospects.

Authority to Request this Information
Depending upon the purpose of your investigation, the U.S. _____ ent is authorized to ask for this information under Executive Or _____ 10865, 12333, and 12356; sections 3301 and 9101 of title 5, U _____ C _____ sections 2165 and 2201 of title 42, U.S. Code; se _____ s 781 to 87 _____ title 50, U.S. Code; and parts 5, 732, and 736 of _____ ʳe of I _____ eral Regulations.

Your Social Security number is needed to keep ι _____ : accι _____ because other people may have the sar _____ ᵐe and birth d _____ xecutιᵛe Order 9397 also asks Federal ageⁱ _____ this numι _____ help identify individuals in agency records.

The Investigative Proces
Background investigatⁱ _____ ∴tional sec _____ positions are conducted to develop informatⁱ _____ show whether you _____ reliable, trustworthy, of good conduct and _____ iracter, a _____ ∴l to _____ United States. The information that y _____ rovⁱ _____ rm _____ confirmed during the investigation. Investⁱ _____ extenᵈ _____ /ond the time covered by this form when necessary ι _____ ᴜⁿlve issueꜞ _____ our current employer must be contacted as part of the investiga _____ even if you have previously indicated on applications or _____ s that you do not want this.

In addition to the questions on this form, inquiry also is made about a person's adherence to security requirements, honesty and integrity, vulnerability to exploitation or coercion, falsification, misrepresentation, and any other behavior, activities, or associations that tend to show the person is not reliable, trustworthy, or loyal.

Your Personal Interview
Some investigations will include an interview with you as a normal part of the investigative process. This provides you the opportunity to update, clarify, and explain information on your form more completely, which often helps to complete your investigation faster. It is important that the interview be conducted as soon as possible after you are contacted.   Postponements will delay the processing of your investigation, and declining to be interviewed may result in your investigation being delayed or canceled.

You will be asked to bring identification with your picture on it, such as a valid State driver's license, to the interview.   There are other documents you may be asked to bring to verify your identity as well. These include documentation of any legal name change, Social Security card, and/or birth certificate.

You may also be asked _____ ing documents about information you provided on the form c _____ ᵉr matters requiring specific attention. These matters includ _____ ᵉⁿ regⁱ ∴tion, delinquent loans or taxes, bankruptcy, judgmᵉⁿᵗ _____ ᵉns, o _____ r financial obligations, agreements involving child cust _____ rt, alimᵉ ᵛ or property settlements, arrests, convictions, pro _____ nd/or pa

Organization of this Form

This _____ ᵃas two parts. Par _____ asks for background information, includinɡ _____ ᵉ you have lⁱ _____ d, gone to school, and worked. Part 2 _____ abouᵗ _____ activitⁱᵉ _____ such matters as firings from a job, _____ histoⁱ _____ rᵈ _____ f illegal drugs, and abuse of alcohol.

In anꜞ _____ ing all qⁱ _____ ⁿs on this form, keep in mind that your answers are _____ ꜞidered together with the information obtained in the ⁱⁿ _____ ɡation to reach an appropriate adjudication.

_____ ᴜctions for Completing this Form
1. _____ ᵒw the instructions given to you by the person who gave you the forᵐ _____ ⁱ any other clarifying instructions furnished by that person to assist you in completion of the form. Find out how many copies of the _____ ᵐ you are to turn in. You must sign and date, in black ink, the _____ ⁱginal and each copy you submit. You should retain a copy of the completed form for your records.

2. Type or legibly print your answers in black ink (if your form is not legible, it will not be accepted). You may also be asked to submit your form in an approved electronic format.

3. All questions on this form must be answered. If no response is necessary or applicable, indicate this on the form (for example, enter "None" or "N/A"). If you find that you cannot report an exact date, approximate or estimate the date to the best of your ability and indicate this by marking "APPROX." or "EST."

4. Any changes that you make to this form after you sign it must be initialed and dated by you.   Under certain limited circumstances, agencies may modify the form consistent with your intent.

5. You must use the State codes (abbreviations) listed on the back of this page when you fill out this form. Do not abbreviate the names of cities or foreign countries.

6. The 5-digit postal ZIP codes are needed to speed the processing of your investigation. The office that provided the form will assist you in completing the ZIP codes.

7. All telephone numbers must include area codes.

8. All dates provided on this form must be in Month/Day/Year or Month/Year format.   Use numbers (1-12) to indicate months.   For example, June 8, 1978, should be shown as 6/8/78.

9. Whenever "City (Country)" is shown in an address block, also provide in that block the name of the country when the address is outside the United States.

10. If you need additional space to list your residences or employments/self-employments/unemployments or education, you should use a continuation sheet, SF 86A. If additional space is needed to answer other items, use a blank piece of paper. Each blank piece of paper you use must contain **your name and Social Security Number at the top of the page.**

Standard Form 86 (EG)
Revised September 1995
U.S. Office of Personnel Management
5 CFR Parts 731, 732, and 736

**QUESTIONNAIRE FOR
NATIONAL SECURITY POSITIONS**

Form approved:
OMB No. 3206-0007
NSN 7540-00-634-4036
86-111

Part 1	Investigating Agency Use Only		Codes			Case Number	

Agency Use Only (Complete items A through P using instructions provided by the Investigating agency).

A Type of Investigation	**B** Extra Coverage		**C** Sensitivity Level	**D** Access	**E** Nature of Action Code	**F** Date of Action	Month	Day	Year

G Geographic Location		**H** Position Code	**I** Position Title	

J SON	**K** Location of Official Personnel Folder	None / NPRC / At SON	Other Address		ZIP Code

L SOI	**M** Location of Security Folder	None / At SOI / NPI	Other Address		ZIP Code

N OPAC-ALC Number	**O** Accounting Data and/or Agency Case Number

P Requesting Official	Name and Title	Signature	Telephone Number	Date

Persons completing this form should begin with the questions below.

1 FULL NAME
• If you have only initials in your name, use them and state (IO).
• If you have no middle name, enter "NMN".
• If you are a "Jr.," "Sr.," "II," etc., enter this in the box after your middle name.

2 DATE OF BIRTH

Last Name	First Name	Middle Name	Jr., II, etc.	Month	Day	Year

3 PLACE OF BIRTH - Use the two letter code for the State.

City	County	Country (if not in the United States)

4 SOCIAL SECURITY

5 OTHER NAMES USED
Give other names you used and the period of time you used them (for example: your maiden name, name(s) by a former marriage, former name(s), alias(es), or nickname(s)). If the other name is your **maiden name**, put "nee" in front of it.

	Name	Month/Year	Month/Year		Name	Month/Year	Month/Year
#1			To	#3			To
#2			To	#4			To

6 OTHER IDENTIFYING INFORMATION

Height (feet and inches)	Weight (pounds)	Hair Color	Eye Color	Sex (Mark one box) Female / Male

7 TELEPHONE NUMBERS

Work (Include Area Code) Day / Night ( )	Home (Include Area Code) Day / Night ( )

8 CITIZENSHIP

a Mark the box at the right that reflects your current citizenship status, and follow its instructions.

I am a citizen or national by birth in the U.S. or U.S. territory/possession. (Answer item d)

I am a U.S. citizen, but I was NOT born in the U.S. (Answer items b, c and d)

I am not a U.S. citizen. (Answer items b and e)

b Your Mother's Maiden Name

c UNITED STATES CITIZENSHIP If you are a U.S. citizen, but were not born in the U.S., provide information about one or more of the following proofs of your citizenship.

Naturalization Certificate (Where were you naturalized?)

Court	City	State	Certificate Number	Month/Day/Year Issued

Citizenship Certificate (Where was the certificate issued?)

City	State	Certificate Number	Month/Day/Year Issued

State Department Form 240 - Report of Birth Abroad of a Citizen of the United States

Give the date the form was prepared and give an explanation if needed.	Month/Day/Year	Explanation

U.S. Passport

This may be either a current or previous U.S. Passport.	Passport Number	Month/Day/Year Issued

d DUAL CITIZENSHIP If you are (or were) a dual citizen of the United States and another country, provide the name of that country in the space to the right.

Country

e ALIEN If you are an alien, provide the following information:

Place You Entered the United States:	City	State	Date You Entered U.S. Month / Day / Year	Alien Registration Number	Country(ies) of Citizenship

Exception to SF85, SF85P, SF85P-S, SF86, and SF86A approved by GSA September, 1995.
Designed using Perform Pro, WHS/DIOR, Sep 95

⑨ WHERE YOU HAVE LIVED

List the places where you have lived, beginning with the most recent (#1) and working back 7 years. All periods must be accounted for in your list. Be sure to indicate the actual physical location of your residence: do not use a post office box as an address, do not list a permanent address when you were actually living at a school address, etc. Be sure to specify your location as closely as possible: for example, do not list only your base or ship, list your barracks number or home port. You may omit temporary military duty locations under 90 days (list your permanent address instead), and you should use your APO/FPO address if you lived overseas.

For any address in the last 5 years, list a person who knew you at that address, and who preferably still lives in that area (do not list people for residences completely outside this 5-year period, and do not list your spouse, former spouses, or other relatives). Also for addresses in the last five years, if the address is "General Delivery," a Rural or Star Route, or may be difficult to locate, provide directions for locating the residence on an attached continuation sheet.

	Month/Year Month/Year	Street Address	Apt. #	City (Country)		State	ZIP Code
#1	To Present						
	Name of Person Who Knows You	Street Address	Apt. #	City (Country)	State	ZIP Code	Telephone Number ( )
#2	Month/Year Month/Year To	Street Address	Apt. #	City (Country)		State	ZIP Code
	Name of Person Who Knew You	Street Address	Apt. #	City (Country)	State	Code	Telephone Number ( )
#3	Month/Year Month/Year To	Street Address	Apt. #	City (Country)		State	ZIP Code
	Name of Person Who Knew You	Street Address	Apt. #	City (Country)	St	de	Telephone Number ( )
#4	Month/Year Month/Year To	Street Address	Apt. #	(Country)		State	ZIP Code
	Name of Person Who Knew You	Street Address	City (try)		State	ZIP Code	Telephone Number ( )
#5	Month/Year Month/Year To	Street Address	#	City (Country)		State	ZIP Code
	Name of Person Who Knew You	Street Address	Apt. #	Country)	State	ZIP Code	Telephone Number ( )

⑩ WHERE YOU WENT TO SCHOOL

List the schools you have attended, beyond Junior High, beginning with the most recent (#1) and working back 7 years. List College or University degrees and the dates they were received. If all of your education occurred more than 7 years ago, list your most recent education beyond high school, no matter when that education occurred.

● Use one of the following codes in the block:

1 - High School   College/University/Military College   **3** - Vocational/Technical/Trade School

● For schools you attended in the past 3 years, list a person who knew you at school (an instructor, student, etc.). Do not list people for education completely outside this period.

● For correspondence schools and extension classes, provide the address where the records are maintained.

	Month/Year Month/Year	Code	Name of School	Degree/Diploma/Other	Month/Year Awarded
#1	To				
	Street Address and City (Country) of School			State	ZIP Code
	Name of Person Who Knew You	Street Address	Apt. # City (Country)	State ZIP Code	Telephone Number ( )
#2	Month/Year Month/Year To	Code	Name of School	Degree/Diploma/Other	Month/Year Awarded
	Street Address and City (Country) of School			State	ZIP Code
	Name of Person Who Knew You	Street Address	Apt. # City (Country)	State ZIP Code	Telephone Number ( )
#3	Month/Year Month/Year To	Code	Name of School	Degree/Diploma/Other	Month/Year Awarded
	Street Address and City (Country) of School			State	ZIP Code
	Name of Person Who Knew You	Street Address	Apt. # City (Country)	State ZIP Code	Telephone Number ( )

Enter your Social Security Number before going to the next page ⟶

⑪   YOUR EMPLOYMENT ACTIVITIES

List your employment activities, beginning with the present (#1) and working back 7 years. You should list all full-time work, part-time work, military service, temporary military duty locations over 90 days, self-employment, other paid work, and all periods of unemployment. The entire 7-year period must be accounted for without breaks, but you need not list employments before your 16th birthday. EXCEPTION: Show all Federal civilian service, whether it occurred within the last 7 years or not.

● **Code.** Use one of the codes listed below to identify the type of employment:

1 - Active military duty stations	5 - State Government (Non-Federal	7 - Unemployment (Include name of 9 - Other
2 - National Guard/Reserve	employment)	person who can verify)
3 - U.S.P.H.S. Commissioned Corps	6 - Self-employment (Include business name	8 - Federal Contractor (List Contractor,
4 - Other Federal employment	and/or name of person who can verify)	not Federal agency)

● **Employer/Verifier Name.** List the business name of your employer or the name of the person who can verify your self-employment or unemployment in this block. If military service is being listed, include your duty location or home port here as well as your branch of service. You should provide separate listings to reflect changes in your military duty locations or home ports.

● **Previous Periods of Activity.** Complete these lines if you worked for an employer on more than one occasion at the same location. After entering the most recent period of employment in the initial numbered block, provide previous periods of employment at the same location on the additional lines provided. For example, if you worked at XY Plumbing in Denver, CO, during 3 separate periods of time, you would enter dates and information concerning the most recent period of employment first, and provide dates, position titles, and supervisors for the two previous periods of employment on the lines below this information.

#1 Month/Year To Present | Code | Employer/Verifier Name/Military Duty Location | Your Position Title/Military Rank

Employer's/Verifier's Street Address | City (Country) | | ZIP Code | Telephone Number ( )

Street Address of Job Location (if different than Employer's Address) | City (Country) | State | Code | Telephone Number ( )

Supervisor's Name & Street Address (if different than Job Location) | City (Country) | | ZIP Code | Telephone Number ( )

PREVIOUS PERIODS OF ACTIVITY (Block #1)
Month/Year To Month/Year | Position Title | Supervisor
Month/Year To Month/Year | Position Title | Supervisor
Month/Year To Month/Year | Position Title | Supervisor

#2 Month/Year To | Code | Employer/Verifier Name/Military Duty Location | Your Position Title/Military Rank

Employer's/Verifier's Street Address | City (Country) | State | ZIP Code | Telephone Number ( )

Street Address of Job Location (if different than Employer's Address) | City (Country) | State | ZIP Code | Telephone Number ( )

Supervisor's Name & Street Address (if different than Job Location) | City (Country) | State | ZIP Code | Telephone Number ( )

PREVIOUS PERIODS OF ACTIVITY (Block #2)
Month/Year To Month/Year | Position Title | Supervisor
Month/Year To Month/Year | Position Title | Supervisor
Month/Year To Month/Year | Position Title | Supervisor

#3 Month/Year To | Code | Employer/Verifier Name/Military Duty Location | Your Position Title/Military Rank

Employer's/Verifier's Street Address | City (Country) | State | ZIP Code | Telephone Number ( )

Street Address of Job Location (if different than Employer's Address) | City (Country) | State | ZIP Code | Telephone Number ( )

Supervisor's Name & Street Address (if different than Job Location) | City (Country) | State | ZIP Code | Telephone Number ( )

PREVIOUS PERIODS OF ACTIVITY (Block #3)
Month/Year To Month/Year | Position Title | Supervisor
Month/Year To Month/Year | Position Title | Supervisor
Month/Year To Month/Year | Position Title | Supervisor

Enter your Social Security Number before going to the next page ──────────►

YOUR EMPLOYMENT ACTIVITIES *(CONTINUED)*

Month/Year — Month/Year To	Code	Employer/Verifier Name/Military Duty Location		Your Position Title/Military Rank		
#4						
Employer's/Verifier's Street Address			City (Country)	State	ZIP Code	Telephone Number ( )
Street Address of Job Location (if different than Employer's Address)			City (Country)	State	ZIP Code	Telephone Number ( )
Supervisor's Name & Street Address (if different than Job Location)			City (Country)	State	ZIP Code	Telephone Number ( )

	Month/Year — Month/Year To	Position Title	Supervisor
PREVIOUS PERIODS OF ACTIVITY *(Block #4)*	Month/Year — Month/Year To	Position Title	Supervisor
	Month/Year — Month/Year To	Position Title	Supervisor
	Month/Year — Month/Year To	Position Title	Supervisor

Month/Year — Month/Year To	Code	Employer/Verifier Name/Military Duty Location		Your Position Title/Military Rank		
#5						
Employer's/Verifier's Street Address			City (Country)	State	ZIP Code	Telephone Number ( )
Street Address of Job Location (if different than Employer's Address)			City (Country)	State	ZIP Code	Telephone Number ( )
Supervisor's Name & Street Address (if different than Job Location)			City (Country)	State	ZIP Code	Telephone Number ( )

	Month/Year — Month/Year To	Position Title	Supervisor
PREVIOUS PERIODS OF ACTIVITY *(Block #5)*	Month/Year — Month/Year To	Position Title	Supervisor
	Month/Year — Month/Year To	Position Title	Supervisor
	Month/Year — Month/Year To	Position Title	Supervisor

Month/Year — Month/Year To	Code	Employer/Verifier Name/Military Duty Location		Your Position Title/Military Rank		
#6						
Employer's/Verifier's Street Address			City (Country)	State	ZIP Code	Telephone Number ( )
Street Address of Job Location (if different than Employer's Address)			City (Country)	State	ZIP Code	Telephone Number ( )
Supervisor's Name & Street Address (if different than Job Location)			City (Country)	State	ZIP Code	Telephone Number ( )

	Month/Year — Month/Year To	Position Title	Supervisor
PREVIOUS PERIODS OF ACTIVITY *(Block #6)*	Month/Year — Month/Year To	Position Title	Supervisor
	Month/Year — Month/Year To	Position Title	Supervisor
	Month/Year — Month/Year To	Position Title	Supervisor

12 PEOPLE WHO KNOW YOU

List three people who know you well and live in the United States. They should be good friends, peers, colleagues, college roommates, etc., whose combined association with you covers as well as possible the last 7 years. Do not list your spouse, former spouses, or other relatives, and try not to list anyone who is listed elsewhere on this form.

Name **#1**	Dates Known Month/Year — Month/Year To	Telephone Number Day ( ) Night		
Home or Work Address		City (Country)	State	ZIP Code

Name **#2**	Dates Known Month/Year — Month/Year To	Telephone Number Day ( ) Night		
Home or Work Address		City (Country)	State	ZIP Code

Name **#3**	Dates Known Month/Year — Month/Year To	Telephone Number Day ( ) Night		
Home or Work Address		City (Country)	State	ZIP Code

Enter your Social Security Number before going to the next page ——————————→

13 YOUR SPOUSE

Mark one box to show your current marital status and provide information about your spouse(s) in items a. and/or b.

☐ 1 - Never married	☐ 3 - Separated	☐ 5 - Divorced
☐ 2 - Married	☐ 4 - Legally Separated	☐ 6 - Widowed

a Current Spouse Complete the following about your current spouse only.

Full Name	Date of Birth	Place of Birth (Include country if outside the U.S.)	Social Security Number
Other Names Used (Specify maiden name, names by other marriages, etc., and show dates used for each name)			Country(ies) of Citizenship
Date Married	Place Married (Include country if outside the U.S.)		State
If Separated, Date of Separation	If Legally Separated, Where is the Record Located? City (Country)		State
Address of Current Spouse, if different than your current address (Street, city, and country if outside the U.S.)		State ZIP Code	

b Former Spouse(s). Complete the following about your former spouse(s), use blank sheets if needed.

Full Name	Date of Birth	Place of Birth (Include co... ...the U.S.)	State
Country(ies) of Citizenship	Date Married	Place Married (Include country if ... the ...)	State
Check one, Then Give Date ☐ Divorced ☐ Widowed	Month/Day/Year	If Divorced, Where is the Record Locate... (Country)	State
Address of Former Spouse (Street, city, and country if outside the U.S.)		ZIP Code	Telephone Number ( )

14 YOUR RELATIVES AND ASSOCIATES

Give the full name, correct code, and other requested information for each of you... ...d associates, living or dead, specified below.

1 - Mother (first)	5 - Foster parent	9 - Sist...	13 - Half-sister	17 - Other Relative*
2 - Father (second)	6 - Child (adopted also)	10 - St...	... - Father-in-law	18 - Associate*
3 - Stepmother	7 - Stepchild	11 - Step...	...other-in-law	19 - Adult Currently Living With You
4 - Stepfather	8 - Brother	12 - Half-br...	1... Guardian	

*Code 17 (Other Relative) - include only foreign natio... ...ot liste... 1 - ... whom you or your spouse are bound by affection, obligation, or close and continuing contact. Code 18 (Associates) - include on... ...n ...l as...iates ... whom you or your spouse are bound by affection, obligation, or close and continuing contact.

Full Name (If deceased, check box on the left before entering name)	C...	Date of Birth ...th/Day/Year	...ountry of Birth	Country(ies) of Citizenship	Current Street Address and City (country) of Living Relatives	State
	1					
	2					

Enter your Social Security Number before going to the next page ⟶ |

15 CITIZENSHIP OF YOUR RELATIVES AND ASSOCIATES

If your mother, father, sister, brother, child, or current spouse or person with whom you have a spouse-like relationship is a U.S. citizen by other than birth, or an alien residing in the U.S., provide the nature of the individual's relationship to you (Spouse, Spouse-like, Mother, etc.), and the individual's name and date of birth on the first line *(this information is needed to pair it accurately with information in items 13 and 14)*.

On the second line, provide the individual's naturalization certificate or alien registration number and use one of the document codes below to identify proof of citizenship status. Provide additional information on that line as requested.

   1 - Naturalization Certificate: Provide the date issued and the location where the person was naturalized (Court, City and State).
   2 - Citizenship Certificate: Provide the date and location issued (City and State).
   3 - Alien Registration: Provide the date and place where the person entered the U.S. (City and State).
   4 - Other: Provide an explanation in the "Additional Information" block.

#1 Association	Name		Date of Birth *(Month/Day/Year)*
Certificate/Registration #	Document Code	Additional Information	

#2 Association	Name		Date of Birth *(Month/Day/Year)*
Certificate/Registration #	Document Code	Additional Information	

16 YOUR MILITARY HISTORY

	Yes	No
a Have you served in the United States military?		
b Have you served in the United States Merchant Marine?		

List all of your military service below, including service in Reserve, National Guard, and U.S. Merchant Marine. Start with the most recent period of service (#1) and work backward. If you had a break in service, each separate period should be listed.

●**Code.** Use one of the codes listed below to identify your branch of service:
1 - Air Force   2 - Army   3 - Navy   4 - Marine Corps   5 - Coast Guard   6 - Merchant Marine   National Guard

●**O/E.** Mark "O" block for Officer or "E" block for Enlisted.
●**Status.** "X" the appropriate block for the status of your service during the time you served. If your service was in the National Guard, do not use an "X": use the two-letter code for the state to mark the block.
●**Country.** If your service was with other than the U.S. Armed Forces, identify the country for which you served.

Month/Year	Month/Year	Code	Service/Certificate #	O	E	Active Reserve	Inactive Reserve	National Guard (State)	Country
	To								
	To								

17 YOUR FOREIGN ACTIVITIES

	Yes	No
a Do you have any foreign property, business connections, or financial interests?		
b Are you now or have you ever been employed by or acted as a consultant for a foreign government, firm, or agency?		
c Have you ever had any contact with a foreign government, its establishments (embassies or consulates), or its representatives, whether inside or outside the U.S., other than on official U.S. Government business? *(Does not include routine visa applications and border crossing contacts.)*		
d In the last 7 years, have you had an active passport that was issued by a foreign government?		

If you answered "Yes" to a, b, c, or d above, explain in the space below: provide inclusive dates, names of firms and/or governments involved, and an explanation of your involvement.

Month/Year	Month/Year	Firm and/or Government	Explanation
	To		
	To		

18 FOREIGN COUNTRIES YOU HAVE VISITED

List foreign countries you have visited, except on travel under official Government orders, beginning with the most current (#1) and working back 7 years. (Travel as a dependent or contractor must be listed.)
●Use one of these codes to indicate the purpose of your visit: **1** - Business   **2** - Pleasure   **3** - Education   **4** - Other
●Include short trips to Canada or Mexico. If you have lived near a border and have made short (one day or less) trips to the neighboring country, you do not need to list each trip. Instead, provide the time period, the code, the country, and a note ("Many Short Trips").
●Do not repeat travel covered in Items 9, 10, or 11.

	Month/Year	Month/Year	Code	Country		Month/Year	Month/Year	Code	Country
#1		To			#3		To		
#2		To			#4		To		

This concludes Part 1 of this form. If you have used Page 9, continuation sheets, or blank sheets to complete any of the questions in Part 1, give the number for those questions in the space to the right:

Enter your Social Security Number before going to the next page ⟶

Page 6

Standard Form 86
Revised September 1995
U.S. Office of Personnel Management
5 CFR Parts 731, 732, and 736

QUESTIONNAIRE FOR
NATIONAL SECURITY POSITIONS

Form approved:
OMB No. 3206-0007
NSN 7540-00-634-4036
86-111

Part 2	OFFICIAL USE ONLY		

		Yes	No
19 YOUR MILITARY RECORD			
Have you ever received other than an honorable discharge from the military? If "Yes," provide the date of discharge and type of discharge below.			

Month/Year	Type of Discharge

20 YOUR SELECTIVE SERVICE RECORD

		Yes	No
a Are you a male born after December 31, 1959? If "No," go to 21. If "Yes," go to b.			
b Have you registered with the Selective Service System? If "Yes," provide your registration number. If "No," show the reason for your legal exemption below.			

Registration Number	Legal Exemption Explanation

21 YOUR MEDICAL RECORD

		Yes	No
In the last 7 years, have you consulted with a mental health professional (psychiatrist, psychologist, counselor, etc.) or have you consulted with another health care provider about a mental health related condition?			

If you answered "Yes," provide the dates of treatment and the name and address of the therapist/doctor below, unless the consultation(s) involved only marital, family, or grief counseling, not related to violence by you.

Month/Year	Month/Year	Name/Address of Therapist/Doctor	State	ZIP Code
	To			
	To			

22 YOUR EMPLOYMENT RECORD

		Yes	No
Has any of the following happened to you **in the last 7 years**? If "Yes," begin with the most recent occurrence and go backward, providing date fired, quit, or left, and other information requested.			

Use the following codes and explain the reason your employment was ended.

1 - Fired from a job
2 - Quit a job after being told you'd be fired

3 - Left a job by mutual agreement following allegations of misconduct
4 - Left a job by mutual agreement following allegations of unsatisfactory performance

5 - Left a job for other reasons under unfavorable circumstances

Month/Year	Code	Specify Reason	Employer's Name and Address (Include city/Country if outside U.S.)	State	ZIP Code

23 YOUR POLICE RECORD

		Yes	No
For this item, report information regardless of whether the record in your case has been "sealed" or otherwise stricken from the court record. The single exception to this requirement is for certain convictions under the Federal Controlled Substances Act for which the court issued an expungement order under the authority of 21 U.S.C. 844 or 18 U.S.C. 3607.			
a Have you ever been charged with or convicted of any felony offense? (Include those under Uniform Code of Military Justice)			
b Have you ever been charged with or convicted of a firearms or explosives offense?			
c Are there currently any charges pending against you for any criminal offense?			
d Have you ever been charged with or convicted of any offense(s) related to alcohol or drugs?			
e In the last 7 years, have you been subject to court martial or other disciplinary proceedings under the Uniform Code of Military Justice? (Include non-judicial, Captain's mast, etc.)			
f In the last 7 years, have you been arrested for, charged with, or convicted of any offense(s) not listed in response to a, b, c, d, or e above? (Leave out traffic fines of less than $150 unless the violation was alcohol or drug related.)			

If you answered "Yes" to a, b, c, d, e, or f above, explain below. Under "Offense," do not list specific penalty codes, list the actual offense or violation (for example, arson, theft, etc.).

Month/Year	Offense	Action Taken	Law Enforcement Authority/Court (Include City and county/country if outside U.S.)	State	ZIP Code

Enter your Social Security Number before going to the next page ⟶

24 **YOUR USE OF ILLEGAL DRUGS AND DRUG ACTIVITY**

	Yes	No

The following questions pertain to the illegal use of drugs or drug activity. You are required to answer the questions fully and truthfully, and your failure to do so could be grounds for an adverse employment decision or action against you, but neither your truthful responses nor information derived from your responses will be used as evidence against you in any subsequent criminal proceeding.

a Since the age of 16 or in the last 7 years, whichever is shorter, have you illegally used any controlled substance, for example, marijuana, cocaine, crack cocaine, hashish, narcotics (opium, morphine, codeine, heroin, etc.), amphetamines, depressants (barbiturates, methaqualone, tranquilizers, etc.), hallucinogenics (LSD, PCP, etc.), or prescription drugs?

b Have you ever illegally used a controlled substance while employed as a law enforcement officer, prosecutor, or courtroom official; while possessing a security clearance; or while in a position directly and immediately affecting the public safety?

c In the last 7 years, have you been involved in the illegal purchase, manufacture, trafficking, production, transfer, shipping, receiving, or sale of any narcotic, depressant, stimulant, hallucinogen, or cannabis for your own intended profit or that of another?

If you answered "Yes" to a or b above, provide the date(s), identify the controlled substance(s) and/or prescription drugs used, and the number of times each was used.

Month/Year	Month/Year	Controlled Substance/Prescription Drug Used	Number of Times Used
	To		
	To		

25 **YOUR USE OF ALCOHOL**

	Yes	No

In the last 7 years, has your use of alcoholic beverages (such as liquor, beer, wine) resulted in any alcohol-related treatment or counseling (such as for alcohol abuse or alcoholism)?

If you answered "Yes," provide the dates of treatment and the name and address of the counselor or doctor below. Do not repeat information reported in response to item 21 above.

Month/Year	Month/Year	Name/Address of Counselor or Doctor	State	ZIP Code
	To			
	To			

26 **YOUR INVESTIGATIONS RECORD**

	Yes	No

a Has the United States Government ever investigated your background and/or granted you a security clearance? If "Yes," use the codes that follow to provide the requested information below. If you cannot recall the investigating agency and/or the security clearance received, enter "Other" agency code or clearance code, as appropriate, and "Don't know" or "Don't recall" under the "Other Agency" heading, below. If your response is "No," or you don't know or can't recall if you were investigated and cleared, check the "No" box.

Codes for Investigating Agency	Codes for Security Clearance Received		
1 - Defense Department	0 - Not Required	3 - Top Secret	6 - L
2 - State Department	1 - Confidential	4 - Sensitive Compartmented Information	7 - Other
3 - Office of Personnel Management	2 - Secret	5 - Q	

Month/Year	Agency Code	Other Agency	Clearance Code	Month/Year	Agency Code	Other Agency	Clearance Code

b To your knowledge, have you ever had a clearance or access authorization denied, suspended, or revoked, or have you ever been debarred from government employment? If "Yes," give date of action and agency. Note: An administrative downgrade or termination of a security clearance is not a revocation.

	Yes	No

Month/Year	Department or Agency Taking Action	Month/Year	Department or Agency Taking Action

27 **YOUR FINANCIAL RECORD**

	Yes	No

a In the last 7 years, have you filed a petition under any chapter of the bankruptcy code (to include Chapter 13)?

b In the last 7 years, have you had your wages garnished or had any property repossessed for any reason?

c In the last 7 years, have you had a lien placed against your property for failing to pay taxes or other debts?

d In the last 7 years, have you had any judgments against you that have not been paid?

If you answered "Yes" to a, b, c, or d, provide the information requested below:

Month/Year	Type of Action	Amount	Name Action Occurred Under	Name/Address of Court or Agency Handling Case	State	ZIP Code

Enter your Social Security Number before going to the next page ————————➤

28	**YOUR FINANCIAL DELINQUENCIES**						**Yes**	**No**
a	In the last 7 years, have you been over 180 days delinquent on any debt(s)?							
b	Are you currently over 90 days delinquent on any debt(s)?							

If you answered "**Yes**" to a or b, provide the information requested below:

Incurred Month/Year	Satisfied Month/Year	Amount	Type of Loan or Obligation and Account Number	Name/Address of Creditor or Obligee	State	ZIP Code

29	**PUBLIC RECORD CIVIL COURT ACTIONS**						**Yes**	**No**
	In the last 7 years, have you been a party to any public record civil court actions not listed elsewhere on this form?							

If you answered "Yes," provide the information about the public record civil court action requested below.

Month/Year	Nature of Action	Result of Action	Name of Parties Involved	Court (Include City and ...y/country ...ide U.S.)	State	ZIP Code

30	**YOUR ASSOCIATION RECORD**						**Yes**	**No**
a	Have you ever been an officer or a member or made a contribution to an organization dedicated to ... nt overthr... he United States Government and which engages in illegal activities to that end, knowing that the or... ...gages ... acti... ...with the specific intent to further such activities?							
b	Have you ever knowingly engaged in any acts or activities designed to overt... ...Unite... ...es Government by force?							

If you answered "Yes" to a or b, explain in the space below.

Use the continuation sheet(s) (SF86A) for additional answers to items 9, 10, ... 1... ...the space below to continue answers to all other items and any information you would like to add. If more space is needed than is provided ... ...a blan... ...eet(... ...per. Start each sheet with your name and Social Security Number. Before each answer, identify the number of the item.

After completing Parts 1 and 2 of this form and any attachments, you should review your answers to all questions to make sure the form is complete and accurate, and then sign and date the following certification and sign and date the release on Page 10.

Certification That My Answers Are True

My statements on this form, and any attachments to it, are true, complete, and correct to the best of my knowledge and belief and are made in good faith. I understand that a knowing and willful false statement on this form can be punished by fine or imprisonment or both. (See section 1001 of title 18, United States Code).

Signature *(Sign in ink)*   Date

Enter your Social Security Number before going to the next page ————————→

Standard Form 86
Revised September 1995
U.S. Office of Personnel Management
5 CFR Parts 731, 732, and 736

Form approved:
OMB No. 3206-0007
NSN 7540-00-634-4036
86-111

UNITED STATES OF AMERICA

AUTHORIZATION FOR RELEASE OF INFORMATION

Carefully read this authorization to release information about you, then sign and date it in ink.

I Authorize any investigator, special agent, or other duly accredited representative of the authorized Federal agency conducting my background investigation, to obtain any information relating to my activities from individuals schools, residential management agents, employers, criminal justice agencies, credit bureaus, consumer reporting agencies ...ection agencies, retail business establishments, or other sources of information. This information may include, but is r ...mited my academic, residential, achievement, performance, attendance, disciplinary, employment history, criminal hist ...ecor ...ormation, and financial and credit information. I authorize the Federal agency conducting my investigation to a... the re... of my background investigation to the requesting agency for the purpose of making a determination of suitability or ...ili... r a security clearance.

I Understand that, for financial or lending institutions, medical institutions, ho ...s, health care rofessionals, and other sources of information, a separate specific release will be needed, and I may be ...ted t... h a re... at a later date. Where a separate release is requested for information relating to mental health trea... ..or ...seling... ...ase will contain a list of the specific questions, relevant to the job description, which the doctor or th... ...st will b ...ked.

I Further Authorize any investigator, special agent ...her du... ...redited representative of the U.S. Office of Personnel Management, the Federal Bureau of Investigation, the ...o...nt of ...se, the Defense Investigative Service, and any other authorized Federal agency, to request criminal ...cord in... ...a... about ...e from criminal justice agencies for the purpose of determining my eligibility for access to classi... ...ation nd/o... ...assignment to, or retention in a sensitive National Security position, in accordance with 5 U.S.C. 9101. I un... ...na... ...y request a copy of such records as may be available to me under the law.

I Authorize custodians of records a... sou... ...formation pertaining to me to release such information upon request of the investigator, special agent, or other dul... ...cre... ...sentative of any Federal agency authorized above regardless of any previous agreement to the contra...

I Understand that info... ...ase by records custodians and sources of information is for official use by the Federal Government only fo... ...poses p... ...ided in this Standard Form 86, and that it may be redisclosed by the Government only as authorized by law.

Copies of this authorization that show my signature are as valid as the original release signed by me. This authorization is valid for five (5) years from the date signed or upon the termination of my affiliation with the Federal Government, whichever is sooner. Read, sign and date the release on the next page if you answered "Yes" to question 21.

Signature *(Sign in ink)*	Full Name *(Type or Print Legibly)*		Date Signed
Other Names Used			Social Security Number
Current Address *(Street, City)*	State	ZIP Code	Home Telephone Number *(Include Area Code)* ( )

FOR OFFICIAL USE ONLY *(When filled in)*

DOD REQUEST FOR PERSONNEL SECURITY INVESTIGATION	*Form Approved* OMB No. 0704-0384 *Expires Aug 31, 2002*

Public reporting burden for this collection of information is estimated to average 15 minutes per response, including the time for reviewing instructions, searching existing data sources, gathering and maintaining the data needed, and completing and reviewing the collection of information. Send comments regarding this burden estimate or any other aspect of this collection of information, including suggestions for reducing this burden, to Department of Defense, Washington Headquarters Services, Directorate for Information Operations and Reports (0704-0384), 1215 Jefferson Davis Highway, Suite 1204, Arlington, VA 22202-4302.
PLEASE DO NOT RETURN YOUR COMPLETED FORM TO THIS ADDRESS. RETURN COMPLETED FORM TO ADDRESS IN ITEM 15.

1. CODE	2. REQUESTER FILE NUMBER *(Optional)*	3. DATE OF REQUEST *(MM/DD/YYYY)*	4. THIS REQUEST IS FOR *(X one)*
			a. SINGLE SCOPE BACKGROUND INVESTIGATION (SSBI)
5a. FROM		5b. TO	b. PERIODIC REINVESTIGATION (PR)
			c. SPECIAL INVESTIGATIVE INQUIRY (SII)
			d. EXPANDED NATIONAL AGENCY CHECK (ENAC)
			e. OTHER *(Specify in Remarks)*

6. DO YOU DESIRE ADVANCE NOTICE OF NAC RESULTS *(X one)*	YES	NO	7. ST___ *(X as applicable)*

8. SUBJECT OF INVESTIGATION / ___ ACCESS TO CLASSIFIED MATERIAL *(X one)*

a. NAME *(LAST, First, Middle Name) (Last name in ALL CAPITALS)*	b. SOCIAL SECURITY NUMBER	CONFIDENTIAL	SECRET
		SECRET	
c. MAIDEN NAME		___ICAL NU___R WEAPON POSITION	
		c. L___ ___SS AUTHORIZATION (LAA)	
d. OTHER NAMES USED OR KNOWN BY		d. SEN___ COMPARTMENTED INFOR___ION (SCI)	
		e. ___-ESI	
		f. PRESIDENTIAL SUPPORT	
		g. CRITICAL SENSITIVE POSITION/DUTIES	
e. DATE OF BIRTH *(MM/DD/YYYY)*	f. PLACE OF BIRTH *(City, County, State and Count___)*	g. SEX	h. ADP-1
			i. NATO ASSIGNMENT
			j. CRYPTO/COMSEC
			k. SPECIAL ACCESS PROGRAM (SAP)
9. U.S. CITIZENSHIP VERIFIED *(X one)*	a. YES	c. VERIFICATION DOCUME___ RE___D	l. OODEP
	b. NO		m. OTHER *(Explain in Remarks)*

10. LOCAL FILES VERIFICATION/PRE-SCREENING ___			11. PRIOR INVESTIGATION *(X a, b, or c)*

TYPE *(X as applicable)* a.	DATE REVIEWED CONDUCTED *(__/MM/DD/YYYY)*	___FILE ___ INFORMATION - UNFAVORABLE ___ REVEALED *(X one)* c.	a. YES *(Type, Date, By Whom, and File Number)*
		YES	NO	
(1) PERSONNEL			
(2) SECURITY			
(3) MEDICAL			
(4) BASE/MILITARY PO___			
(5) AUTHORIZED P___ ___REENING INTERVIEW			
(6) OTHER			b. NO	c. UNKNOWN

12. TITLE OR POSITION ___ ___UBJECT *(I___tary, list rank and service; if U.S. Government employee, list grade; and if contractor employee, list job titl___.)*	13. TS BILLET NUMBER

14. ENCLOSURES *(Please list. Use continuation sheets, if necessary.)*

15. RETURN RESULTS TO: *(Read instructions before completing this item.)*

	FOR DSS USE ONLY	
	CCN (Case Control Number) (1 - 15)	DSS CLOSING STAMP
	(16 - 22)	
	PB (72 - 73)	PC (74 - 75)	
Investigations conducted on Army, Navy, and Air Force military personnel will be returned only to the parent service for adjudication regardless of the source of the original request.	SV (76)	CR (77 - 78)	
	R	A	I	N	COMPLETED
					DATE COMPLETED

DD FORM 1879, AUG 1999 PREVIOUS EDITION MAY BE USED. **FOR OFFICIAL USE ONLY** *(When filled in)* Page 1 of 4 Pages

FOR OFFICIAL USE ONLY *(When filled in)*

16. REASON ACCESS TO CLASSIFIED INFORMATION OR INVESTIGATION IS REQUIRED *(Provide description of duties warranting access/ investigation. Contractors must list contract number.)*

17. HISTORY OF GOVERNMENT EMPLOYMENT AND/OR CURRENT MILITARY SERVICE INDICATED ON ATTACHED SF 85P/SF86 IS *(X one)*

	a. CORRECT		b. PARTIALLY CORRECT *(Explain in Remarks)*		c. COULD NOT BE VERIFIED *(Explain in Remarks)*

18. REMARKS *(Use continuation sheet(s), if necessary.)*

19. INVESTIGATION VALIDITY CERTIFICATION
   I certify that the information provided on this form ... ... of my knowledge and that the above named individual has the need for the indicated clearance to perform assigned duties.

a. TYPED NAME OF CERTIFIER *(Last, Firs... ...ame)*	b. TITLE OF CERTIFIER	
c. SIGNATURE OF CERTIFIER	d. DATE SIGNED BY CERTIFIER *(MM/DD/YYYY)*	e. TELEPHONE NUMBER *(Include Area Code)*

20. EMPLOYEE'S IMM...IATE S... ...R'S ...RTIFICATION

	I am aware of a... ...matio... ...ncerning the individual named on the front of this form.
	I am not aware of ... adverse in ...ation concerning the individual named on the front of this form.

   If you are aware of adverse ... ...on, you must reflect that information in the space below. Use continuation sheets, if necessary. Complete items 20.a. through ...

a. ADVERSE INFORMATION *(If none, indicate "None.")*

b. IMMEDIATE SUPERVISOR *(Last, First, Middle Name)*	c. TITLE	
d. SIGNATURE	e. DATE SIGNED *(MM/DD/YYYY)*	f. TELEPHONE NUMBER *(Include Area Code)*

DD FORM 1879, AUG 1999   FOR OFFICIAL USE ONLY *(When filled in)*   Page 2 of 4 Pages

FOR OFFICIAL USE ONLY *(When filled in)*

GENERAL INSTRUCTIONS

1. DD Form 1879 is used to request a Single Scope Background Investigation (SSBI), Expanded NAC (ENAC) and Additional Investigation, Periodic Reinvestigation (PR), Special Investigative Inquiry (SII). Its use is restricted to actions involving individuals and it will not be used to request investigations of incidents, events or organizations.

2. The following documents must accompany each request for investigation on military, civilian, and contractor personnel.

- Standard Form 85P, "Questionnaire for Public Trust Positions," is to be used by all Federal agencies as the basis for investigations concerning suitability for positions requiring special public trust where such positions do not involve access to national security information.

- Standard Form 86, "Questionnaire for National Security Positions," is to be used by all Federal agencies as the basis for investigations preliminary to granting an individual access to classified national security information or access to sensitive nuclear information or materials.

- FD Form 258, "Fingerprint Card." Submit one signed copy.

3. The original and two copies of DD Form 1879 will be forwarded to the Defense Security Service (DSS) or the Defense Industrial Security Clearance Office (DISCO). See Detailed Instructions below.

4. The Detailed Instructions for completing Items 1, 4 through 6, 10 through 17, and 19 are different depending on whether the subject is military personnel, U.S. Government employee, or contractor personnel.

5. If the Electronic DD Form 1879 is utilized, the requester must sign the electronically generated DD Form 1879 and retain until the clearance processing is complete. The signed DD Form 1879 shall be released to DSS upon request.

DETAILED INSTRUCTIONS

1. CODE.
   MILITARY/U.S. GOVERNMENT EMPLOYEES. Enter the Unit Identification Code (UIC) or Personnel Accounting System (PAS) code.
   CONTRACTOR EMPLOYEES. Enter the Commercial and Government Entity (CAGE) code for current employment.

2. **REQUESTER FILE NUMBER.** To be used by the requester for internal filing system. This item is optional.

3. **DATE OF REQUEST.** Date you dispatched the request to DSS. Enter date in MM/DD/YYYY format. October 30, 2000 would be 10/30/2000.

4. THIS REQUEST IS FOR.
   MILITARY/U.S. GOVERNMENT EMPLOYEES. Mark only one block. Requesters requiring additional investigation will mark block 4.e. and indicate "Added Coverage" in remarks.
   CONTRACTOR EMPLOYEES. Mark only one block (a., b., c. or d.). Do NOT mark block e.

5. ADDRESSES.
   a. FROM.
   MILITARY/U.S. GOVERNMENT EMPLOYEES. Enter name and address (including ZIP Code) of the headquarters, unit, or activity submitting the request for investigation.
   CONTRACTOR EMPLOYEES. Enter your facility's name and address (including ZIP Code).
   b. TO.
   MILITARY/U.S. GOVERNMENT EMPLOYEES. Send DD Form 1879 and enclosures to:

   Defense Security Service
   P.O. Box 18585
   Baltimore, Maryland 21240-8585

   CONTRACTOR EMPLOYEES. This block MUST be left blank. The DD Form 1879 and enclosures must be sent to:

   Defense Security Service
   Defense Industrial Security Clearance Office
   P.O. Box 2499
   Columbus, Ohio 43216-5006

   NOTE: This address must not be entered into block 5.b.

6. DO YOU DESIRE ADVANCE NOTICE OF NAC RESULTS?
   MILITARY/U.S. GOVERNMENT EMPLOYEES. If advance notice of the NAC results is desired prior to the completion of the investigation, mark "Yes."
   CONTRACTOR EMPLOYEES. This item MUST be left blank.

7. STATUS.
   a. **ACCESS TO CLASSIFIED MATERIAL.** Place an "X" beside the highest level of classified material to which the subject of the investigation will have access.
   b. through m.
   MILITARY/U.S. GOVERNMENT EMPLOYEES. Mark the appropriate block indicating the reason for investigation. If there are unusual circumstances involving the request, indicate this information in Item 18. If block 7.m. is marked, outline in Item 18 the exact reason for the investigation.
   Do not use the same DD Form 1879 to request additional investigation on a subject after DSS has completed his/her case. If investigative results are inadequate, provide a new DD Form 1879 specifically state in Item 18 what investigation you want and substantiate the need for it. Information on the new DD Form 1879 must be accurately transferred from the old DD Form 1879.
   CONTRACTOR EMPLOYEES. If request is for an OODEP, mark block 7.l. and indicate "OODEP" in Item 18. If request is for Special Access, mark block 7.k. and indicate "Special Access" and the program name (if unclassified) in Item 18.

8. SUBJECT OF INVESTIGATION.
   a. **NAME.** Enter the subject's name in the following order: LAST name, first name, middle name. The LAST name will appear in all CAPITAL letters.
   b. **SOCIAL SECURITY NUMBER.** Enter subject's Social Security Number.
   c. **MAIDEN NAME.** List maiden name, if applicable. Enter name as shown below:
      Nee - GUNTER, Amy Elizabeth
   d. **OTHER NAMES USED OR KNOWN BY.** List all other names used or known by. Each name entered will be identified as to type, e.g.:
      Also Known As (AKA) - HAHN, Joseph A., Mrs.
      Alias - GLADHILL, Christine
   e. **DATE OF BIRTH.** Enter subject's birth date in MM/DD/YYYY format, e.g., March 13, 1948 would be 03/13/1948.
   f. **PLACE OF BIRTH.** Enter city, county, and state (or country if not U.S.). Do not abbreviate City or Country.

9. **U.S. CITIZENSHIP VERIFIED.** If "Yes" is marked, indicate in block 9.c. which document from the below list was reviewed for verification. If U.S. Citizenship was verified in a previous investigation, mark "Yes" and explain in 9.c. that citizenship has been previously verified. If Naturalizaton Certificate was reviewed, list, in block 9.c., the certificate number. If "No" is marked, explain in Item 18 why citizenship was not verified.
   - Birth Certificate
   - Naturalization Certificate
   - Citizenship Certificate
   - Passport
   - Report of Birth Abroad of a U.S. Citizen

FOR OFFICIAL USE ONLY *(When filled in)*

DETAILED INSTRUCTIONS *(Continued)*

10. LOCAL FILES VERIFICATION/PRE-SCREENING INTERVIEW.
Include a review of appropriate indices and files maintained by or for the military or employing agency/activity concerning its person- nel. Examples are organization, management, and supervisor files; personnel, disciplinary, performance and counseling files; medical files; special security and special program files; security, law en- forcement and intelligence indices or files (excluding state and local civilian law enforcement agencies); and legal and legal assistance files (excluding statutorily restricted information). Included are files, forms or records executed by persons having knowledge of the individual being considered for a personnel security investigation. Local files include files maintained by other elements of a corpora- tion or its parent company in support of the employing entity.

a. TYPE.
MILITARY/U.S. GOVERNMENT EMPLOYEES. The review of local files will be indicated by marks in the appropriate blocks. If a particular record was not reviewed, indicate, in Item 18, the reason why and state where the record is located. Complete block (5) if an Authorized Pre-Screening Interview was conducted; if not conducted when appropriate, indicate the reason in Item 18. Complete block (6) if other records are reviewed that do not fall into categories (1) through (5).
CONTRACTOR EMPLOYEES. Mark blocks (1), (2), and (6), if appropriate. Also, mark block (3) if the information is available to you; if not, so indicate. Do not mark blocks (4) or (5).
b. DATE REVIEWED/CONDUCTED. Enter date review was completed for each record and, if applicable, date Pre-Screening Interview was conducted.
c. FILES VERIFICATION - UNFAVORABLE INFORMATION REVEALED.
MILITARY/U.S. GOVERNMENT EMPLOYEES. Mark as [applicable] for each type of record and/or Pre-Screening Interview. If unfavorable information is developed, provide pertinent deta[ils in] Item 18.
CONTRACTOR EMPLOYEES. Mark as applic[able for] each ty[pe] of record. If unfavorable information is develop[ed, provide] [pert]in[ent] details in Item 18.

11. PRIOR INVESTIGATION.
MILITARY/U.S. GOVERNMENT E[MPLOYE]ES, AND CONTRACTOR EMPLOYEES. If "Yes[," indicate] the type [of] investigation, date, who conducted th[e invest]ig[ation, an]d the [fi]le number are listed.

12. TITLE OR POSITION [OF SU]BJECT.
MILITARY OR U.[S. GOVER]NMENT EM[PLO]YEES. If military service member, lis[t ran]k, service [and] write [in "]Military Applicant." If U.S. Government [e]mployee, [list rank] and [wri]te in "U.S. Government Applic[ant."]
CONTRACTOR [EMPLOYE]ES. List [job] title.

13. TS BILLET NUMBER.
MILITARY/U.S. GOVER[NMENT E]MPLOYEES. If request is for a Top Secret clearance, list the Billet Number if such a system has been implemented.
CONTRACTOR EMPLOYEES. This item should be left blank.

14. ENCLOSURES. List and identify all enclosures attached to this form (i.e., SF 85P, SF 86, FD Form 258, copies of local files verification, results of Pre-Screening Interview, etc.).

15. RETURN RESULTS TO.
MILITARY PERSONNEL. Enter the name of the parent military service which will adjudicate the investigation. <u>NOTE:</u> Investiga- tions conducted on military personnel, who are assigned to a DoD Component, will be returned <u>only</u> to the Subject's parent military service for adjudication, regardless of the Component making the original request. The adjudicating facility will then be responsible for expeditiously transmitting the results of the clearance deter- mination to the Component who requested the investigation.
U.S. GOVERNMENT EMPLOYEES. Enter the name of the organization and mailing address that the investigation should be sent to upon completion.
CONTRACTOR EMPLOYEES. This item MUST be left blank.

16. REASON ACCESS TO CLASSIFIED INFORMATION OR INVESTIGATION IS REQUIRED.
MILITARY/U.S. GOVERNMENT EMPLOYEES. List unclassified description of duties which warrant access to classified information or which warrant the investigation.
CONTRACTOR EMPLOYEES. List unclassified description of duties which warrant access to classified information or which warrant the investigation. Also, the applicable contract number MUST be listed.

17. HISTORY OF GOVERNMENT EMPLOYMENT AND/OR CURRENT MILITARY SERVICE INDICATED ON ATTACHED SF 85P/SF 86 IS:
MILITARY/U.S. GOVER[NME]NT EMPLOYEES. Complete as appropriate. If block 17[.b. or] 17.c. i[s] marked, provide explanation in Item 18.
CONTRACTOR E[MPLO]YEE[S. Th]is item MUST be left blank.

18. REMARKS. Enter info[rmati]on neces[sary t]o clarify entries in other items and to list additio[nal inf]orm[atio]n when there is insufficien[t] space. This item m[ay be con]tinued on plain bond paper with a h[eadi]ng containing subject [na]me, Social Security Number, and the n[otation] "Continuation Sheet - 1879."

[19. INVE]STIG[ATION VALI]D[ITY] CERTIFICATION.
a. TY[PE] NAME [OF CER]TIFIER. Type full name of individual certifyi[ng v]alidity of t[he] request for investigation.
[**CO]NTRACTOR EMPLOYEES.** If the request is for a Top Secret [cleara]nce, this individual must be the Facility Security Officer (FSO) or [K]OODEP. For all other requests, this individual must be the FSO [or de]signee.
b. TITLE OF CERTIFIER. List the title of individual certifying the [requ]est for investigation.

c. SIGNATURE OF CERTIFIER. Signature of individual authorized to request investigation.

d. DATE SIGNED BY CERTIFIER. Enter the date this form is signed.

e. TELEPHONE NUMBER. List the telephone number, including area code and/or Defense Switched Network (DSN) of the certifying official.

20. EMPLOYEE'S IMMEDIATE SUPERVISOR'S CERTIFICATION.
If request is for an upgrading of a currently held clearance or for a Periodic Reinvestigation (PR), the subject's immediate supervisor MUST complete the certification. Certification by the immediate supervisor does not require review of the completed SF 85P/SF 86 by the supervisor.
If the electronic DD Form 1879 is utilized, the requester must retain an originally signed document from the employee's immediate supervisor certifying the absence or presence of any adverse information. This documentation must be retained with a copy of the electronically generated DD Form 1879, signed by the requester, until the clearance process is complete. The employee's immediate supervisor documentation must contain the following:

a. ADVERSE INFORMATION. Self-explanatory.

b. IMMEDIATE SUPERVISOR. Type full name of immediate supervisor.

c. TITLE. List the title of immediate supervisor.

d. SIGNATURE. Signature of immediate supervisor.

e. DATE SIGNED. Enter the date this form is signed.

f. TELEPHONE NUMBER. List the telephone number, including area code and/or DSN number of the immediate supervisor.

DD FORM 1879, AUG 1999   FOR OFFICIAL USE ONLY *(When filled in)*

GLOSSARIES

- ☐ Description
- ☐ Homeland Security Terms
- ☐ Military Terms
- ☐ Law Enforcement Terms
- ☐ Immigration Terms

DESCRIPTION

This section contains four glossaries that contain definitions of homeland security terms, military terms, law enforcement terms, and immigration terms. Although this section is subdivided, all these terms are actually interconnected with the missions and functions of homeland security. Readers should become familiar with the meanings of these words and terms. They are provided to assist candidates in their examinations and interviews for careers in homeland security.

HOMELAND SECURITY TERMS

> The following selected homeland security terms are provided to assist candidates in understanding their options and opportunities. "Homeland-speak" is a unique language that relies on other unique and special terms. The use of the glossary may help you to become familiar with words and their meaning.
>
> *Definitions were abstracted from the "Homeland Security Briefing Document" and from the Critical Infrastructure Assurance Office (CIAO).

A

Attack A discrete malicious action of debilitating intent inflicted by one entity upon another. A threat might attack a critical infrastructure to destroy or incapacitate it.

B

Biological agent A microorganism that causes disease in humans, plants, or animals or causes the deterioration of material.

Biological warfare The use, for military or terrorist purposes, of living organisms or materials derived from them to cause death or incapacitation in humans, animals, or plants.

Biological warfare agent Living organisms or their derivatives that can be used in weapons to cause incapacitation or death. Biological agents have the ability to reproduce themselves; thus they are less predictable than chemical agents.

Biosensor An electronic device that uses biological molecules to detect specific compounds.

C

Chain reaction A series of reactions in fissionable material in which neutrons that are the product of a fission reaction induce subsequent fissions. A fission chain reaction is self-sustaining when an average of one fission is produced by each previous fission.

Chemical agent A chemical substance that is intended for use in military operations to kill, seriously injure, or incapacitate people through its physiological effects. Excluded from consideration are riot control agents, chemical herbicides, and smoke and flame materials. Included are blood, nerve, choking, blister, and incapacitating agents.

Chemical warfare (cw) All aspects of military operations involving the employment of lethal and incapacitating munitions/agents and the warning and protective measures associated with such offensive operations. The term "chemical warfare weapons" may be used for both lethal and incapacitating munitions/agents of either chemical or biological origin.

Chemical warfare agent A chemical substance intended for use in military operations to kill, seriously injure, or incapacitate people through physiological effects. Generally separated by severity of effects: lethal (choking, nerve, and blood agents), blistering, and incapacitating.

Consequence management Includes measures to protect public health and safety, restore essential government services, and provide emergency relief to governments, businesses, and individuals affected by the consequences of terrorism. The laws of the United States assign primary authority to the states to respond to the consequences of terrorism; the federal government provides assistance as required.

Contingency plan Plan maintained for emergency response, backup operations, and post-disaster recovery, to ensure availability of critical resources and facilitate the continuity of operations in an emergency.

Cyberattack Exploitation of the software vulnerabilities of information technology-based control components.

Cyberspace Describes the world of interconnected computers and the society that surrounds them. Commonly known as the Internet.

D

Defense The confidence that Americans' lives and personal safety, both at home and abroad, are protected and the United States' sovereignty, political freedom, and independence, with its values, institutions, and territory, are maintained intact (synonymous with national security).

E

Economic security The confidence that the nation's goods and services can successfully compete in global markets while maintaining or boosting the real incomes of its citizens.

Emergency services A critical infrastructure characterized by medical, police, fire, and rescue systems and personnel that are called upon when an individual or community is experiencing an emergency. These services are typically provided at the local level (county or metropolitan area). In addition, state and federal response plans define emergency support functions to assist in response and recovery.

N

Natural disaster A physical capability with the ability to destroy or incapacitate critical infrastructures. Natural disasters differ from threats due to the absence of intent.

Nuclear detonation A nuclear explosion resulting from fission or fusion reactions in nuclear materials, such as from a nuclear weapon.

Nuclear device Nuclear fission (or fission and fusion) together with the arming, fusing, firing, chemical explosive, canister, and diagnostic measurement equipment, that have not reached the development status of an operational nuclear weapon.

Nuclear emergency search team (nest) A cadre of highly trained technical personnel that maintains on-call, deployable search, identification, and diagnostic capabilities to respond to lost or stolen nuclear weapons and special nuclear materials, nuclear explosive threats, and radiation dispersal threats.

P

Physical security Actions taken for the purpose of restricting and limiting unauthorized access. Specifically, reducing the probability that a threat will succeed in exploiting critical infrastructure vulnerabilities, including protection against direct physical attacks, e.g., through use of conventional or unconventional weapons.

R

Rad (radiation absorbed dose) Unit of absorbed dose radiation. One rad represents the absorption of 0.01 joule of nuclear (or ionizing) radiation energy per kilogram of absorbing material or tissue.

Radiation High-energy particles or gamma rays that are emitted by an atom as the substance undergoes radioactive decay. Particles can be charged alpha or beta particles, neutral neutrons, or gamma rays.

Risk The probability of a particular critical infrastructure's vulnerability being exploited by a particular threat weighed against the impact of that exploitation.

Risk assessment Produced from the combination of threat and vulnerability assessments. Characterized by analyzing the probability of destruction or incapacitation resulting from a threat's exploitation of a critical infrastructure's vulnerabilities.

T

Terrorism The calculated use of unlawful violence or threat of unlawful violence to inculcate fear. Intended to coerce or to intimidate governments or societies in the pursuit of goals that are generally political, religious, or ideological.

Terrorist An individual who uses violence, terror, and intimidation to achieve a result.

Terrorist groups Any element, regardless of size or espoused cause, that commits acts of violence or threatens violence in pursuit of its political, religious, or ideological objectives.

Thermonuclear weapon A nuclear weapon in which the main contribution to the explosive energy results from fusion of light nuclei, such as deuterium and tritium. The high temperatures required for such fusion reactions are obtained by means of an initial fission explosion. Also referred to as a hydrogen bomb.

Threat conditions Conditions that characterize the risk of terrorist attack. Protective measures are the steps that will be taken by the government and the private sector to reduce vulnerabilities. The Homeland Security Advisory System (HSAS) establishes five threat conditions with associated suggested protective measures:

Low condition green: Low risk of terrorist attacks. The following protective measures may be applied:

- Refining and exercising preplanned protective measures.
- Ensuring personnel receive training on HSAS, departmental, or agency-specific protective measures.
- Regularly assessing facilities for vulnerabilities and taking measures to reduce them.

Guarded condition blue: General risk of terrorist attacks. In addition to the previously outlined protective measures, the following may be applied:

- Checking communications with designated emergency response or command locations.
- Reviewing and updating emergency response procedures.
- Providing the public with necessary information.

Elevated condition yellow: Significant risk of terrorist attacks. In addition to the previously outlined protective measures, the following may be applied:

- Increasing surveillance of critical locations.
- Coordinating emergency plans with nearby jurisdictions.
- Assessing further refinement of protective measures within the context of the current threat information.
- Implementing, as appropriate, contingency and emergency response plans.

High condition orange: High risk of terrorist attacks. In addition to the previously outlined protective measures, the following may be applied:

- Coordinating necessary security efforts with armed forces or law enforcement agencies.
- Taking additional precautions at public events.
- Preparing to work at an alternate site or with a dispersed workforce and restricting access to essential personnel only.

Severe condition red: Severe risk of terrorist attacks. In addition to the previously outlined protective measures, the following may be applied:

- Assigning emergency response personnel and prepositioning specially trained teams; monitoring, redirecting, or constraining transportation systems.
- Closing public and government facilities.
- Increasing or redirecting personnel to address critical emergency needs.

MILITARY TERMS

> The following selected military terms are provided to assist in understanding the options and opportunities available in the military. "Military-speak" is a unique and complex language. For that reason, additional terms have been provided. The use of the glossary may help you to become familiar with military words and their meaning.
>
> *Definitions were abstracted from the D.O.D. Military Term Dictionary and various previously cited official military materials.*

A

Active duty Continuous duty on a daily basis. Comparable to "full time" as used in reference to a civilian job. Full-time duty in a uniformed service, including duty on the active list, full-time training duty, annual training duty, and attendance while in the active service at a school designated as a service school by law or by the secretary concerned.

Actual strength The number of personnel in, or projected to be in, an organization or account at a specified point in time.

Allowances Money, other than basic pay, to compensate in certain specified situations for expenses such as meals, rent, clothing, and travel. Also, compensation is given for maintaining proficiency in specific skill areas such as flying or parachuting.

Annual training The minimal period of annual active duty for training or annual field training a member performs each year to satisfy the annual training requirement associated with a reserve component assignment. It may be performed during one consecutive period or in increments of one or more days depending upon mission requirements.

Appointee A qualified candidate who has been offered an appointment to a military academy.

Appointment An offer of admission to a military academy to a candidate.

Armed Forces of the United States Includes the Army, Navy, Air Force, Marine Corps, and Coast Guard, and all components thereof.

Armed services vocational aptitude battery (ASVAB) A test that provides students with academic and vocational aptitude scores to assist them in career exploration and decision making. ASVAB scores are used by the military services to determine enlistment eligibility and to assign occupational specialties.

Army National Guard The army portion of the organized militia of several states, the Commonwealth of Puerto Rico, and the District of Columbia whose units and members are federally recognized.

Army National Guard of the United States A reserve component of the army, all of whose members are members of the Army National Guard.

Artillery Large cannons or missile launchers used in combat.

Assigned strength Actual strength of an entire service, not necessarily equal to combined unit actual strengths since individuals may be assigned but not joined.

Authorized strength The total strength authorized by Congress.

B

Barracks Building where military personnel live.

Base A locality or installation on which a military force relies for supplies or from where it initiates operations.

Basic pay The amount of pay a military member receives, as determined by pay grade and length of service. Basic pay does not include other benefits such as allowances and bonuses.

Basic training A rigorous orientation to the military, which provides a transition from civilian to military life.

BDU Battle dress uniform.

Below Downstairs.

Boot Seaman recruit in boot camp; historic slang from the days in which the recruits wore leggings that resembled boots.

Briefing A verbal military communication method used to provide or exchange information, to obtain a decision, or to review important mission details. It should include an introduction, body, conclusion, and audience question and answer period. There are four types of briefing formats: information, decision, staff, and mission. Also, the act of giving in advance specific instructions or information.

Brightwork Brass or shiny metal.

Bulkhead Wall.

Bunk Bed.

C

Cadet An appointee who has been admitted to a military academy and has taken the oath of allegiance.

Candidate A precandidate for a military academy who has a nomination in an authorized category (also referred to as a nominee).

Chain of command The succession of commanding officers from a superior to a subordinate through which command is exercised. Also called command channel.

Civil functions Functions primarily associated with the Civil Works program of the Army Corps of Engineers. This program encompasses planning, programming, designing, constructing, and operating federal water resource projects for navigation, flood control, hydroelectric power, water supply, recreation, and related activities. Civil functions also include cemetery workers (army) and conservation management employees (air force).

Civilian Anyone not on active duty in the military.

Combat information Unevaluated data, gathered by or provided directly to the tactical commander that, due to its highly perishable nature or the critical nature of the situation, cannot be processed into tactical intelligence in time to satisfy the user's tactical intelligence requirements.

Command A specifically designated organization with direct line authority from the next higher commander or the chief of staff of the United States Army. It must have a clearly identifiable headquarters and organizational structure composed of a variety of units, agencies, activities, depots, arsenals, or installations. The headquarters of a command may be organized under either table(s) of organization and equipment (TOE) or tables of distribution and allowances (TDA). An organization composed of one or relatively few separate TDA/TOE units would not normally be termed a command.

Command channel *See* CHAIN OF COMMAND.

Commissary A store on a military base that sells groceries and other items at a substantial discount to military personnel.

Commissioned officer A member of the military holding the rank of second lieutenant or ensign or above. This roll in the military is similar to that of a manager or executive.

Concealment The protection from observation or surveillance. A position that cannot easily be detected from the front or from the air. For example, a position that blends well enough with its surroundings that an approaching soldier approximately 115 feet (35 m) to the front or within hand grenade range cannot detect it.

Continental United States Unless otherwise qualified, the 48 contiguous states and the District of Columbia.

Cook off Functioning of a chambered round of ammunition, initiated by the heat of the weapon.

Cover A natural or man-made protection from enemy observation and fire. An example of this would be a frontal parapet high and thick enough to protect the soldier's head completely while he or she fires a weapon. It should afford protection from direct frontal small arms fire and from the effects of indirect fire.

Cryptomaterial All material, including documents, devices, or equipment, that contains crypto information and is essential to the encryption, decryption, or authentication of telecommunications.

D

Danger close In artillery and naval gunfire support, information in a call for fire to indicate that friendly forces are within 2,000 feet (600 m) of the target.

Dead space An area within the maximum effective range of a weapon, surveillance device, or observer that cannot be covered by fire or observation from a particular position because of intervening obstacles, the nature of the ground, the characteristics of the trajectory, or the limitations of the pointing capabilities of the weapons.

Delayed entry program (DEP) A military program that allows an applicant to delay entry into active duty for up to a year, for such things as finishing school, and so on.

Direct fire Fire directed at a target that is visible to the aimer. To avoid direct fire, the soldier moves from cover to cover, using the "rush" technique.

Direct hire civilians Employees hired directly by an agency of the Department of Defense (DOD). Includes foreign nationals hired by DOD to support DOD activities in their home countries.

Drill To train or exercise in military operations. A disciplined, repetitious exercise to teach and perfect a skill or procedure, for example, fire, person overboard, abandon ship, lifeboat, and damage control drills on watercraft.

Duty Assigned task or occupation.

E

Enlisted member A person enlisted, enrolled, or conscripted into the military service. Also includes enlisted personnel currently enrolled in an officer-training program. Military personnel below the rank of warrant or commissioned officers. This role is similar to that of a company employee or supervisor.

Enlistee A service member, not a warrant or commissioned officer, who has been accepted by the military and has taken the Oath of Enlistment.

Enlistment 1. Voluntarily entering military service under enlisted status, as distinguished from induction through selective service. 2. A period of time, contractual or prescribed by law, that enlisted members serve between enrollment and discharge.

Enlistment agreement (enlistment contract) A legal contract between the military and an enlistment applicant, which contains information such as enlistment date, term of enlistment, and other options such as a training program guarantee or a cash bonus.

F

Field of fire The area which a weapon or group of weapons may cover effectively with fire from a given position.

Frocked Incumbent authorized to wear the next higher insignia of rank before being officially promoted to that rank.

G

GI Bill benefits A program of education benefits for individuals entering the military. This program enables service persons to set aside money to be used later for educational purposes.

H

Hostile, hostile conditions, or hostile actions Meets the requirements of a battle casualty. A battle casualty is any casualty incurred in action. "In action" characterizes the casualty status as having been the direct result of hostile action, sustained in combat or relating thereto, or sustained going to or returning from a combat mission, provided that the occurrence was directly related to hostile action. Included are persons killed or wounded mistakenly or accidentally by friendly fire directed at a hostile force or what was thought to be a hostile force. However, injuries due to the elements or self-inflicted wounds and, except in unusual cases, wounds or deaths inflicted by a friendly force while the individual is in an absent without leave or dropped from the rolls status, or when the individual is voluntarily absent from a place of duty, are not to be considered as sustained in action and are, thereby, not to be interpreted as battle casualties.

I

Inactive reserve duty Affiliation with the military in a nontraining, nonpaying status after completing the minimum obligation of active-duty service.

Infantry Units of people trained, armed, and equipped to fight on foot.

Intelligence (military) The product resulting from the collection, processing, integration analysis, evaluation, and interpretation of available information concerning foreign countries or areas.

L

Leave paid time off for vacation, personal time, or sick time.

Liberty Time off ashore.

Logistics The science of planning and carrying out the movement and maintenance of forces. In its most comprehensive sense, those aspects of military operations that deal with design development, acquisition, storage, movement, distribution, maintenance, evacuation, and disposition of material; movement, evacuation, and hospitalization of personnel; acquisition or construction, maintenance, operation, and disposition of facilities; and acquisition or furnishing of services.

M

Midshipman *See* SERVICE ACADEMY CADET.

Military afloat Navy and Marine Corps military personnel aboard ship. Also includes Navy and Marine Corps military personnel who are assigned to afloat and mobile units, such as aircraft squadrons, construction battalions, and fleet and air command staffs, and those who are aboard ship.

Military Entrance Processing Stations (MEPS) One-stop processing stations located around the country that provide aptitude testing, medical and physical exams, and provide career counseling to candidates entering the military.

Military functions Activities typically associated with the uniformed services.

Military occupational specialty (MOS) A specific job or occupation in one of the five services. A term used to identify a group of duty positions possessing such a close occupational or functional relationship that an optimal degree of interchangeability among persons so classified exists at any given level of skill. An advanced MOS means that specialized occupational qualifications are required to perform that duty. Positions with an advanced MOS require journeyman, supervisory, or leadership levels of skill.

A duty MOS is a position in which the soldier is actually performing duty. An entry MOS reflects the occupational qualifications required for performing a duty position that represents the lowest level of skill within an entry group. A primary MOS (entry or advanced) represents the highest or most significant job skill that the individual can best perform.

Military occupational specialty (MOS) code A fixed number that indicates a given military occupational specialty. Also known as military occupational number and specification serial number.

Military qualification standards The system for establishing the standards and responsibilities for the professional development, training, and education of officers at appropriate levels/grades in order to execute our war-fighting doctrine.

Military temporarily shore based Navy and Marine Corps military personnel assigned to afloat and mobile units, such as aircraft squadrons, construction battalions, and fleet and air command staffs, and who are temporarily based ashore for a period that exceeds 30 days.

Missing Active-duty military personnel who are not present at their duty station due to apparent involuntary reasons and whose location is not known. Excluded are personnel who are in an absent without leave or deserter status or those who have been dropped from the rolls of their military servce.

Musters Assembling in formation.

N

Nomination The selection of a precandidate as an official candidate for admission to a military academy by a legal nominating authority.

Nominee *See* CANDIDATE.

Noncommissioned officer (NCO) An enlisted member in pay grades E-4 or higher.

O

Obligation The period of time one agrees to serve on active duty, in the reserve, or a combination of both.

Obstacle Any obstruction that stops, delays, or diverts movement. Obstacles may be natural: deserts, rivers, swamps, or mountains; or they may be artificial: barbed-wire entanglements, pits, or concrete or metal antimechanized traps. Artificial obstacles may be ready-made or they may be constructed in the field.

Officer A commissioned or warrant officer.

Officer candidate school (OCS) A program for college graduates with no prior military training who wish to become military officers. Also, qualified enlisted members who wish to become officers may attend OCS. After successful completion, candidates are commissioned as military officers.

Officer training school (OTS) *See* OFFICER CANDIDATE SCHOOL.

Operating location The geographic location where military or civilian employees of the Department of Defense are physically located for the performance of duties.

Operation order A directive, usually formal, issued by a commander to subordinate commanders for the purpose of effecting the coordinated execution of an operation.

P

Pay grade A level of employment, as designated by the military. There are 9 enlisted pay grades and 10 officer pay grades through which personnel can progress during their career. Pay grade and length of service determine a service member's pay.

Precandidate A student interested in attending a military academy who has returned a completed application/precandidate questionnaire.

Principal nominee A nominee whom the member of Congress ranks as first choice for an authorized vacancy in a military academy.

Q

Qualified alternate A qualified candidate not chosen to fill any specific nomination category but placed into a nationwide pool from which additional appointments are made to fill the entering class of a military academy.

Qualified candidate A candidate to a military academy who has met all admissions requirements.

Quarters Living accommodations or housing.

R

Rack Bed.

Ready reserve The selected reserve and individual ready reserve liable for active duty as prescribed by law.

Recorded duty station The actual physical location where active-duty military personnel perform duty on a permanent basis.

Recruit *See* ENLISTEE.

Regular military compensation The total value of basic pay, allowances, and tax savings a service member receives, which represents the amount of pay a civilian worker would need to earn to receive the same take-home pay.

Reserve components The Army National Guard of the United States, Army Reserve, Naval Reserve, Marine Corps Reserve, Air National Guard of the United States, Air Force Reserve, and Coast Guard Reserve.

Reserve officers' training corps (ROTC) Training given to undergraduate college students who plan to become military officers. Often they receive scholarships for tuition, books, fees, and uniforms and also a monthly allowance.

Reserves Those people in the military who are not presently on full-time, active duty. In a national emergency, reservists can be called up immediately to serve on active duty because they are highly trained by the services and drill regularly. During peacetime, they perform functions in support of the active-duty forces in our country's defense, such as installing and repairing communications equipment. Reservists are also entitled to some of the employment benefits available to active military personnel.

Retired reserve Those individuals whose names are placed onto the reserve retired list by proper authority in accordance with law or regulations. Members of the retired reserve may, if qualified, be ordered to active duty involuntarily in time of war or national emergency declared by the Congress, or when otherwise declared by the Congress, or when otherwise authorized by law. This occurs only when the secretary of the army determines that adequate numbers of qualified individuals in the required categories are not readily available in the ready reserve or in an active status in the standby reserve.

S

Security classification A category to which national security information and material is assigned to denote the degree of damage that unauthorized disclosure would cause to national defense or foreign relations of the United States and to denote the degree of protection required. There are three such categories:

Top secret: National security information or material that requires the highest degree of protection and the unauthorized disclosure of which could reasonably be expected to cause exceptionally grave damage to national security. Examples of "exceptionally grave damage" include armed hostilities against the United States or its allies, disruption of foreign relations vitally affecting the national security, the compromise of vital national defense plans or complex cryptological and communications intelligence systems, the revelation of sensitive intelligence operations, and the disclosure of scientific or technological developments vital to national security.

Secret: National security information or material that requires a substantial degree of protection and the unauthorized disclosure of which could reasonably be expected to cause serious damage to national security. Examples of "serious damage" include disruption of foreign relations significantly affecting the national security, significant impairment of a program or policy directly related to the national security, revelation of significant military plans or intelligence operations, and compromise of significant scientific or technological developments relating to national security.

Confidential: National security information or material that requires protection and the unauthorized disclosure of which could reasonably be expected to cause damage to national security.

Security clearance An administrative determination by competent national authority that an individual is eligible, from a security standpoint, for access to classified information.

Service academy cadet A person in training at one of the service academies to become a commissioned officer.

Service classifier A military information specialist who helps applicants select a military occupational field.

Service obligation The amount of time an enlisted member agrees to serve in the military, as stated in the enlistment agreement.

Standby reserve Those units and members of the reserve components (other than those in the ready reserve or retired reserve) who are liable for active duty.

Station A place of assigned duty.

Subsistence Food.

T

Tentative candidate A precandidate to a military academy who appears to have the potential to be a qualified candidate, based upon self-reported information.

Tour of Duty A period of obligated service. Also used to describe a type of duty tour, such as a "Mediterranean tour."

Transients All military members who are available for duty while executing permanent change of station (PCS) orders. Transients shall comprise all military personnel in a travel, proceed, leave enroute, or temporary duty enroute status on PCS orders to execute an accession, separation, training, operational, or rotational move.

W

Warrant officer A person who holds a commission or warrant in a warrant officer grade.

X

XO Executive officer.

LAW ENFORCEMENT TERMS

> The following words may appear on various law enforcement examinations and interconnect with homeland security. Using the glossary may help you to become familiar with these words and their meanings.

A

Abduct To restrain a person with intent to prevent his or her liberation by either secreting or holding that person in a place where he or she is not likely to be found or using or threatening to use deadly physical force.

Abusive Using harsh words.

Accomplice A person who knowingly, voluntarily, and with a common intent with the principal offender unites in the commission of a crime; someone equally concerned in the commission of a crime.

Acquit To set free, release, or discharge as from an accusation of crime. Opposite in meaning is to convict.

Addict One who has acquired the habit of using narcotics to such an extent as to deprive him or her of reasonable self-control.

Adjourn To put off, postpone.

Admissible Pertinent and proper to be considered in reaching a decision. As applied to evidence, the term means that it is of such character that the court is bound to receive it and allow it to be introduced.

Admission In a criminal prosecution, any act or declaration of the accused inconsistent with his or her claim of innocence is admissible against that person. If a defendant makes a statement not amounting to a confession but constituting an admission of acts in issue against him or her, or of facts relevant to the issue, such statement is admissible.

Admonish To caution or advise.

Admonition A reprimand from a judge to a person accused, upon being discharged, warning him or her of the consequences of conduct and intimating to that person that a repetition of the offense will bring more severe punishment. Also, any authoritative oral communication or statement by way of advice or caution by the court.

Affidavit A sworn written statement. The affidavit is divided into three parts. The location is entered at the upper left corner—this is the venue. Below this is the statement itself—the body of the affidavit. At the bottom, the officer who administers the oath certifies that the statement was sworn to before him or her—this is the jurat.

Affirmant A person who testifies on affirmation, or one who affirms instead of taking an oath.

Affirmation A pledge given by the person taking it "that his or her attestation or promise is made under an immediate sense of his or her responsibility to God."

Aforethought In criminal law, deliberate: planned, premeditated.

Aggression The practice of making attacks.

Aggressor One who first employs hostile force. The party who first offers violence or offense.

Agitator One who stirs up, excites, ruffles, perturbs. One who incessantly advocates a social change.

Alias Any name by which one is known other than his or her true name.

Alibi A claim that one was in a place different from that charged.

Appeal The removal of a cause from an inferior court to one of superior jurisdiction for the purpose of obtaining a review and retrial.

Apprehend To seize, take, or arrest a person on a criminal charge.

Arraign To bring an arrested person before the court, where the charge against him or her is explained and the plea is taken. If the person is later indicted, the same process is repeated in a higher court.

Arrest Taking a person into custody so he or she may be held to answer for a crime. An arrest, to be binding, does not require physical seizure of the person. If the individual voluntarily submits to the custody of the officer, he or she is arrested just as if that person were handcuffed.

Arson An intentional damaging of property by fire or explosion.

Assault An unlawful offer or attempt to do injury to another with force or violence.

Authorize Give legal power to.

Autopsy The dissection of a dead body for the purpose of inquiring about the cause of death.

B

Bail The release of a prisoner from custody on the written guarantee that he or she will appear in court at a specified time or forfeit property of some kind.

Bail bond The agreement signed by the released prisoner and the surety guaranteeing that the prisoner will appear at the specified time and place or will forfeit property.

Barricade An obstruction or block to prevent passage or access.

Blackmail The obtaining of something of value from a person by means of threatening to expose that person to injury, disgrace, libel, and so on.

Bodily harm Any touching of another person against his or her will with physical force, in an intentional, hostile, and aggressive manner or a projecting of such force against his or her person.

Bribery The offering, giving, receiving, or soliciting of anything of value to influence an action.

Burden of proof The burden of proving the fact in issue. In a criminal case, the prosecutor has the duty of proving beyond a reasonable doubt the guilt of the person charged.

Burglary Entering or remaining unlawfully in a building with the intent to commit a crime therein.

Bystander One who stands near, a chance looker-on; hence one who has no concern with the business being transacted, one present but not taking part, a spectator.

C

Cadaver A dead human body, a corpse.

Capacity Function or position.

Coercion Compelling a person to do (or omit) that which he or she does not have to (or may legally) do, by some illegal means such as threat, force, and so on.

Collision An impact or sudden contact of a moving body with an obstruction, which may or may not be stationary, in its line of motion.

Collusion An agreement between two or more persons for fraudulent or deceitful purposes.

Commitment The written order by which a court or magistrate directs an officer to take a person to prison. Authority for holding in jail one accused of crime.

Common knowledge Matters that the court may declare applicable to action without necessity of proof. It is knowledge that every intelligent person has.

Common law As distinguished from law created by the enactment of legislatures, the body of those principles and rules of action, relating to the government and security of persons and property, that derive their authority solely from usages and customs of immemorial antiquity or from the judgments and decrees of the courts recognizing, affirming, and enforcing such usages and customs.

Competency In the law of evidence, the presence of those characteristics, or the absence of those disabilities, which render a witness legally fit and qualified to give testimony in a court of justice; this can be applied, in the same sense, to documents or other written evidence.

Complainant One who instigates prosecution or who makes accusation against a suspected person.

Complaint A sworn written allegation that a specified person committed a crime.

Compulsion Forcible inducement to the commission of an act; an impulse or feeling of being irresistibly driven toward the performance of some act.

Concur To agree, accord, act together.

Conduct Personal behavior, deportment.

Confess To admit as true; to admit the truth of a charge or accusation.

Confession A voluntary statement made by a person charged with crime wherein he or she acknowledges guilt of the offense charged.

Confrontation The act of setting a witness face-to-face with the prisoner in order that the latter may make any objections to the witness or that the witness may identify the accused.

Consent A concurrence of wills, agreement; voluntarily yielding the will to that of another.

Conspiracy In criminal law, a combination of two or more persons formed for the purpose of committing, by their joint efforts, some unlawful or criminal act.

Constitutional right A right guaranteed to the citizens by the Constitution and so guaranteed to prevent legislative interference therewith.

Contempt of court Any act that is calculated to embarrass, hinder, or obstruct a court in the administration of justice or that is calculated to lessen the court's authority or dignity.

Convict To find a person guilty of a criminal charge.

Corporal punishment Physical punishment as distinguished from monetary punishment or a fine; any kind of punishment inflicted on the body.

Corpus delicti The body of a crime; the substance or foundation of a crime; the substantial fact that a crime has been committed.

Corroborate To strengthen; to add weight or credibility to a thing by additional and confirming facts or evidence.

Corruption The act of an official who unlawfully and wrongfully uses his or her position to procure some benefit for himself or herself or for another person contrary to that person's duty and the rights of others.

Counterfeit In criminal law, to forge; to copy or imitate, without authority or right, and with the intent to deceive or defraud, by passing the copy or thing forged for that which is original or genuine.

Credibility Worthiness of belief; that quality of a witness that renders his or her evidence worthy of belief.

Crime An act or omission, forbidden by law, and punishable upon conviction as the law may prescribe.

Crimes *mala in se* Acts immoral or wrong in themselves, such as burglary, larceny, arson, rape, murder; those acts that are wrong by their very nature.

Crimes *mala prohibita* Acts prohibited by statute that infringe on others' rights, though no moral turpitude may attach, and that are crimes only because they are so prohibited.

Criminal One who has committed a crime; one who has been legally convicted of a crime. Also, that which pertains to or is connected with the law of crimes, or the administration of penal justice, or that relates to or has the character of crime.

Criminal negligence An offense when someone fails to perceive a substantial and unjustifiable risk that such result will occur or that such circumstance exists. The risk must be of such nature and degree that the failure to perceive it constitutes a gross deviation from the standard of care that a reasonable person would observe in the situation.

Cross-examination Examining a witness upon a trial or hearing, or upon taking a deposition, by the party opposed to the one who produced the witness, upon his evidence to test its truth, to develop it further, or for other purposes.

Cruel and unusual punishment Such punishment not known to the common law, and also any punishment so disproportionate to the offense as to shock the moral sense of the community.

Culpable Blamable; censurable, involving the breach of a legal duty or the commission of a fault.

Custody In the keeping of officers of the law.

D

Deadly weapon Weapons or instruments made and designed for offensive or defensive purposes or for the destruction of life or the infliction of injury.

Death The cessation of life; the ceasing to exist; defined by physicians as a total stoppage of the circulation of the blood and a cessation of vital functions, such as respiration and pulsation.

Defendant In a criminal action, the party charged with a crime.

Defraud To practice fraud; to cheat or trick; to deprive a person of property by fraud, deceit, or artifice.

Degree In criminal law, a division or classification of one specific crime into several grades of guilt, according to the circumstances attending its commission.

Delinquency Failure, omission, violation of duty; the state or condition of one who fails to perform his or her duty; synonymous with misconduct and offense.

Demeanor One who deposes to the truth of certain facts; one who gives under oath testimony that is reduced to writing.

Deposition The testimony of a witness taken upon interrogatories, not in open court, reduced to writing and duly authenticated, and intended to be used upon the trial of an action in court; subject to cross-examination.

Detain Keep in custody.

Direct evidence Proof that tends to show the existence of a fact in question, without the intervention of the proof of any other fact, and is distinguished from circumstantial evidence, which is often called "indirect."

Disorderly conduct A term of loose and indefinite meaning (except as occasionally defined in statutes) but generally signifying any behavior that is contrary to law and, more particularly, tends to disturb the public peace or decorum, scandalize the community, or shock the public sense of morality.

Double jeopardy The act of being subjected to a second prosecution for a crime for which the defendant has once been prosecuted and duly convicted or acquitted; this is barred by the Constitution of the United States, Fifth Amendment.

Doubt Uncertainty of mind; the absence of a settled conviction or opinion.

Due process of law Law in its regular course of administration through courts of justice.

Duress Unlawful constraint exercised upon a person whereby he or she is forced to do some act that the person otherwise would not have done. Duress may also include the same injuries, threats, or restraint exercised upon the person's spouse, child, or parent.

E

Entrapment The act of officers or agents of the government in inducing a person to commit a crime not contemplated by that person, for the purpose of instituting a criminal prosecution against that person.

Ethical Of or relating to moral action, motive, or character, as ethical emotion; related to moral feelings, duties, or conduct; conforming to professional standards of conduct.

Evidence All the means by which any alleged matter of fact, the truth of which is submitted to investigation, is established or disproved.

Expert evidence Testimony given in relation to some scientific, technical, or professional matter by experts, persons qualified to speak authoritatively by reason of their special training, skill, or familiarity with a subject.

Extortion The obtaining of property from another, with his or her consent, induced by a wrongful use of force or fear or under color of official right.

Extradition The surrender by one state to another of an individual accused or convicted of an offense outside its own territory and within the territorial jurisdiction of the other, which, being competent to try and punish that person, demands the surrender.

F

Fabricate To invent; to devise falsely. "Invent" is sometimes used in a bad sense, but "fabricate" is never used in any other.

False pretenses Designed misrepresentation of existing facts or conditions whereby a person obtains another's money or goods.

Felon A person who commits a felony.

Felony A crime of a graver or more atrocious nature than those designated as misdemeanors. Generally an offense punishable by death or imprisonment in a state prison.

Forensic medicine That science that teaches the application of every branch of medical knowledge to the purposes of the law; hence its limits are, on the one hand, the requirements of the law, and, on the other, the whole range of medicine.

Forgery The false making or material altering, with intent to defraud, of any writing that, if genuine, might apparently be of legal efficacy or the foundation of a legal liability.

Fraud A generic term, embracing all multifarious means that human ingenuity can devise and that are resorted to by one individual to get advantage over another by false suggestions or by suppression of truth, and includes all surprise, trick, cunning, dissembling, and any unfair way by which another is cheated.

Frisk The running of hands rapidly over another's person, as distinguished from "search," which is to strip and examine contents more thoroughly.

Fruits of crime In the law of evidence, material objects acquired by means and in consequence of the commission of crime and sometimes constituting the subject matter of the crime.

Fugitive One who flees; always used in law with the implication of flight, evasion, or escape from some duty or penalty or from the consequences of a misdeed.

G

Graft The popular meaning is the fraudulent obtaining of money, position, and so on, by dishonest or questionable means, as by taking advantage of one's official position; also anything thus gained.

Guilty Having committed a crime; the word used by a prisoner in pleading to the indictment when he or she confesses the crime of which he or she is charged, and by the jury in convicting.

H

Hearing In criminal law, the examination of a prisoner charged with a crime and of the witnesses for the accused.

Hearsay Evidence not proceeding from the personal knowledge of the witness but from the mere repetition of what that person has heard others say; generally inadmissible except from certain specified circumstances.

Homicide The killing of one human being by the act, procurement, or omission of another. Homicide is not necessarily a crime. It is a necessary ingredient of the crimes of murder and manslaughter, but there are other cases where homicide may be committed without criminal intent and without criminal consequences. The term "homicide" is neutral; while it describes the act, it pronounces no judgment on its moral or legal quality.

Hung jury A jury so irreconcilably divided in opinion that they cannot agree upon any verdict.

I

Identification Proof of identity; the proving that a person, subject, or article before the court is the very same that he, she, or it is alleged, charged, or reputed to be.

Illegal Not authorized by law, unlawful.

Immoral Contrary to good morals; inconsistent with the rules and principles of morality; inimical to public welfare according to the standards of a given community, as expressed in law or otherwise.

Immunity A particular privilege; freedom from duty or penalty.

Imprison To put in a prison; to put in a place of confinement. To confine a person, or restrain his or her liberty, in any way.

Inadmissible That which, under the established rules of law, cannot be admitted or received.

Incriminate To charge with crime; to expose to an accusation or charge of crime; to involve oneself or another in a criminal prosecution or the danger thereof; as in the rule that a witness is not bound to give testimony that would tend to incriminate him or her.

Indictment An accusation in writing, presented by a grand jury to a competent court, charging a person named therein with a crime.

Insane Unsound in mind; of unsound mind; deranged, disordered, or diseased in mind.

Insubordination State of being insubordinate; disobedience to constituted authority; refusal to obey lawful order of a superior officer.

Integrity As occasionally used in statutes prescribing the qualifications of public officers and others with responsibility, the soundness of moral character and principle, as shown by one person's dealing with others, and fidelity and honesty in discharge of trusts; synonymous with probity, honesty, and uprightness.

Intent Design, resolve, or determination with which a person acts; being a state of mind, it is rarely susceptible of direct proof but must ordinarily be inferred from the facts. Intent shows the presence of will in the act that consummates a crime.

Intoxicated Drunk.

Investigation To follow up step-by-step by patient inquiry or observation; to trace or track mentally; to examine and inquire into with care and accuracy; the taking of evidence; a legal inquiry.

Involuntary Without will or power of choice; opposed to volition or desire; an act is involuntary when done under duress.

J

Jail A building designated by law, or regularly used, for the confinement of persons held in lawful custody.

Jurisdiction Sphere of authority; area of legal operation.

Justifiable Rightful; warranted or sanctioned by law.

K

Knowingly With knowledge; consciously, intelligently, wilfully, intentionally. The word imports a perception of facts requisite to make a crime.

L

Larceny Taking away possessions of someone else illegally.

Latent Hidden, concealed, not apparent, dormant, as a latent fingerprint.

Law That which is laid down, ordained, or established; that which must be obeyed and followed by citizens, subject to sanctions or legal consequences; rule of conduct prescribed by law-making body of state.

Legal evidence A broad general term meaning all admissible evidence, including both oral and documentary, but with a further implication that it must be of such a character as tends reasonably and substantially to prove the point, not to raise a mere suspicion or conjecture.

Lie detector A machine that records by a needle on a graph varying emotional disturbances when answering questions truthfully or falsely as indicated by fluctuations in blood pressure, respiration, or perspiration.

M

Magistrate An officer having the power to issue a warrant of arrest for a person charged with a crime.

Mala Bad; evil; wrongful.

Mala in se Wrong in themselves; acts morally wrong; offenses against conscience.

Mala prohibita Prohibited wrongs or offenses; acts that are made offenses by positive laws and prohibited as such.

Malfeasance Evildoing; ill conduct; the commission of some act that is positively unlawful; the doing of an act that is wholly wrongful and unlawful. Comprehensive term including any wrongful conduct that affects, interrupts, or interferes with the performance of official duties.

Mandatory Containing a command; imperative.

Marshal An officer pertaining to the organization of the federal judicial system whose duties are similar to those of a sheriff. This person is to execute the process of the U.S. courts within the district for which he or she is appointed.

Material evidence Evidence relevant and that goes to the substantial matters in a dispute or has a legitimate and effective influence or bearing on the decision of a case.

Medical jurisprudence *See* FORENSIC MEDICINE.

Mens rea A guilty mind; a guilty or wrongful purpose; a criminal intent.

Misconduct A transgression of some established and definite rule of action, a forbidden act, a dereliction from duty, unlawful behavior, willful in character.

Misdemeanor Offenses lesser than a felony and generally punishable by fine or imprisonment in penitentiary.

Mistrial An erroneous, invalid, or nugatory trial; a trial of an action that cannot stand in law because of want of jurisdiction, a wrong drawing of jurors, or disregard of some other fundamental requisite.

Mitigating circumstances Circumstances that do not constitute a justification or excuse of the offense in question but that, in fairness and mercy, may be considered as extenuating or reducing the degree of moral culpability.

Morgue A place where the bodies of persons found dead are kept for a limited time and exposed to view so they may be identified.

Murder The unlawful killing of a human being by another with malice aforethought, either express or implied.

N

Naturalize To confer citizenship upon an alien; to make a foreigner the same, in respect to rights and privileges, as if he or she were a native citizen or subject.

Negligence The ommission to do something that a reasonable person, guided by those considerations that ordinarily regulate human affairs, would do, or the doing of something that a reasonable or prudent person would not do.

Not guilty A plea of general issue in criminal prosecutions. The form of the verdict in criminal cases, where the jury acquits the defendant.

O

Obstruct To hinder or prevent from progress, to check, to stop, also to retard the progress of, make accomplishment of difficult and slow. To impose impediments, to the hindrance or frustration of some act or service, as to obstruct an officer in the execution of his or her duty.

Officer The incumbent of an office; one who is charged by a superior power (and particularly by government) with the power and duty of exercising certain functions.

Overt Open; manifest; public; an action as distinguished from a thought.

P

Pathology In medical jurisprudence, the science or doctrine of diseases. That part of medicine that explains the nature of diseases, their causes, and their symptoms.

Peace officers Generally includes sheriffs and their deputies, constables, members of the police forces of cities, and other officers whose duty is to enforce and preserve the public peace.

Penal laws Those laws that specify the persons who are capable of committing crimes and that specify those liable to punishment therefore. Laws that define the nature of the various crimes and prescribe the kind and measure of punishment to be inflicted for each crime.

Penitentiary A penal institution, run by a county, to which are sentenced misdemeanants and other lesser offenders.

Perjury In criminal law, the willful assertion as to a matter of fact, opinion, belief, or knowledge made by a witness in a judicial proceeding as part of evidence, either upon oath or in any form allowed by law to be substituted for an oath, whether such evidence is given in open court, in an affidavit, or otherwise, such assertion being material to the issue or point of inquiry and known to such witness to be false.

Perpetrator Someone who commits a crime.

Police The function of that branch of the administrative machinery of government that is charged with the preservation of public order and tranquility; the promotion of the public health, safety, and morals; and the prevention and detection of crimes.

Police power That inherent and absolute power in state over persons and property that enables the people to prohibit all things inimical to comfort, safety, health, and welfare of society.

Possess To have control of.

Postmortem After death. A term usually applied to an autopsy or examination of a dead body to ascertain the cause of death.

Premeditate To think of an act beforehand; to contrive and design; to plot or lay plans for the execution of a purpose.

Premeditation The act of meditating in advance; deliberation upon a contemplated act; plotting or contriving; a design formed to do something before it is done. A prior determination to do and act, but such determination need not exist for any particular period before it is carried into effect.

Premises Property.

Prima facie case Such as will suffice until contradicted and overcome by other evidence. A case that has proceeded upon sufficient proof to that stage where it will support the verdict if evidence to the contrary is disregarded.

Prison A penal institution, run by the state, to which are sentenced those convicted of felonies.

Prisoner One who is deprived of his or her liberty; one under arrest and confined upon a charge of violating the law.

Probable cause Reasonable cause. There is no fixed formula for determining probable cause. Probable cause is held to exist where the facts and circumstances within the arresting officer's knowledge and of which he or she has reasonably trustworthy information are sufficient in themselves to warrant a person of reasonable caution to believe that an offense has been or is being committed. Simply stated, probable cause may be defined as reasonable grounds for the belief of guilt.

Probation Trial; test; the act of proving. In modern criminal administration, allowing a person convicted of an offense to go at large, under a suspension of sentence, during good behavior and generally under the supervision or guardianship of a probation officer.

Probation officer An officer of the court that assists in the administration of the probation system for offenders against the criminal laws.

Prohibit To forbid by law; to prevent; not synonymous with "regulate."

Proof The effect of evidence; the establishment of a fact by evidence.

Prosecute To follow up; to carry on an action or other judicial proceeding; to proceed against a person criminally. To prosecute an action is not merely to commence it but includes following it to an ultimate conclusion.

Public trial A trial held in public, in the presence of the public, or in a place accessible and open to the attendance of the public at large or of persons who may properly be admitted. The requirement of a public trial is for the benefit of the accused; that the public may see that he or she is fairly dealt with and not unjustly condemned, and that the presence of interested spectators may keep his or her peers keenly alive to a sense of their responsibility and to the importance of their functions.

Punishment In criminal law, any pain, penalty, suffering, or confinement inflicted upon a person by the authority of the law and the judgment and sentence of a court, for some crime or offense committed by that person, or for his or her omission of a duty enjoined by law.

R

Real evidence Evidence furnished by things themselves, on view or inspection, as distinguished from a description of them by the words of a witness. For instance, the weapons or instruments used in a crime, and other inanimate objects, and evidence of the physical appearance of a place (crime scene) as obtained by a jury when they are taken to view it.

Reasonable doubt After jurors have compared and considered all the evidence, the condition when they cannot decide whether or not the defendant is guilty. If reasonable doubt remains, the accused is entitled to the benefit of it by an acquittal. A reasonable doubt is a doubt that would cause a reasonable and prudent person to pause and hesitate to act.

Reckless driving Operation of a motor vehicle manifesting reckless disregard of possible consequences and indifference to others' rights.

Resisting an officer In criminal law, the offense of obstructing, opposing, and endeavoring to prevent (with or without actual force) a peace officer in the execution of a writ or in the lawful discharge of his or her duty while making an arrest or otherwise enforcing the peace.

Rigor mortis In medical jurisprudence, a rigidity or stiffening of the muscular tissue and joints of the body, which sets in at varied intervals after death, but usually within a few hours, and which is one of the recognized tests of death.

Robbery Forcible stealing.

S

Search In criminal law, an examination of a person's house or other buildings or premises, or of his or her person, with a view to the discovery of contraband or illicit or stolen property, or some evidence of guilt to be used in the prosecution of a criminal action for some crime or offense with which that person is charged.

Search warrant An order in writing in the name of the people, signed by a judge, justice, or magistrate of a court of criminal jurisdiction, directed to a peace officer, commanding him or her to search for personal property and bring it before the judge, justice, or magistrate.

Sentence The judgment formally pronounced by the court or judge upon the defendant after his or her conviction in a criminal prosecution, awarding the punishment to be inflicted. Judgment formally declaring to the accused the legal consequences of guilt that he or she has confessed to or has been convicted of.

Statute An act of the legislature declaring, commanding, or prohibiting something; a particular law enacted and established by the will of the legislative department of government.

Subdue Overpower.

Subordinate Placed in a lower order, class, or rank; occupying a lower position in a regular descending series.

Subpoena A process to cause a witness to appear and give testimony, commanding him or her to lay aside all pretenses and excuses and to appear before a court or magistrate therein named at a time therein mentioned to testify for the party named under a penalty therein mentioned.

Superior One who has a right to command; one who holds a superior rank.

Suspect To have a slight or even vague idea concerning, not necessarily involving knowledge, belief, or likelihood. Also used to designate the person wanted for the commission of a crime.

T

Testify To bear witness; to give evidence as a witness; to make a solemn declaration, under oath or affirmation, in a judicial inquiry for the purpose of establishing or proving some fact.

Trial A judicial examination, in accordance with the law of the land, of a cause, either civil or criminal, of the issues between the parties, whether of law or fact, before a court that has jurisdiction over it.

V

Venue The place or county in which an injury is declared to have been done or fact declared to have happened. Also, the county in which an action or prosecution is brought for trial and that is to furnish the panel of jurors.

Verdict The formal and unanimous decision or finding made by a jury, impaneled and sworn for the trial of a cause, and reported to the court, upon the matters or questions duly submitted to them upon the trial.

Victimize To make someone suffer.

Violation The breaking of a law.

W

Waiver The intentional or voluntary relinquishment of a known right.

Warrant A writ or precept from a competent authority in pursuance of law, directing the doing of an act, addressed to an officer or person competent to do the act, and affording that person protection from damage if he or she does it.

Witness To subscribe one's name to a document for the purpose of attesting its authenticity and proving its execution, if required, by bearing witness thereto. In general, one whom, being present, personally sees or beholds a thing; a spectator or eyewitness. One who testifies to what he or she has seen, heard, or otherwise observed.

IMMIGRATION TERMS

The following contains selected immigration-related terms. The U.S. Border Patrol, INS, Customs Service, FBI, U.S. Coast Guard, and a host of other agencies use these terms. For that reason, additional terms have been provided. The use of the glossary may help you to become familiar with these words and their meanings.

Definitions were abstracted from an INS Web briefing document.

A

Acquired citizenship Citizenship conferred at birth on children born abroad to a U.S. citizen parent(s).

Agricultural worker As a nonimmigrant class of admission, an alien coming temporarily to the United States to perform agricultural labor or services, as defined by the secretary of labor.

Alien Any person not a citizen or national of the United States.

Asylee An alien in the United States or at a port of entry who is found to be unable or unwilling to return to his or her country of nationality or to seek the protection of that country because of persecution or a well-founded fear of persecution.

B

Beneficiaries Aliens on whose behalf a U.S. citizen, legal permanent resident, or employer have filed a petition for such aliens to receive immigration benefits from the U.S. Immigration and Naturalization Service.

Border crosser An alien resident of the United States reentering the country after an absence of less than six months in Canada or Mexico, or a nonresident alien entering the United States across the Canadian border for stays of no more than six months or across the Mexican border for stays of no more than 72 hours.

Border patrol sector Any one of 21 geographic areas into which the United States is divided for the Immigration and Naturalization Service's border patrol activities.

Born out of wedlock *See* OUT OF WEDLOCK.

Business nonimmigrant An alien coming temporarily to the United States to engage in commercial transactions that do not involve gainful employment in the United States.

C

Certificate of citizenship Identity document proving U.S. citizenship. Certificates of citizenship are issued to derivative citizens and to persons who acquired U.S. citizenship.

Citizenship The country in which a person is born or naturalized and to which that person owes allegiance and by which he or she is entitled to be protected.

Crewman A foreign national serving in a capacity required for normal operations and service on board a vessel or aircraft. Crewmen are admitted for 29 days, with no extensions.

D

Deportable alien An alien in and admitted to the United States subject to any grounds of removal specified in the Immigration and Nationality Act.

Deportation The formal removal of an alien from the United States when the alien has been found removable for violating the immigration laws.

M

Migrant A person who leaves his or her country of origin to seek residence in another country.

N

National A person owing permanent allegiance to a state.

Nationality The country of a person's citizenship or the country in which the person is deemed a national.

Naturalization The conferring, by any means, of citizenship upon a person after birth.

Nonimmigrant An alien who seeks temporary entry to the United States for a specific purpose.

O

Out of wedlock A child born of parents who were not legally married to each other at that time.

P

Parolee An alien, appearing to be inadmissible to the inspecting officer, allowed into the United States for urgent humanitarian reasons or when that alien's entry is determined to be for significant public benefit.

Permanent resident alien An alien admitted to the United States as a lawful permanent resident.

Port of entry Any location in the United States or its territories that is designated as a point of entry for aliens and U.S. citizens. All district and file control offices are also considered ports since they become locations of entry for aliens adjusting to immigrant status.

Preinspection Complete immigration inspection of airport passengers before departure from a foreign country. No further immigration inspection is required upon arrival in the United States other than submission of INS Form I-94 for nonimmigrant aliens.

R

Refugee Any person who is outside his or her country of nationality who is unable or unwilling to return to that country because of persecution or a well-founded fear of persecution.

Removal The expulsion of an alien from the United States. This expulsion may be based on grounds of inadmissibility or deportability.

Resettlement Permanent relocation of refugees in a place outside their country of origin to allow them to establish residence and become productive members of society there.

S

Safe haven Temporary refuge given to migrants who have fled their countries of origin to seek protection or relief from persecution or other hardships until they can return to their countries safely or, if necessary, until they can obtain permanent relief from the conditions they fled.

Stateless Having no nationality.

Stowaway An alien coming to the United States surreptitiously on an airplane or vessel without legal status of admission. Such an alien is subject to denial of formal admission and return to the point of embarkation by the transportation carrier.

Student As a nonimmigrant class of admission, an alien coming temporarily to the United States to pursue a full course of study in an approved program in either an academic (college, university, seminary, conservatory, academic high school, elementary school, other institution, or language-training program) or a vocational or other recognized nonacademic institution.

T

Transit alien An alien in immediate and continuous transit through the United States, with or without a visa. This includes aliens who qualify as persons entitled to pass in transit to and from the United Nations Headquarters District and foreign countries. It also includes foreign government officials, their spouses, and their unmarried minor (or dependent) children in transit.

V

Visa waiver program Allows citizens of certain selected countries, traveling temporarily to the United States under the nonimmigrant admission classes of visitors for pleasure and visitors for business, to enter the United States without obtaining nonimmigrant visas.

Voluntary departure The departure of an alien from the United States without an order of removal.

Index

ABOUT THE AUTHORS

Donald B. Hutton
Donald B. Hutton serves as an executive staff member for the New York State Thruway Authority and New York State Canal Corporation. He worked progressively for several law enforcement agencies; with the New York State Office of Inspector General as executive deputy inspector general, as a Delaware & Hudson Railroad Police Department special agent, as a United States Department of Veterans Affairs police officer, and as a United States Customs Service inspector.

Mr. Hutton served in the United States Coast Guard as a reservist from 1976 until 1992 in the following capacities: as a boatswains mate, a pollution investigator, a special agent in intelligence, and in mobilization/augmentation administration. In 1992, Mr. Hutton received an honorable discharge *semper paratus*.

He has a master's degree from the State University of New York College at Buffalo. In 1994, he served on the National Assessment of Educational Progress Panel (NAEP), also known as the "nation's report card." In 2001, he was elected to serve on the Board of Trustees for Daeman College in Amherst, New York.

Mr. Hutton is also the author of numerous articles and the following books published by the prestigious Barron's Educational Series: *Guide to Law Enforcement Careers* (1997), *Guide to Military Careers* (1998), and *Guide to Law Enforcement Careers,* 2nd Edition (2001). In addition, he is author of the maritime suspense thriller, *A Deep Blue Sounding: Dark Voyage with the U.S. Coast Guard* (Edgewater Press, 2000).

Anna Mydlarz
Anna Mydlarz has been a career law enforcement officer, serving with the City of Buffalo Police Department for over 20 years. She has had experience in patrol work and has been promoted to detective, serving with the burglary task force, vice squad, and narcotics squad. She currently serves in the communication crime unit, which specializes in high-tech crimes, stalking, telephone harassment, and Internet crimes. Furthermore, she serves on several task forces that are at the forefront of emerging issues.

NOTES

NOTES

NOTES